Contents

Macmillan Education Limited
4 Crinan Street
London N1 9XW

Companies and representatives throughout the world

Ferris Wheel Level 3 Teacher's Book 978-1-380-02679-8
Ferris Wheel Level 3 Teacher's Book with Navio App 978-1-380-02678-1

First published 2019

Teacher's Book credits:
Designed by emc design ltd
All character artwork and main illustrations by Jose Ignacio Gómez (Nacho Gómez); others by Animation Group Sp. z o.o. pp208, 210, 212, 214, 216, 218, 220, 222, 224, 226, 228, 230, 232–243; and Conor Rawson (Beehive Illustration) pp44, 66, 70, 88, 92, 110, 114, 132, 136, 154, 158, 176, 180, 198, 202
Cover design by emc design ltd
Cover illustration by Jose Ignacio Gómez (Nacho Gómez)
Picture research by Lorraine Beck

Author's acknowledgements
I would like to thank everyone at Macmillan Education in the UK, Spain and Mexico who has contributed to the development and production of these materials. I would also like to thank all the teachers who have taken time to read and pilot the materials, and given invaluable feedback at every stage of writing the course. Special thanks as ever go to my husband, Alan, for his encouragement and support, and to our son and daughter, Jamie and Hannah, from whose early childhood days I learnt so much.

Student's Book credits:
Text © Carol Read 2019
Design and illustration © Macmillan Education Limited 2019

The author has asserted their right to be identified as the author of this work in accordance with the Copyright, Designs and Patents Act 1988.

Original design by Clare Webber
Page make-up by emc design ltd
Illustrated by Jose Ignacio Gómez (Nacho Gómez) pp3–100 (all character artwork and main illustrations), 101–112 (Mimi).
Other illustrations by Animation Group Sp. z o.o. pp101–112; Conor Rawson (Beehive Illustration) pp12, 24, 26, 36, 38, 48, 50, 60, 62, 72, 74, 84, 86, 96, 98.
Cover design by emc design ltd
Cover illustration by Jose Ignacio Gómez (Nacho Gómez) with additional artwork by Conor Rawson (Beehive Illustration)
Picture research by Lorraine Beck

The publishers would like to thank Alex Tamulis, São Paulo, Brazil; Ayşegül Sezer, INO Schools, Turkey; Daniela Araujo Pielli, Alt Idiomas, São Bernardo Do Campo, Brazil; Daniela Pugliese, Milton's College, Buenos Aires, Argentina; Esra Ezici, Turkey; Fernanda Domeniconi Nery Amorim, São Paulo, Brazil; Gabriela Iocolari, English Schoolhouse, Buenos Aires, Argentina; Gulbin Cin, Bahcesehir College, Turkey; Mariana Pastorino, Em Pi Instituto de Inglés, Santa Fe, Argentina; Mariné Ortiz, Warrington, Buenos Aires, Argentina; Paola Daniela Tuninetti, Academia Argüello, Córdoba, Argentina; Silvana Paola Accardo, Escuela Cooperativa Mundo Nuevo Instituto Casa de Jesús, Buenos Aires, Argentina.

The author and publishers would like to thank the following for permission to reproduce their photographs :

Alamy Stock Photo/Frankie Angel p36(dinner), Alamy Stock Photo/Stefan Ember pp35, 43(brushing hair), Alamy Stock Photo/Freer Law p74(card tubes), Alamy Stock Photo/GeoStills p81(butterfly), Alamy Stock Photo/Victor Gladkiy p16(trees), Alamy Stock Photo/Esa Hiltula pp15, 23(merry-go-round), Alamy Stock Photo/Idea studio pp55, 56, 63(pool), Alamy Stock Photo/IMAGEMORE Co. Ltd pp35, 43(brushing teeth), Alamy Stock Photo/James Jackson p36(breakfast), Alamy Stock Photo/Juniors Bildarchiv GmbH p81(eggs), Alamy Stock Photo/David Lee p46(tl), Alamy Stock Photo/Roel Meijer pp15, 23(slide), Alamy Stock Photo/Monkey Business p29(parrots), Alamy Stock Photo/Pixavril p101(sticker – painting), Alamy Stock Photo/Apisit Sriputtirut pp25, 29, 33(crocodile), Alamy Stock Photo/Anna Stowe pp55, 63(toyshop), Alamy Stock Photo/Martin Sudzina pp81, 83(caterpillar), Alamy Stock Photo/Wavebreak Media Ltd p56(zoo), Alamy Stock Photo/John White Photos p59(m), Alamy Stock Photo/Sergey Yarochkin p74(yoghurt pots), Alamy Stock Photo/Zoonar GmbH pp46, 49(spaghetti); **Getty Images** pp26(monkey), 31(t), Getty Images/ac_bnphotos p46(pizza), Getty Images/ AlasdairJames pp51, 53(crisps), Getty Images/Ale-ks pp75, 76, 79, 83(ladybird), Getty Images/AlexStar p84(modelling clay), Getty Images/Steve Allen p59(l), Getty Images/allFOOD p103(sticker – rice), Getty Images/aluxum pp51, 53(plums), Getty Images/ amriphoto pp25, 26, 29, 33(elephant), Getty Images/aopsan p54(plate), Getty Images/artisteer p36(lunch), Getty Images/bgfoto pp16(grass), Getty Images/ David Bishop Inc. pp45, 53(chicken), Getty Images/brentmelissa pp65, 69, 73(maracas), Getty Images/Carlsson, Peter p56(restaurant), Getty Images/cenkertekin pp15, 23(seesaw), Getty Images/ChiccoDodiFC p39(preschool), Getty Images/cjmckendry pp15, 16, 23(pond), Getty Images/Clover No.7 Photography pp11, 13(running), Getty Images/CT757fan p74(colored paper), Getty Images/DarioEgidi p56(supermarket), Getty Images/Peter Dazeley p36(shower), Getty Images/Dorling Kindersley pp65, 69, 73(recorder), Getty Images/Elva Etienne pp5, 13(drawing), Getty Images/EyeEm/Vesna Jovanovic p51(icecream), Getty Images/EyeEm/Alexander Palm p51(market background), Getty Images/EyeEm/Adzahar Saini pp15, 23(swing), Getty Images/EyeEm/Kazuki Tsune p81(chrysalis), Getty Images/fanjianhua p16(path), Getty Images/ FatCamera p11(cr), Getty Images/Floortje pp45, 53(pancake), p46(br), Getty Images/fotoedu p74(sellotape), Getty Images/Stephen Frink p59(r), Getty Images/GalapagosFrame pp16, 19, 23(bench), Getty Images/GlobalP pp25, 33(hippo, lion, parrot), p26(hippo, parrot, snake, zebra), p29(monkeys), Getty Images/GrashAlex pp65, 69, 73(tambourine), Getty Images/hallojulie pp19, 23(park), Getty Images/Hemera Technologies pp14, 24, 64(paper), Getty Images/Hero Images pp55, 63(museum), Getty Images/HHelene pp75, 76, 79, 83(bee), Getty Images/ImagesBazaar p11 (cl), Getty Images/Image Source p39(house), Getty Images/indigolotos p49(bl), Getty Images/iStockphoto p26(giraffe), 45, 46, 53(yoghurt), 65, 69, 73(guitar), Getty Images/iStockphoto/Thinkstock pp29(hippo), 74(rice), Getty Images/ithinksky p51(peas), Getty Images/Juanmonino p46(fish), Getty Images/Kaphoto p76(ant), Getty Images/KidStock pp35, 43(getting dressed), Getty Images/Dave King pp45, 46, 53(toast), Getty Images/ kivoart p49(br), Getty Images/kk2s pp65, 69, 73(piano), Getty Images/kristianbell pp31(b), 33(br), Getty Images/Philippe Lissac pp5, 13(counting), Getty Images/losw pp16, 19, 23bmr(merry-go-round), Getty Images/luamduan p26(tiger), Getty Images/lucielang pp34, 44, 64(crayons), Getty Images/magnetcreative pp51, 53(oranges), Getty Images/malcolm_grima pp75, 79, 83(snail), Getty Images/Rob Maynard p56(park), Getty Images/MilaDrumeva p101(sticker – bench), Getty Images/monkeybusinessimages pp35, 43(washing hands), 55, 63(movie theater), Getty Images/Marvin E. Newman pp55, 56, 63(shops), Getty Images/Neyya pp11(tl), Getty Images/photohampster p16(flowers), Getty Images/photka p16 (seesaw), Getty Images/pioneer111 pp16, 19, 23 bmr(swings), Getty Images/Raffalo pp75, 79, 83(worm), Getty Images/RedHelga p51(carrots), Getty Images/RuthBlack p51(cupcakes), Getty Images/Serg_Velusceac pp14, 24, 74, 84(paints), Getty Images/Sergiy1975 p16(slide), Getty Images/Sidekick p11(tr), Getty Images/somethingway pp5, 13(singing), Getty Images/Spaces Images p56(bookstore), Getty Images/Chris Stein p11(bl), Getty Images/travellinglight p46(soup), Getty Images/Udomsook pp44(pencil), Getty Images/Martin Wahlborg p16(park background), Getty Images/Wavebreakmedia pp35, 43(getting up), Getty Images/YinYang p69(drum), Getty Images/Priscila Zambotto pp5, 13(building); **Getty Images Plus/**iStock pp45, 53(lettuce); **iStockphoto/**alex_kz pp14, 24, 34, 44, 54, 64, 74, 84(glue); **MACMILLAN MEXICO/**Tony Sanchez pp75, 76, 83(butterfly); **Macmillan Education Limited/**Paul Bricknell pp5, 13(coloring), 102(sticker – washing face); **Shutterstock/**Serhii Bobyk p56(cinema), Shutterstock/Chursina Viktoriia pp51, 53(candy); **Spectrecom** pp9, 12, 13(bmr), 22, 29(c), 32, 33(bmr), 39(tr), 42, 43(bmr), 49(t), 52, 59(tr), 62, 63(bmr), 69(c), 72(tr), 73(bmr), 79(tr), 82, 83(bmr); **www.imagesource.com** p34(string).

Commissioned photos by Helen Marsden/Spectrecom pp4, 6, 7, 11(Alex,Lucy,Auntie Vicky), 14(1,2,3), 16(Alex and Lucy), 17, 19(tr), 21, 24(1,2,3), 26(Alex and Lucy), 27, 31(tr), 34(wool,tissue paper,hanger,1,2,3), 36 (Alex,Lucy), 37, 41, 43(br), 44(1,2,3), 46(Alex,Lucy), 47, 51(Alex,Lucy,Auntie Vicky), 53(bmr), 54(tissue paper,1,2,3), 56(Alex and Lucy), 57, 61, 63(br), 64(1,2,3), 66, 67, 71, 72(Alex,Lucy), 73(br), 74(tissue paper,stickers,1,2,3), 76(tr), 77, 81(tr), 84(tissue paper,1,2,3).

Printed and bound in Brazil

2025
24

A letter from the author

Dear Teacher,

I'm delighted to welcome you to *Ferris Wheel*. Get ready to hop on with your children for what I hope will be a truly enjoyable and successful learning journey!

Before we start, I'd like to introduce you to the imaginary world of the meerkats. The delightful Mimi and her family accompany us through the course and provide a rich source of engaging, and often humorous, stories that young children will want to hear again and again.

Mimi is curious about the world, full of fun, at times mischievous, but also sensible, helpful, loving and kind.

Mimi's younger brother, Dylan, is funny, adorable and sometimes a little silly. Together they make an appealing and loveable pair.

Mimi and Dylan's mommy and daddy work at the Ferris Wheel next to the meerkats' house. Mommy and Daddy share roles such as shopping and cooking, and love sports and dancing, too.

In contrast to the fantasy world of the meerkats, *Ferris Wheel 3* also features two real-life children, Lucy and Alex, whose favorite animated stories are about the meerkat family. Together with Auntie Vicky, Lucy and Alex extend the natural contexts in which children are exposed to English. We meet them in lively videos where they interact in everyday situations, or act out traditional rhymes and songs. These provide a realistic and motivating model that supports children as they learn to communicate in English.

The Ferris Wheel, with its brightly colored pods, represents the course's innovative Hop on & Hop off approach to learning. Instead of working through the units in a linear way, you can teach them in the order that best suits your educational context and the children's curriculum, interests and needs. This gives you flexibility and allows your English program to be in sync with children's learning in other areas of the curriculum.

Before writing *Ferris Wheel*, I carried out extensive research to find out what teachers really need and want from a pre-school English language course. My findings led me to adopt a methodological approach for *Ferris Wheel* that takes into account the priorities and everyday concerns of classroom practitioners, as well as applying what we know from academic research about young children's overall development and language learning. It also incorporates many practical techniques from my own experience of teaching young children.

This is reflected in the methodology of *Ferris Wheel* in the following ways:

- Units with a clear, logical structure that build children's linguistic competence and self-confidence.
- Lesson procedures and activities that are easy to implement and manage, even with large classes.
- A wealth of content to foster children's motivation and develop language skills, including stories, songs, culture, values, real-world content and projects.
- A focus on the development of the whole child, including metacognitive, cognitive, psychological and physical development, social and emotional learning (SEL), life skills and values education.
- A balance between fantasy, which builds on children's natural capacity for creativity and play, and reality, which develops children's curiosity in learning about the real world.
- A wide range of resources to ensure lessons are engaging and dynamic, including the Mimi puppet, the *Ferris Wheel* mat, animated stories, videos, songs, Teacher's and Student's Apps, flashcards, story cards and posters.

Ferris Wheel is dedicated to every pre-school teacher who shares a passion for early language learning and believes in the unique learning potential of every child. I hope you and your children enjoy using *Ferris Wheel* as much as I enjoyed writing it!

All the best,
Carol

Ferris Wheel 3 Syllabus

Unit	Main vocabulary	Key language	Values	Content-based learning	Culture	Project
Hello	Mommy, Daddy, Mimi, Dylan; Ferris Wheel; blue, green, orange, pink, red, yellow; numbers 1–6	Hello. How are you? I'm fine, thank you. Where's number (one)? It's on (red). I'm (sleepy). Hurry up. Here's your (hat). Goodbye.				
School	color, count, dance, draw, jump, paint, play, run, sing, think	What do you do at school? I (draw) at school. Do you want to (color)? Yes, I do. / No, I don't. I want to (jump). I don't want to (draw). I like/don't like (school). I'm (happy). What exercise do you do? I (play soccer).	**Being kind:** help, play, share, sit down	**Doing exercise:** play soccer, ride my bike, swim, walk (to school)	***Go in and out the window:*** go, shake hands, stand; partner, window	A chart of our favorite school activities
The park	bench, flowers, grass, merry-go-round, path, pond, seesaw, slide, swing, trees	There's (a path). There are (trees). It's (windy). Is there (a slide)? Are there (swings)? Where's (Mommy)? Under the (tree). On the (bench). Put your (trash) in the (trash can). I put my trash in the trash can.	**Looking after the environment:** park, trash, trash can; clean	**The life cycle of a plant:** leaves, plant, roots, seed, sun, water	***Little Red Riding Hood:*** cake, wolf	A model of a park
Wild animals	crocodile, elephant, giraffe, hippo, lion, monkey, parrot, snake, tiger, zebra	What's that? It's a (snake). What are those? They're (monkeys). It's (black and white). It has (big teeth). I'm a (crocodile). I'm hungry. I can help you! Thank you. (Five) little monkeys sitting in a tree. You can't catch me! Along comes Mr. Crocodile.	**Saying 'thank you':** mouse; head, teeth	**Animal body parts:** claws, fur, tail, whiskers	***Five little monkeys***	A safari park mobile
Daily routines	brush my hair/teeth, get dressed, get up, have breakfast/lunch/dinner, take a shower, wash my face/hands	What do you do every day? I (get up). Do you (wash your hands) (at school)? Yes, I do. / No, I don't. It's time to (get dressed). What do you do at (home)? I (have breakfast) at (home). I don't (have dinner) at (school). I wash my hands with soap. This (bowl) is (small).	**Having a daily routine:** drink water, eat, learn, play, sleep	**How and when to wash your hands:** faucet, soap, towel, water; clean	***Goldilocks and the three bears:*** bed, bowl, tiny; Baby Bear	Our book, *Giant Joe's Day*

Unit	Main vocabulary	Key language	Values	Content-based learning	Culture	Project
Meals	chicken, fish, pancake, pizza, rice, salad, soup, spaghetti, toast, yogurt	What do you have for (dinner)? I have (soup). Do you want (pancakes)? Yes, please. / No, thank you. I want/don't want (toast). I like/don't like (soup). (Oranges) are/aren't good for you. (Candy) isn't good for you. (Mix) the pancake.	**Willingness to try food:** food, peas, tomatoes	**Healthy and unhealthy food:** fruit, vegetables; candy, carrots, chips, cupcakes, ice cream, oranges, peas, plums, tomatoes	***Mix a pancake:*** pan, pancake; catch, cook, mix, toss	Plates of healthy food
Town	bookstore, mall, movie theater, museum, park, restaurant, supermarket, swimming pool, toy store, zoo	Do you want to (go to the zoo)? Yes, I do. / No, I don't. Where do you want to go? I want to (go to the museum). Let's (go to the mall). The (stoplights) are (red). Do you want to help? Yes, of course. The (man) pulls the (woman).	**Interest in learning:** ask questions, find out about my world, go to school, look at books, play games, talk to friends, watch movies/TV	**Crossing the street safely:** crosswalk, sidewalk, stoplights, street; stop, look, listen	***The enormous carrot:*** man, woman; pull	A map of Mimi's town
Music	drum, guitar, maracas, piano, recorder, tambourine; clap, dance, listen, sing	What are you doing? I'm (playing the piano). Do you like (playing the maracas)? Yes, I do. / No, I don't. I like (playing the drum). It's (loud). Clap the rhythm. What can you play? I play the (violin).	**Willingness to practice:** practice	**Different rhythms:** fast, slow, loud, quiet	***I am the music man:*** trombone, violin	Maracas to play different rhythms
Bugs	ant, bee, butterfly, ladybug, snail, worm; legs, spots, stripes, wings	Does (a snail) have (spots)? Yes, it does. / No, it doesn't. Where are the (bees)? I don't know. Ask the (ladybug), please. It doesn't have (stripes). I care for (nature). They're eggs on a leaf.	**Caring for our world:** animals, bugs, family, flowers, friends, nature, trees	**The life cycle of a butterfly:** caterpillar, chrysalis, egg, leaf	***The ant and the grasshopper:*** grasshopper; summer, winter; play, work; food	A bug diorama

Unit	Main vocabulary	Key language
Endmatter	black, blue, brown, gray, green, orange, pink, purple, red, white, yellow numbers 1–100 circle, diamond, oval, rectangle, square, star, triangle hungry, thirsty, clean, dirty, old, young	It's (red). It's a (star). I can see (three) (diamonds). I'm (hungry). He's/She's/It's (old).
Festivals	animals, people, pictures, stories, words, world; elephant, gorilla, panda, polar bear, rhino, tiger; beach, countryside, forest, mountains	I like books about (people). I like books with (pictures). Save the (panda). I go to the (countryside). Let's protect the (beach).

Ferris Wheel 1 Syllabus

Unit	Main vocabulary	Key language	Content-based learning
Hello	Mimi, Dylan, Mommy, Daddy, boy, girl; red; Ferris Wheel	Hello, I'm (Mimi).	
Family	mommy, daddy, grandma, grandpa, brother, sister; blue, green, orange, pink, red, yellow	Where's your (grandma)? Here. This is my (mommy). Here we go. Round and round.	**Wheels go round and round:** round, wheel
Classroom	book, chair, crayon, eraser, pencil, table	Sit down. Stand up. Look! It's a (chair). I don't know. I'm (happy). What color is your (book)? It's (red).	**Putting classroom objects where they belong:** shelf, tray
My face	ear, eye, hair, mouth, nose, teeth	I have (a nose). I have (two) (eyes). It's (a boy) in the water.	**What we do with our ears and eyes:** hear, see
Clothes	boots, coat, hat, shoes, shorts, T-shirt	Put on your (hat). Take off your (shoes). Where are your (boots)? Here.	**Clothes for sunny and rainy weather:** rainy, sunny
Toys	ball, car, doll, scooter, teddy, train	What's this? It's a (train). Let's play with the (ball). What's your favorite toy? It's my (teddy).	**Where we play and where we work:** classroom, playground; play, work
Food	apple, banana, cookie, juice, sandwich, water	I like (bananas). I'm hungry. Can I have (a sandwich), please? Here's (a sandwich) for you. / Here you go. Thank you. Are you hungry?	**Things we drink and things we eat:** drink, eat
Pets	bird, cat, dog, fish, mouse, rabbit	I have a (mouse). Is this your (mommy)? Yes, it is. / No, it isn't. My (fish) is (orange).	**Animals that fly and animals that swim:** fly, swim
Beach	bucket, crab, ocean, sand, shell, shovel	I can see (a crab). Me too. How many (little crabs)? (Five). What color are the (shells)? They're (pink).	**Where animals live:** land, water
Endmatter	blue, brown, green, orange, pink, purple, red, yellow; numbers 1–10; circle, rectangle, square, triangle; happy, sad, big, small, up, down		
Festivals	Carnival, mask, parade; dance, sing happy, family; mommy, daddy, grandma, grandpa, brother, sister eyes, feet, fur; teddy bear		

Ferris Wheel 2 Syllabus

Unit	Main vocabulary	Key language	Content-based learning
Hello	Mommy, Daddy, Mimi, Dylan, Ferris Wheel blue, green, orange, pink, red, yellow numbers 1–6 ball, car, doll, teddy, train, scooter	Hello, I'm (Mimi). Where's the (ball)? Here's the (ball)! It's (blue).	
Classroom	backpack, crayons, glue, paints, paper, pencil, pencil case, scissors	Do you have your/a (pencil)? Yes, I do. / No, I don't. I have (red) (paint). I don't have (scissors).	**Places at school and what we do there:** cafeteria, classroom, library, playground
My body	arms, feet, fingers, hands, head, legs, toes, tummy	I can/can't move my (head). Can you? Can you move your (head)? Yes, I can. / No, I can't. What can you do? I can/can't (dance). Move your (head).	**Things we can do with our bodies:** climb, hop, jump, run
Clothes	coat, dress, pants, shirt, shoes, skirt, socks, sweater	This is my (skirt). These are my (shoes). What are you wearing? I'm wearing (a white) (hat).	**Clothes for hot and cold weather:** gloves, sandals, scarf; cold, hot
Home	bathroom, bedroom, dining room, garage, house, kitchen, living room, yard	Is (Sam) in the (garden)? Yes, he/she is. / No, he/she isn't. Where's (Dylan)? In the (dining room). He's/She's in the (house). He/She isn't in the (garage).	**Putting things away where they belong:** box, closet, recycling bin, shelf
Food	apples, bananas, bread, carrots, cereal, eggs, ice cream, milk	I like (carrots). I don't like (cereal). How about you? Do you like (bananas)? Yes, I do. / No, I don't. Put the (eggs) in the cart.	**Food that grows in the garden:** pears, peas, potatoes, tomatoes
Farm animals	cow, dog, duck, goat, hen, horse, rooster, sheep	There's a (horse). There are (cows). How many (hens)? (Four). The (sheep) goes (baa).	**Animals and their babies:** calf, foal, lamb, puppy
Transportation	bike, boat, bus, car, motorcycle, plane, train, truck	Let's go by (bus)! Yes. / No. I want to go by (car). Do you want to go by (bus)? Yes, I do. / No, I don't.	**Different forms of transportation and where they go:** air, road, track, water
Space	astronaut, Earth, moon, planet, rocket, sky, star, sun	What's this? It's (the sun). Can you see (the moon)? Yes, I can. / No, I can't. What can you see? How many (stars) can you see?	**What we can see in the sky at night and in the day:** day, night; clouds, rainbow
Endmatter	black, blue, brown, green, orange, pink, purple, red, white, yellow; numbers 1–20; circle, diamond, oval, rectangle, square, star, triangle; hot, cold, noisy, quiet, clean, messy		
Festivals	animals, bird, children, fly, happy, peace, world Carnival, clown, crown, king, pirate, queen; happy children; hug, play, run, talk	I'm a (pirate). I love to (play).	

What's in *Ferris Wheel*?

Student's Book
The *Ferris Wheel* Student's Book has a flexible, Hop on & Hop off approach that allows you to adapt to the unique needs and requirements of your class, and align children's English learning with the content and sequence of the wider curriculum. Hop on and off the Ferris Wheel wherever you wish or follow the unit sequence given in the book – it's up to you! Each unit has ten lessons that follow a logical structure in order to develop children's language skills and understanding of the chosen topic.

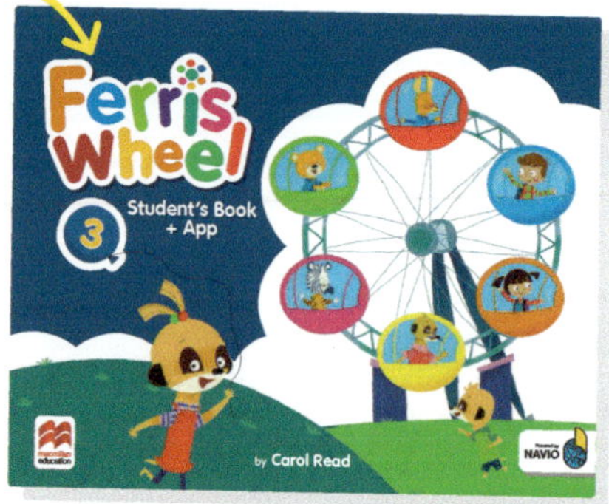

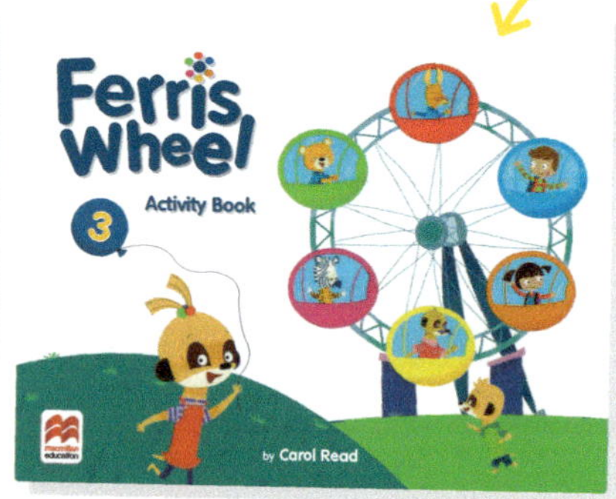

Activity Book
The full-color Activity Book mirrors the Student's Book structure and provides additional practice of key language and content. Activities such as visual discrimination, matching, pre-literacy and numeracy support and develop children's cognitive and fine motor skills.

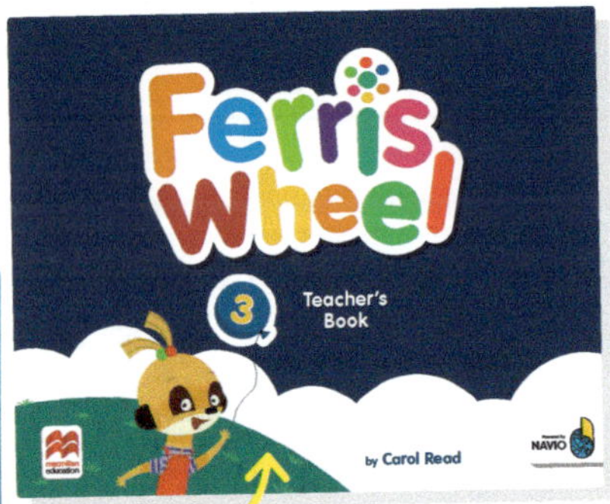

Teacher's Book
Detailed lesson plans, interleaved with the Student's Book pages, allow you to navigate the course with ease. Learning objectives, materials, teacher's tips and audioscripts are all at your fingertips.

***Ferris Wheel* mat**
The *Ferris Wheel* mat is a flexible teaching resource. Place it on the floor during Circle time, or hang it on the wall or board, and put flashcards or real objects in the pockets to play motivating language games. Practical ideas for using the mat can be found on p20.

Mimi puppet
Mimi the meerkat is an engaging puppet who will bring your classes to life. The use of a puppet has a positive impact on children's motivation and participation. Practical ideas for using the puppet can be found on p21.

Teacher's App on Navio
The Teacher's App on Navio offers one-stop access to the digital resources, including Tap & Teach Lessons with integrated audio and video, the Rewards tool to award points for good behavior or success, and a Progress Tracker. You'll also find additional resources in the Resource Bank, including posters, story cards, word cards, worksheets, evaluation materials, extra flashcards, alternative festivals, and letters to parents.

Student's App on Navio
The Student's App allows students to explore Navio's immersive worlds. They complete game-based activities designed to practice and review language and content. The App also includes all the songs, videos and animated stories from the course. The access code can be found on the inside front cover of the Student's Book.

Class CDs
All the audio material, including stories, songs, rhymes, chants, games and dialogues, can be found on the Class CDs.

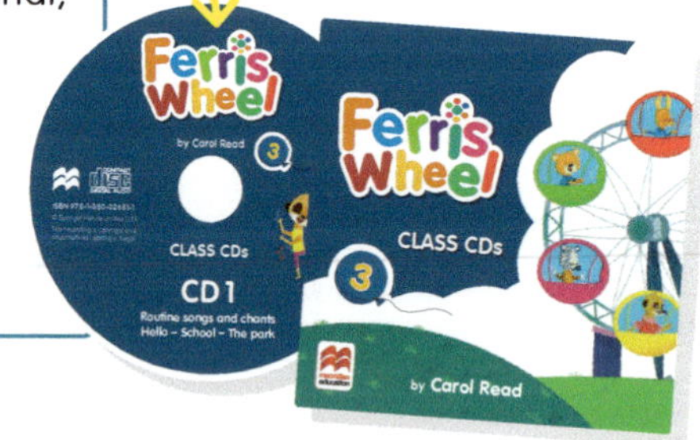

Flashcards
Photographic flashcards are provided for every key vocabulary item. See page 19 for ideas for using the flashcards.

Ferris Wheel's Hop on & Hop off approach

Ferris Wheel's **unique and innovative Hop on & Hop off approach** offers teachers the flexibility to teach the eight core units in any order. Topics can be aligned with the wider curriculum, or sequenced according to your and your class's preferences.

Wherever possible, recycled language comes either from **within the same unit, or from the previous level**. This ensures that children are not expected to use language that they haven't yet covered. If recycled language is taken from other units in the same level, it is for receptive understanding only.

This overall approach to the teaching of generic vocabulary and the recycling of known language allows for **regular and systematic review**, while removing the need to work through the units in chronological order.

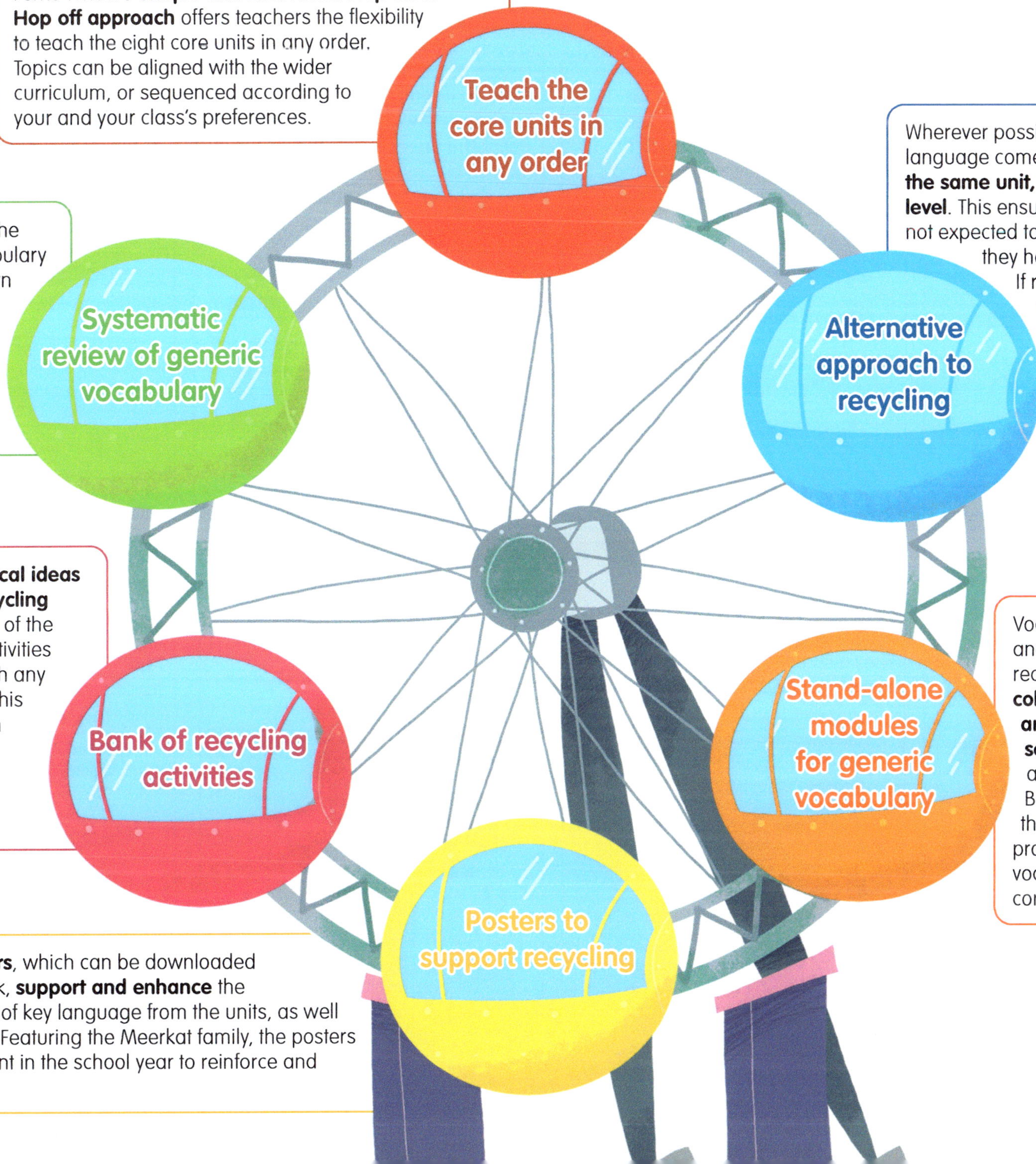

There is a **bank of practical ideas and suggestions for recycling known language** on p19 of the Teacher's Book. These activities are designed to work with any vocabulary set or topic. This means you can use them to recycle vocabulary and language from any unit that you have previously covered.

Vocabulary that is generic and can be applied and recycled in any unit, such as **colors**, **numbers**, **shapes and concepts**, appear in **separate short modules** at the back of the Student's Book. This gives teachers the flexibility to present, practice and review this vocabulary outside of the core units.

The *Ferris Wheel* **posters**, which can be downloaded from the Resource Bank, **support and enhance** the teaching and recycling of key language from the units, as well as generic vocabulary. Featuring the Meerkat family, the posters can be used at any point in the school year to reinforce and recycle key language.

About the Student's Book and Activity Book

The *Ferris Wheel* Student's Book and Activity Book have eight core units, plus a *Hello* unit. The course's Hop on & Hop off approach allows you to teach the core units in the order you prefer. Each unit features ten varied lessons to consistently develop a range of skills, as well as motivating children and promoting the use of English in their daily classroom interactions.

Student's Book

Lesson 1, Vocabulary

Six new topic-based vocabulary items are introduced by Mimi and Dylan. Children practice saying the new words, stick the vocabulary stickers on the Ferris Wheel while they say a rhythmic chant, and play a memory game.

Lesson 2, Language

The **target language structure and four additional vocabulary items** are introduced through an appealing and memorable song.

Lesson 3, Story

Children listen to the story using the printable story cards, or watch a **delightful animated version.** They then do a comprehension activity and stick the story sticker.

Lesson 4, Story Song

Children listen to, sing and act out the story song using the audio or an animated version. This **reinforces and reviews the concepts and key language in the story**. They then do a comprehension activity related to the song.

Lesson 5, Speaking

Children watch a **video** showing Lucy, Alex and Auntie Vicky using the **unit language in a realistic context.** Children are then encouraged to use some of the key language in a speaking activity that also practices **life skills.**

Lesson 6, Values

Children sing a song that develops their awareness of a specific value related to the story. They also practice **social and emotional (SEL) skills**.

Lesson 7, Content

Children are introduced to new vocabulary items and learn about **content from the wider world** related to the unit topic.

Lesson 8, Culture

Children are introduced to culture from the English-speaking world through listening to or watching the video of Lucy, Alex and Auntie Vicky. They either sing and act out a **traditional song**, or Auntie Vicky reads the children a **traditional story**.

Review

With the help of Mimi and Dylan, children **review their learning**, including key language and the main activities they did. They then complete a **self-evaluation** activity.

Project

The unit culminates in a creative and **cooperative project** related to the topic, providing a natural context in which to practice and review known language.

Endmatter

Colors, numbers, shapes and **key concepts** are covered in short modules at the back of the Student's Book. This allows frequently-used vocabulary to be introduced, practiced and reviewed at any stage of the course. This supports *Ferris Wheel*'s Hop on & Hop off approach and facilitates regular recycling. There are also three **Festivals** pages and pull-out **Stickers** pages.

Activity Book

Lessons 1–8, Review and Project

The Activity Book **mirrors the Student's Book unit structure** exactly. The activities are designed to **consolidate children's understanding** of the new language and content presented in the Student's Book, whilst **simultaneously developing skills** such as visual discrimination, pre-literacy, matching, coloring, sequencing, and numeracy.

Endmatter

The Activity Book endmatter provides **further practice of the frequently-used vocabulary** presented in short modules at the back of the Student's Book: **colors, numbers, shapes** and **key concepts**. There are also three Festivals pages with activities to extend and develop this content.

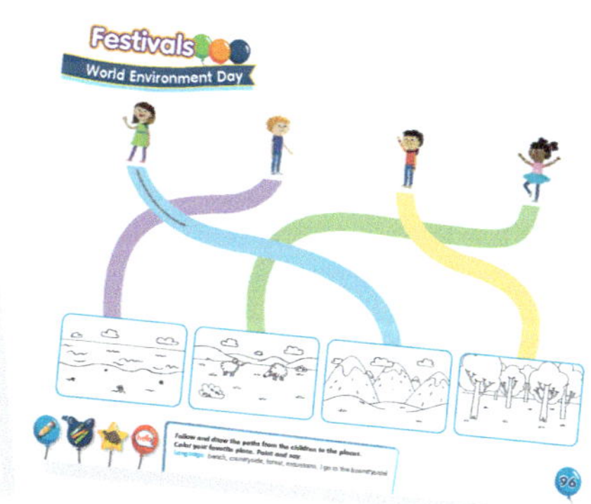

Teacher's and Student's Apps on Navio

The Navio app that accompanies this course offers one-stop access to the wide range of resources that come with *Ferris Wheel*. Tap & Teach Lessons enable you to move seamlessly between the book and digital components. You can track your students' progress using the Progress Tracker and find additional resources in the Resource Bank.

Accessing the app

To access Navio, go to www.macmillaneducationeverywhere.com to create a Macmillan Education account, or log in with your existing account. Then you can enter your access code and download the app for your device (see system requirements at www.macmillaneducationeverywhere.com/system-requirements).

Setting up a class

You can use Navio's Learning Management System to set up a class and register your students with their names and the email address of their parents or guardians. You can then provide login details to parents so that they can log in to the Student's App and enter the code from the inside front cover of the Student's Book to access the 3D worlds and practice activities. Alternatively, parents can register their children directly at www.macmillaneducationeverywhere.com and students can then join your class using a class code.

Managing your downloads

Navio makes it easy to manage the storage space on your device, as you can control how much material you download at one time. Navio makes it clear how much storage space your chosen content will need. You can download the complete Teacher's and Student's Apps at once or, if your device has limited storage capacity, you can choose to download only one or two units. When you complete a unit, you can safely delete the content from your device. You won't lose your students' data, as this information is stored online.

Using the Progress Tracker

All the work your students complete in the app is recorded in the Progress Tracker. You can monitor the progress of a whole class or any individual student. Every activity in the app is mapped against the course learning objectives and skills, so you can easily identify where your students need extra support.

Teaching a lesson

Navio makes it easy to plan and teach your lessons with fully interactive **Tap & Teach Lessons**. Find the lesson you want to teach and click to open it. A thumbnail view of all activities in the lesson is available via the toolbar at the bottom of the page. The toolbar also contains the Tap & Teach tools you need to teach heads-up, whole-class activities, including a timer, pen tool, and mask tool. Lessons include all the audio and video you need for the lesson, as well as some extra tools such as digital flashcards.

Using the Rewards tool

Navio's Rewards tool is a great way to keep your students engaged in class. Much more than just a record of attendance, you can also use it to award points for good behavior or success in activities. You can even organize your class into teams, and you can award points to individuals, groups or the whole class at any time. When students earn points, they appear in the Student's App the next time they log in, so parents can see their performance.

Student's App

As a teacher you can also access a version of the Student's App from the main menu of the Teacher's App. This has all the same content that your students can access at home, but your version is set in teacher mode. This means that all the activities and worlds are already unlocked, and the app does not record any scores to the Progress Tracker. We recommend using teacher mode when students share devices to avoid mixing up students' grades and progress. However, if students have individual devices or are using the app at home, they should always log in with their own username and password. In this way they can earn points and badges, set up and customize their avatar and build a record of their progress in the Progress Tracker.

Features of the Teacher's Book

The *Ferris Wheel* Teacher's Book lesson plans are interleaved with the Student's Book pages. Each lesson plan follows the same structure: **Circle time**, **Table time** and **Closing time**.

Each unit begins with an overview of the **vocabulary, language** and **objectives** for the unit.

The audioscripts for the **unit story** and **songs** are also provided at the start of the unit for easy reference.

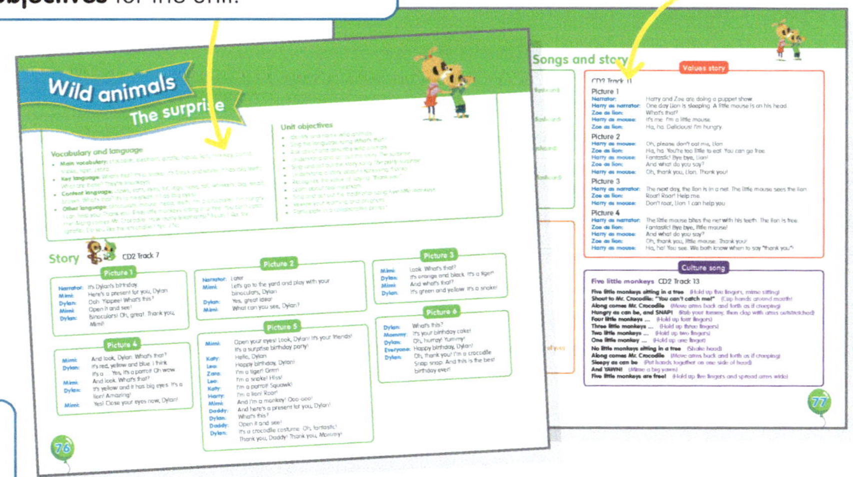

The detailed lesson plans are **interleaved** with full-size reproductions of the Student's Book pages.

Each lesson plan has an overview of the lesson's **learning objectives** and **language aims**, along with the **materials** you need.

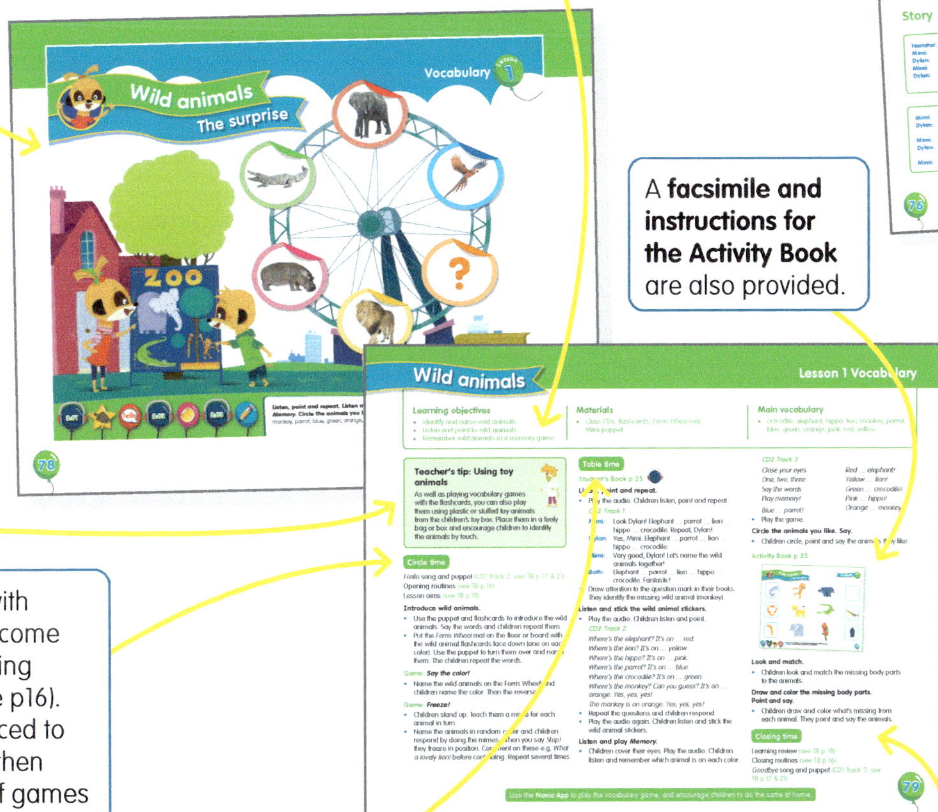

A **facsimile and instructions for the Activity Book** are also provided.

Teacher's tips provide helpful advice and suggestions to enrich the teaching experience.

Each lesson begins with **Circle time**. Children come together for the opening learning routines (see p16). They are also introduced to the lesson aims and then engage in a variety of games and activities using the Mimi puppet and the *Ferris Wheel* mat. Circle time focuses children's attention and is an opportunity for key input and new learning.

During **Table time**, children do a range of language and skills activities in the Student's Book. Step-by-step instructions, as well as audioscripts for the listening activities and chants, allow you to guide children through these activities smoothly and effectively.

Closing time ends the lesson with a learning review (see p18) and closing routines (see p16). Children then sing the *Goodbye song* as they wave goodbye to the Mimi puppet.

Additional resources

Activities Banks with ideas on how to use the Mimi puppet and *Ferris Wheel* mat in class, as well as recycling activities, and ways to specifically promote social and emotional learning, life skills and learning enrichment, can be found on pp19–25. There are also guidelines for how to incorporate **learning reviews** and **learning routines** into your lessons, along with audioscripts for the *Ferris Wheel* routine songs, on pp16–18.

Photocopiable templates specifically designed for the **Project** lessons can be found at the back of the Teacher's Book.

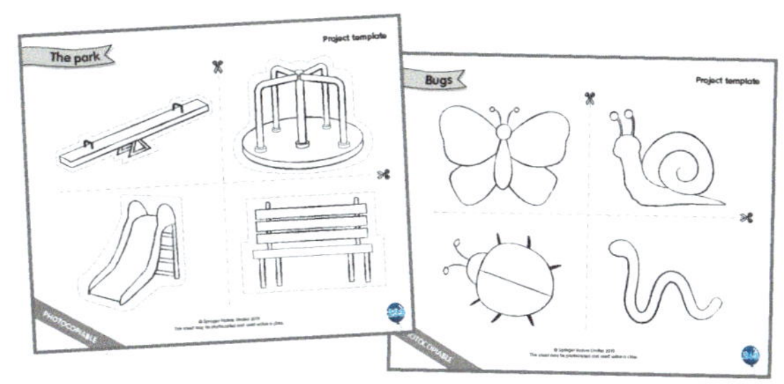

Whole child development

What is whole child development?

Many educators believe that children's learning success, both now and in the future, depends as much on their overall development as on their academic achievements. Developing the whole child means that we not only rely on traditional classroom-based learning, but give children the space and the opportunity to develop their creativity, physical, social and emotional expression, empathy, and understanding of the world around them.

A child's emotional, social, physical, creative and cognitive capacities are all intertwined and of equal importance. As language teachers, we also need to give all aspects of a child's development equal attention in order to achieve well-being, and create the optimal conditions for learning and growth. The development of a child's sense of self-worth and self-determination during the pre-school years is likely to be much more influential on positive long-term outcomes than a focus on standard academic achievements alone.

Ferris Wheel and whole child development

Ferris Wheel aims to integrate whole child development in a holistic way, including natural exposure to meaningful language, with the systematic development of age-appropriate language, thinking and social skills. This ensures that children are given the opportunities they need to develop all aspects of themselves, while simultaneously working towards the language and academic objectives in each unit.

Each level of *Ferris Wheel* was written to reflect the ages and stages of social, emotional, psychological, physical and cognitive development of pre-schoolers. Key child development goals, such as the development of creative thinking, personal autonomy, social and emotional learning, life skills, values, cognitive and metacognitive skills, and deliberate memory, are integrated and addressed throughout the course. On-the-page activities include ordering, matching, sequencing, tracing and visual discrimination to encourage effort, persistence, concentration and the development of early cognitive skills. Many of the songs in *Ferris Wheel* have accompanying actions to develop gross motor skills and coordination. There is a focus on creativity and personal expression, e.g. in the Story and in the Project lessons, and on emotional intelligence, self-esteem and autonomy, e.g. in the Values lessons. Metacognitive skills are developed through regular learning reviews, reflection and self-assessment.

Life skills

Life skills are the strategies needed to deal effectively with the challenges of everyday life. Life skills enable children to effectively problem-solve, adapt, take responsibility for their actions, cooperate and collaborate with others, make decisions, and interact with their peers.

Life skills are integrated across all levels of *Ferris Wheel*. In the Speaking lessons, children watch videos demonstrating how the real-life characters respond and behave in a variety of typical, everyday scenarios that are relevant to young children. On page 23 of the Teacher's Book, you will also find a bank of practical activities to help children develop and practice age-appropriate life skills.

Social and emotional learning (SEL)

Social and emotional learning (SEL) is essential for success at school and in life. Children who develop social and emotional awareness and skills find it easier to manage themselves, relate to others and resolve conflict. This creates positive self-esteem and provides a healthy foundation for children's learning and well-being.

Pre-schoolers are naturally egocentric and are still in the process of learning how to understand and interpret other people's emotions and intentions. This ability to "de-center" or move away from their own limited viewpoint to integrate other people's perspective is a skill that requires practice. SEL is an integrated part of the methodology of *Ferris Wheel* and is also reflected in the learning routines (see p16), unit stories and Values lessons, in which children rehearse strategies for handling their emotions, having empathy for others and making good choices about behavior. On p22, you can also find a bank of activity ideas for the development of social and emotional skills, including self-awareness, self-management, social awareness, relationship skills, responsible decision-making and autonomy.

Values education

The Values education lessons in every unit of *Ferris Wheel* encourage children to think about a range of age-appropriate values in relation to themselves, other people and their immediate environment. The Values lessons link back to a theme or issue that arose in the unit story. Children sing and act out a values-related song and are given options and choices that encourage them to reflect on specific values and apply them to their own lives.

About the projects

Each unit of *Ferris Wheel* culminates with an enjoyable and motivating project, which acts as a final outcome to children's learning in the unit. The projects are simple and achievable, and require only basic materials. The *Ferris Wheel 3* projects include making a model of a park, creating a plate of healthy food, making a map of Mimi's town, and assembling a bugs diorama. Photocopiable templates for the projects can be found in the back of the Teacher's Book.

Cooperative learning, or working together to accomplish **shared goals**, can be beneficial for both the group and the individual. By encouraging children to work with others, we nurture their ability to be **considerate, patient, kind and collaborative**. By following the simple steps in each Project lesson, children work individually, and then in small groups or with the class, to contribute towards a shared outcome. This brings **a sense of satisfaction and boosts self-esteem**.

Three numbered photographs clearly demonstrate **the steps children must follow** to achieve the final outcome, developing **logic and sequencing skills**, and giving them the confidence to attempt the project with **minimal teacher intervention**.

Activities such as painting, gluing and decorating promote the development of **fine motor skills**.

By showing **images of the materials**, rather than a written list, children are empowered to identify and collect the materials they need independently. This promotes **organizational skills and autonomy**.

In the Activity Book, children complete a motivating **art and craft activity** that practices **the key language** from the unit.

There are **photocopiable templates** provided at the back of the Teacher's Book so only **minimal forward planning** is needed.

The project creates a natural context for **production of the unit language**, and any other known language. This opportunity is fully exploited through a group discussion in which children express their personal opinions and give each other positive feedback.

The Teacher's Book provides **step-by-step guidance** on how to prepare children before they embark on their project, as well as **classroom management techniques** to ensure your project lessons run smoothly.

Simpler alternatives are suggested for most projects.

Learning routines

Learning routines are established procedures and patterns of behavior that you teach children and then use to signal and punctuate everyday classroom activities. Learning routines impact positively on children's behavior, participation, and social and emotional well-being, as well as on your ability to manage your classes and hold children's attention. Audioscripts for *Ferris Wheel*'s learning routine songs and chants can be found on p17.

Some typical learning routines include:

- **Opening routines** at the start of lessons, such as greeting the puppet, singing the *Hello song* (see p17), taking the register, identifying the day of the week, or talking about the weather.
- **Activity routines** to create the appropriate atmosphere for specific activities, such as Circle time and Story time.
- **Transition routines** to help children make the transition from one stage of the lesson to another in an orderly way.
- **Classroom routines** for specific tasks, such as giving out and collecting materials.
- **Energy-building routines** to use when children are losing concentration and need a short, physical break.
- **Settling routines** to use when children need to calm down and refocus their attention, e.g. after doing a lively, physical activity.
- **Thinking and feeling routines** to foster certain skills and attitudes, such as explicit thinking, cooperation, mindfulness, and social and emotional learning (SEL).
- **Closing routines** at the end of lessons, such as learning reviews (see p18), cleaning up and singing the *Goodbye song* (see p17).

For **children**, learning routines:

- give security and confidence about what they are expected to do;
- help them manage and regulate their behavior;
- provide frequent, repeated exposure to the same language in a meaningful context;
- provide opportunities for guided interaction and turn-taking in a familiar context;
- develop a sense of responsibility and autonomy in carrying out everyday classroom tasks;
- foster active participation in a safe environment;
- create a sense of community and positively develop social and emotional skills.

For **the teacher**, learning routines:

- allow you to create a safe and caring learning environment;
- allow you to manage your class positively and effectively;
- enable you to carry out essential routine classroom tasks more quickly and efficiently;
- provide for smoother transitions between activities;
- provide opportunities for you to communicate naturally with children;
- cut down on lesson preparation time;
- help you create a positive socio-affective atmosphere in your lessons and develop relationships with all children based on care, respect and trust.

The following guidelines will help you make the most of learning routines in your lessons:

- Decide on the learning routines that you are going to introduce in your lessons and the exact procedure and language you will use to carry out each one. For example, as part of your opening routines, you could:
  i) Hold up a feely bag with the puppet inside. Ask children *Who's here?*
  ii) Encourage children to answer *Mimi* and call to the puppet to come out of the bag.
  iii) Use the puppet to say *Hello, children!* and get children to respond *Hello, Mimi!*
  iv) Get the puppet to greet individual children, e.g. *Hello, Lucía. How are you today?*, and encourage children to respond *Hello, Mimi. I'm fine.*
- Repeat the learning routines in every lesson. To begin with, use exactly the same procedure and language pattern each time. Explicitly model language and be ready to support children in either non-verbal or verbal responses until they become familiar with the routine.
- Once children are responding confidently to a learning routine, you can start to gradually adjust the procedure and extend the language.
- Use opening and closing routines to provide a clear framework and structure to lessons. However, be careful not to spend too long on these stages of the lesson.
- Be aware that although learning routines may feel repetitive for you, children will love to do them over and over again!
- If you have an English Language Area (ELA) (see p25) in your classroom, it is a good idea to resource it with materials you use for learning routines, such as the *Ferris Wheel* mat, flashcards and Mimi puppet, so children can use the learning routines as a starting point for improvisation and free play.

Ferris Wheel 3 learning routine audioscripts

Hello song CD1 Track 2

Hello, hello, how are you? (Wave to the Mimi puppet)
How are you today?
Hop on the Ferris Wheel. (Draw a circle in the air)
It's time to learn and play.

Verse 2: **Hello, hello, I'm fine, thanks.**
I'm fine, I'm fine today.

Goodbye song CD1 Track 3

Goodbye, goodbye, goodbye. (Wave to the Mimi puppet)
We're finished for today.
Hop off the Ferris Wheel. (Draw a circle in the air)
See you another day! (Wave to the Mimi puppet)
[Repeat]

Story rhyme CD1 Track 4

It's time for a story. (Open palms of hands as if opening a book)
One, two, three. (Hold up three fingers one by one)
Are you ready? (Hold out hand to the class)
Listen to me! (Hold hand to your ear)

Let's find out what happens
In our story today. (Open palms of hands)
Look, listen and think. (Point to eyes, ears and forehead)
Be ready to say! (Point to mouth)

Mindfulness chant CD1 Track 5

I breathe in. (Breathe in slowly)
I breathe out. (Breathe out slowly)
One, two, three. (Hold up three fingers one by one)
I **close** my eyes. (Close eyes)
I listen.
I'm as calm as can be.

Verse 2: **open** (Open eyes)

Thinking hat song CD1 Track 6

Let's put on our thinking hats, (Mime putting hat on)
Think, remember, guess. (Point to forehead)
Let's put on our thinking hats (Mime putting hat on)
And try our very best!
[Repeat]

Circle time chant CD1 Track 7

Sit down,
Cross your legs,
Hands together,
Just like me!
Ready to learn,
Ready to play,
Let's start our lesson,
One, two, three!
[Repeat]

Table time train chant CD1 Track 8

It's table time, it's table time! (Form a train and lead children to their tables)
Ch-ch-ch-ch, ch-ch-ch-ch
Off we go, off we go!
Ch-ch-ch-ch, ch-ch-ch-ch
[Repeat]

Mimi's action rhyme CD1 Track 9

Follow, follow, follow me. (Signal for children to copy you)
Walk, walk, walk. (Walk purposefully around the classroom)
One, two, three!

Verse 2: **Run, run, run.** (Run slowly around the classroom)
Verse 3: **Jump, jump, jump.** (Jump around the classroom)
Verse 4: **Sit down, shhh …** (Sit down and put your finger to your mouth)

Weather chant CD1 Track 10

What's the weather like today? (Point to the window)
Look and see. Can you say?
Is it sunny? Is it cloudy? (Point to pictures of the weather)
Is it rainy? Is it windy?
Is it foggy? Is it snowy?
Is it hot? Is it cold? (Mime being hot and cold)
What's the weather like today? (Point to the window)
Look and see. Can you say?

Clean up song CD1 Track 11

Let's clean up, clean up,
And put our things away.
Let's clean up, clean up,
It's time to stop today!
[Repeat]

Days of the week chant CD1 Track 12

Monday, Tuesday,
Wednesday, Thursday,
Friday, Saturday, Sunday!
[Repeat]
And today is …! (Children say the correct day)

Mimi's recycling chant CD1 Track 13

Remember, remember,
One, two, three.
Look and say
The words with me! (Hold up six flashcards in turn for children to say the words)

Very good! Very good!
Great! Hurray!
For all the words
That we can say!

Mimi's recycling song CD1 Track 14

Ask a question, Ask a question.
Say the answer.
"Yes" or "No"!
Take turns
With your partner.
Here we go! Here we go!

Feelings song CD1 Track 15

Be kind to your friends
When they're **happy, happy, happy**. (Draw a smile on your face with a finger and smile)
Be kind to your friends
When they're **sad, sad, sad**. (Draw a sad mouth on your face with a finger and frown)

Verse 2: **sleepy** (Yawn and stretch)
scared (Put fingers to face and look scared)

Be kind to your friends
As they're kind to you.
Remember your friends
Have feelings too.

Cooperation song CD1 Track 16

Let's work together! (Have the class join hands in a circle)
Let's cooperate!
I help you,
You help me.
It's great! It's great!

Verse 2: **I share with you.**
You share with me.

Learning reviews

Much of children's learning during the pre-school years takes place in an implicit, natural way when children are engaged in meaningful and enjoyable activities. However, as teachers, we also need to encourage children to reflect on their learning in child-friendly ways. This helps develop metacognitive skills – children's ability to think about, plan, monitor, reflect on and evaluate their learning. It also allows you to introduce a range of learning strategies that, over time, will inform and support children's learning. As well as providing immediate benefits, such as giving children agency and choice in their learning, this also lays the foundations for becoming responsible and motivated learners in the future.

The learning reviews in *Ferris Wheel* offer children an opportunity to think about both what they are learning (the product) and how they are learning (the process). It is recommended that a short learning review is carried out as a regular part of the Closing time routines at the end of every lesson. At the end of each unit, the Review lesson also offers an opportunity for children to evaluate their learning during the whole unit.

Learning reviews are most effective when they form part of a three-stage learning cycle:

- **Before:** understand the aim and purpose of the lesson;
- **During:** participate in the lesson;
- **After:** think about the outcomes of the lesson and how they were achieved.

Establishing lesson aims

At the start of lessons, briefly explain the lesson aims in simple, child-friendly language. You may like to use the Mimi puppet to do this. Examples of generic lesson aims are as follows:

- **Lesson 1 (Vocabulary):** *Today we're going to learn words for … . We're also going to do some activities to help us learn to say and remember the words.*
- **Lesson 3 (Story):** *Today we're going to listen to, and watch, a story about Mimi and Dylan. We're also going to do activities to check that we understand the story.*

Conducting a learning review

At the end of the lesson, conduct a learning review either in English or in the children's shared language, or using a mixture of the two. Initially, you may wish to use English to name activities and the learning content, and the children's shared language to express ideas about the learning process. You can either do all or select only some of the steps described below:

i) Refer back to the lesson aims communicated to children at the start of the lesson.

ii) Ask children *What did we do first/next/then?* Elicit their ideas. Be ready to use prompts and reminders as necessary.

iii) Ask further questions about each activity, e.g. *What did you learn when we played the* Ferris Wheel *mat game?* Encourage personal responses and make sure it's clear that there are no correct answers.

iv) Extend children's thinking by asking further questions about each activity, e.g. *How did the* Ferris Wheel *mat game help you learn?* Be prepared for children to find questions about the learning process challenging, especially at first. Model possible responses to clarify what you mean, e.g. *The* Ferris Wheel *mat game helped me see pictures of the words in my head.*

v) Ask children for their personal views of the activities they have done, e.g. *Did you like the* Ferris Wheel *mat game? Why? / Why not?* Again make it clear that there are no correct answers.

vi) Refer back to the lesson aims and ask, e.g. *How well did you learn to say and remember the words?* Encourage children to evaluate their work in the lesson positively with a focus on what they have achieved.

vii) Ask children to talk about their progress in the lesson when they go home. Brief parents and carers to show interest, ask further questions and respond positively. When children do the Review lesson, add your own comment, stamp and/or signature to endorse the children's self-evaluation, and make sure that this is shared with parents.

Activities Bank: Recycling

1. Slow reveal

Hide some flashcards from previous units behind a book. Slowly reveal a flashcard so it is just visible over the top of the book. Children say the word as soon as they recognize it.

2. Quick flash

Hold flashcards from previous units facing you. Quickly, show children the top flashcard, then turn it back to you again. Children name the item they saw. If they can't name it, quickly show the same flashcard a second time.

3. Odd one out

Choose three flashcards from two different units, e.g. *chicken, fish, slide*. Display the flashcards and encourage children to point and say the odd one out.

4. Point to the …

Display some flashcards from previous units around the classroom. Choose one of the words at random and say *Point to the (bench)*. Children point to the correct flashcard.

5. What's in the bag?

Use the flashcards to review vocabulary from a previous unit. Then choose four of the flashcards (or real objects) and place them in a bag without the children seeing. Children talk to a partner and guess which four items are in the bag. Ask different pairs to share their guesses. When children guess correctly, remove the flashcard or object from the bag and show it to the class.

6. Can you remember?

Display six flashcards from different units and allow children to observe them for about 30 seconds. Remove the flashcards and place them face down. Ask children to name the items they remember. Each time a child remembers a word, show the corresponding flashcard to the class.

7. Secret word

Use the flashcards to review vocabulary from a previous unit. Put the flashcards away. If you have space, sit all the children in a circle. If not, have children play this game at their desks in small teams. Choose one of the words you reviewed and whisper it to the child on your left or to one child in each team. That child then whispers the same word to the child on their left. Continue around the circle or team until the word reaches the final child. Ask him/her to say the word aloud. If it is the correct word, show the corresponding flashcard. If not, ask the other children to say the word. (You could also try the game with full sentences, e.g. *I'm wearing a dress.*)

8. Order the flashcards

Choose flashcards from previous units and place them on the floor or board. Slowly say three of the words at random. Ask a volunteer to pick up the three corresponding flashcards and put them in the correct order.

9. Stand up!

Give all or some of the children a flashcard from any previous unit and tell them to sit down. Name one of the flashcards. The child holding that flashcard stands up and says the word. If necessary, the rest of the class can help by saying *Stand up, (Jack)!* Ask the class to repeat the word.

10. Which side?

Use the flashcards to review the words from two previous units. Place one flashcard from each set on opposite sides of the room and ask children to stand in the middle of the room. Shuffle the remaining flashcards and place them face down. Take a flashcard from the pile and show it to the class. Children run, jump or walk to the side of the room that has a flashcard from the same unit.

11. I spy

Choose flashcards from previous units that show different-colored objects. Display them around the classroom. Choose a color and say *I spy something (blue)*. Children name the item of that color. Allow a child who answers correctly to take your role and play again.

12. Question chain

Choose flashcards from previous units and sit in a circle with the children if you have space. If not, have children play this game in small teams. Take a flashcard and make a question using that word, e.g. *Do you want to go to the (zoo)? Does a (worm) have (legs)? Do you (brush your teeth) every day?* Pass the flashcard to the child on your left, or the first child in each team, and encourage them to answer the question. They then turn to the child on their left, ask the same question, and pass the flashcard. Children continue asking and answering questions as they pass the flashcards around the circle or team.

13. 20-second time bomb

Use the flashcards to review the vocabulary from several previous units. Put the flashcards away. Set a timer to 20 seconds and name a unit topic, e.g. *Meals/Town/Bugs*. Children must say as many words as they can from that unit before the timer goes off. As children name the words, show the corresponding flashcards.

14. Which one's missing?

Choose five flashcards from previous units and display them on the board. Ask children to close or cover their eyes. Remove one of the flashcards. Ask children to open their eyes and name the missing flashcard.

15. Relay race

Display flashcards from previous units on the board at the children's height. Divide the class into two teams. Ask a child from each team to stand next to each other a few meters away from the board. Name one of the flashcards. The two children race to touch the correct flashcard. The first child to touch the named flashcard wins a point for their team.

16. What do I have?

Place flashcards from previous units face down on the floor or board. Ask a volunteer to pick one up and show it to the class without you seeing it. Ask questions to help you identify the flashcard, e.g. *Is it big? Is it green? Is it an animal?* When you are ready to guess, ask *Do you have a (crocodile)?*

17. Twister

Choose flashcards from previous units and stick them face up on the floor so they are secure. Name a flashcard and ask a volunteer to put one hand or foot on that flashcard. Repeat until both the child's hands and feet are touching flashcards, and he/she is in a position that is difficult to maintain. Count to ten with the class and tell the child to try to stay in the same position until you reach number 10. Repeat with different volunteers.

18. No!

Use the flashcards to review vocabulary from different units. Put the flashcards away. Start to name items from the same topic, e.g. *hippo, lion, elephant, parrot*. Then say an item from a different topic, e.g. *pond*. When you say an item from a different topic, the children shout *No!*

19. Yes or no?

Choose flashcards from previous units. Hold up each flashcard in turn and either say the correct name or an incorrect name. If you say the correct name, the children say *Yes* and wave their arms in the air. If you say the incorrect name, they say *No* and fold their arms.

20. Karaoke

Place one flashcard from each previous unit on the board. Ask a child to touch the flashcard from their favorite unit. Play the songs from that unit. Encourage children to sing along and do the actions.

Activities Bank: The *Ferris Wheel* mat

Note: For larger classes, create a *Ferris Wheel* mat learning station (see p25) and do these activities with small groups. When demonstrating a new mat activity, ensure the other learning stations are familiar activities so the rest of the class can work independently.

1. Where's the …?
Hide six flashcards or objects in different pockets of the mat. Ask *Where's the (salad)?* Children take turns guessing, e.g. *It's in the (blue) pocket!* or *Is it in the (green) pocket?* When a child guesses correctly, remove the object and show it to the class. Alternatively, ask children *What's in the (blue) pocket?* and encourage them to guess, e.g. *It's the salad.*

2. Listen and do!
Display some objects or flashcards. Put children in pairs and give each pair an instruction, e.g. *Put the pencil in the pink pocket!* If they follow the instruction correctly, encourage the class to clap and say *Fantastic!* You can also instruct each pair to remove an object, e.g. *Give me the pencil, please.*

3. Remember, remember!
Put six flashcards or objects in different pockets of the mat. Talk to the children as you do this, e.g. *Let's put the ball in the yellow pocket.* Then ask *Can you remember where the (ball) is?* Ask children to raise their hands if they remember. Choose a child and encourage them to say *It's in the (yellow) pocket.* Ask the child to remove the object and show it to the class.

4. My favorite color
Write each child's name on a small piece of white construction paper. Ask children to color their card using their favorite color from the Ferris Wheel. Children take turns naming the color and putting their card inside the corresponding pocket. At the end, count the cards in each pocket. Ask children which pocket has the most cards and say *(Red) is our favorite color!*

5. Hide and seek
Ask children to turn around as you place the Meerkat family flashcards in different pockets of the mat. Leave a small part of each character's body visible. Have children turn around. Ask *Where's (Dylan)?* Ask a volunteer to point and say *(Dylan) is in the (blue) pocket!*

6. Mimi's magic
Hold up the mat. Ask individual children to check the pockets are empty, e.g. *Please look in the green pocket. Nothing there? Thank you!* Turn the mat around so the pockets are facing you and hide a flashcard or object in one of them. Show the mat to the class and have the Mimi puppet wave a "wand" (a ruler or pencil) as you say *Abracadabra! Listen to me. Look in the (red) pocket. What can you see?* Invite a child to remove and name the object.

7. *Ferris Wheel* ride
You will need small passport-sized photos of the children with reusable sticky tac on the back for this activity. Children choose the pod they want to ride in and stick their photo on it. Encourage them to say *I'm in (red)!* Then ask them to make big circles with their arms as they say the following rhyme: *Round and round and round we go! Oh, Ferris Wheel, we love you so!* Alternatively, ask children to bring in a favorite doll or teddy from home. Invite children to place their toys inside the pockets and say *My (teddy) is in (green)!*

8. Color swat!
You will need two plastic fly swatters for this activity. Hang the mat on the wall. Ask two children to stand either side of the mat and give each child a fly swatter. Name a color. The children should swat the correct color on the mat. Alternatively, place the mat on the floor and ask two or three children to walk around the mat. When you name a color, children must quickly touch the correct color.

9. Action game
Hang the mat on the wall. Over several lessons, teach children an action for each color, e.g. *When I say red, jump!* Introduce no more than two actions per lesson, and review the previous colors and actions each time. Once children are familiar with the colors and associated actions, point to a pocket on the mat and say *(Red)!* Children respond by doing the action and saying the word, e.g. *Jump!*

10. Odd one out
Arrange flashcards in six groups of four – three of the items in each group should be from the same lexical set and one should be from a different set. Put each group of flashcards inside a pocket on the mat. Invite a child to choose a color and remove the flashcards from that pocket. The child names each flashcard and then identifies the odd one out.

11. Sorting shapes
Ahead of time, cut out a selection of shapes from construction paper in the colors from the Ferris Wheel. Put children in small groups and give each group a variety of shapes. Ask them to organize them by color. Have a volunteer from each group place the shapes in the same-colored pocket as they say *A (green) (circle).*

12. Musical mat
Place six flashcards in different pockets and lay the mat on the floor. Ask six children to stand around the mat, one next to each pocket. Play music and ask children to dance around the mat. Pause the music and have children stand still. Say a color and ask the child next to that pocket to take out the flashcard and name the item. Ask the class to shout *Yes* and wave their arms if the child is correct and shout *No* and fold their arms if the child is incorrect.

13. Number game
You will need a big dice for this activity (you can make this out of construction paper). Hide a flashcard in each pocket of the mat. Write the numbers 1–6 on pieces of paper and place these clockwise on the pockets of the mat. Ask children to take turns throwing the dice and counting and saying the number. The child then removes the flashcard from the pocket with that number and names the item.

14. Mood mat
You will need pictures of emojis, e.g. happy, sad, scared, surprised, angry, calm, for this activity. Show each emoji and ask children to act out the emotion using facial expression and body language. Ask a child to choose an emoji and place it in the pocket with the color they associate with that emotion. Encourage them to name the emotion and the color. Make sure children understand that there are no correct answers.

15. *Ferris Wheel* role-play
If you like, prepare simple "tickets" for the role-play. Hang the mat on the wall and ask a small group of children to make a line in front of the mat. Use the Mimi puppet to act out a simple role-play with each child. For example: Mimi: *Hello, (David).* / Child: *Hello, Mimi.* / M: *Welcome to the Ferris Wheel! Choose a color.* / C: *(Orange), please.* [the child touches the correct pocket] / M: *Here's your ticket!* / C: *Thank you.*

Activities Bank: The Mimi puppet

The use of a puppet helps create a positive and warm environment for learning and playing in English. Children will develop a familiarity and fondness for Mimi, making the course materials even more engaging and appealing. Using the Mimi puppet as an integral part of your daily activities and routines brings fantasy, magic and humor into the classroom and creates opportunities for children to use English as part of their real-life interactions. Children will feel more secure and confident speaking English to Mimi and are more likely to actively participate, especially as they know she doesn't understand their first language!

1. Daily routines
Use the puppet to greet and say goodbye to children in every lesson. You can also use her for other classroom routines, such as the weather, the day of the week and taking attendance.

2. Social and emotional learning
Use the puppet to show affection towards the children and encourage the children to show affection back. Establish that the puppet has feelings and moods, e.g. happy, sad, tired. Encourage them to empathize with and respect these feelings, as well as telling Mimi how they feel.

3. Boosting confidence and self-esteem
Use the puppet to encourage and praise children. Ask children to show Mimi their work and get her to show interest and give positive feedback. If the class does a task well, use the puppet to praise and reward them with stickers or similar.

4. Demonstrating and modeling activities
Demonstrate and model activities with the puppet, e.g. act out a conversation or role-play. Do a cooperative activity using the puppet as your partner so children can see what to do. You can also use Mimi to drill vocabulary or short sentences. Children repeat what Mimi said in exactly the same way.

5. Linking fantasy and reality
Use the puppet as a bridge between the imaginative world of the Meerkat family and the real world. For example, use the puppet to show how language introduced in the stories is also applicable and relevant to the context of the classroom.

6. Introducing humor
Use the puppet to introduce an element of humor to lessons, e.g. when you want to surprise children or need to get their attention. For example, the puppet can be naughty, moody, make mistakes, answer questions incorrectly, or refuse to follow your instructions.

7. Learning reviews
Use the Mimi puppet when conducting learning reviews and have her take on the role of teacher. Alternatively, pretend she forgot what the children learned and ask them to remind her, or have Mimi answer your questions incorrectly and encourage children to correct her.

8. Managing your class positively
Use the puppet to help you manage your class, e.g. tell children that Mimi's sleeping or has a headache so they need to be quiet, or have Mimi give them instructions to form a line or a circle, e.g. *Come here, please, (Alex).* Similarly, when conflicts arise, have Mimi ask children to say sorry and be friends again. When selecting children to participate in activities, use Mimi to point to children and say a little rhyme, e.g. *Red, yellow, blue. I love YOU!*

9. Role-play and drama
You can use the puppet to act out simple role-plays or short versions of the unit stories, with the puppet taking on Mimi's role and children acting out the other parts.

10. Games and play
Have Mimi take your role in games to engage children's interest. If you have learning stations or an English Language Area (ELA) in your classroom (see p25), put the puppet there along with other resources, such as flashcards, for use during child-led play.

11. Hello, Mimi!
Ask children to sit in a circle. Play music as children pass the puppet around the circle. Whenever you pause the music, the child who has the puppet holds it up and says *Hello, Mimi!* If you wish, encourage the child to tell the puppet something about themselves, e.g. *I'm Maria. I have a ball.* You could also ask children to bring a stuffed animal from home and have their toys greet Mimi.

12. Do what Mimi says
Use the puppet to give instructions for children to follow, e.g. *Stand up. Sit down. Jump. Run. Stop.* Alternatively, display some flashcards and use the puppet to say, e.g. *Touch the (apple).*

13. Guess what Mimi's thinking
Display 3–6 flashcards on the floor or board. Hold up Mimi and put her in a thinking pose. Encourage children to guess which flashcard Mimi is thinking about. Have Mimi nod or shake her head and say *Yes/No.* When a child guesses correctly, Mimi gives them a high five.

14. Guess what's in Mimi's bag
Put several different objects or flashcards in a non-transparent bag. Make the puppet hold up the bag and ask *What's in my bag?* Children take turns guessing. If a child guesses correctly, Mimi removes the object or flashcard from the bag and shows it to the children.

15. Hide and seek
Choose two children and ask them to cover their eyes. Hide the puppet somewhere in the classroom so it is still partially visible. Ask the two children to open their eyes. Ask *Where's Mimi?* As the two children search, encourage the class to say *no, no, no* softly when they are far from the puppet, and *YES, YES, YES!* loudly when they get close to the puppet.

16. Mimi's song choice
When children learn a new song, draw a picture to illustrate it on a piece of construction paper. Keep the cards in a box. Use the puppet to take a card, show it to the class and say *Please sing this song.* Use Mimi as a conductor while children sing by having her hold a pencil or ruler. Hold her high for children to sing more loudly and low for children to sing quietly.

17. Taking Mimi home
Allow children to take turns taking the puppet home. When children bring the puppet back, encourage them to tell the class about the visit, e.g. where Mimi slept and where she went. If you wish, you could ask parents/carers to take photos of the visit and add them to a shared photo album, *Mimi's Travel Diary.*

Activities Bank: Social and emotional learning (SEL)

By integrating the development of social and emotional learning (SEL) skills into your teaching, you will enable children to deal confidently with the psychological, social and academic demands of pre-school, and lay the foundations for their future educational and life success.

1. Social development

Show that you value the way children relate to each other. Encourage children to think through any social difficulties that arise by asking questions such as *How do you feel when someone …?* This will help children see situations from other people's point of view.

2. Emotional development

Observe children's body language, eye contact, behavior and participation in class. Acknowledge children's emotions, while also making it clear that certain behavior is not acceptable. Provide a positive role model in the way that you express and manage your own emotions. Make discussing your feelings (happy, sad, angry, calm, sleepy, etc.) part of your daily class routine. Sharing your feelings will facilitate an emotional connection with children and give them the confidence to talk about how they feel.

3. Curiosity and confidence

Create a warm and supportive environment in which children feel secure about taking risks, asking questions, sharing ideas or making mistakes. Ask questions to scaffold children's understanding and promote further learning. Give praise and feedback that honestly acknowledges children's achievements and efforts. Make it clear that making mistakes is an important part of learning. Establish regular routines in class so that children feel secure about what is expected of them.

4. Resilience

Resilience is the ability to bounce back and keep going after a difficult or stressful experience. Two significant ways to help children develop resilience are i) to foster positive self-esteem and ii) to reinforce and promote self-belief. A safe and caring learning environment allows children to try to achieve their goals independently while always feeling that they are supported by the adults around them.

5. Responsible decision-making

Children need to practice making positive choices about both their personal and social behavior, and their academic work. Start with simple choices and decisions that are age-appropriate, e.g. the order in which to do activities or which materials to use. Model thinking through the options, making it clear that there are no correct answers. Avoid making decisions for children as, although this may often be quicker and easier, it denies children the opportunity to consider the different options and select the most appropriate action.

6. Self-management

Giving children strategies to control and manage their behavior will contribute to a positive atmosphere in the classroom. After a lively activity, introduce a calming technique to regain children's attention. Ask the children to sit down very slowly while you count down from six. By the time you reach number one, the children should be seated and calm enough to move on to the next activity. Teach children to use language, e.g. *I don't like it when …*, rather than physical actions to express displeasure. Provide them with strategies to calm down, such as relaxing and breathing deeply or deliberately moving away from the upsetting situation. If possible, create a "peace corner" where children can go when they feel angry or upset. Provide cushions, books and stuffed animals to help children relax and process their emotions.

7. Cooperation and empathy

Pair and group work gives children the opportunity to interact positively and show empathy towards their peers. It is also helpful in developing cooperation skills. Encourage children to listen to and show an interest in others and see things from their point of view. When a child shares something about themselves, encourage them to ask a classmate to do the same by asking *How about you?* Be inclusive at all times and encourage children to behave respectfully towards their classmates by using language such as *please*, *thank you* and *sorry*.

8. Supportiveness and self-esteem

Encourage children to support and help their classmates. Pairing shy children with a more confident classmate can be beneficial for the self-esteem of both children. Encourage children to help and guide each other throughout the day, not only with academic tasks, but also with daily routines, such as putting on coats and shoes, etc. When playing games or doing other activities, remind children to use positive language. If the answer is incorrect, encourage them to say, e.g. *Try again*. If the answer is correct, encourage them to offer praise, e.g. *Great job! Very good!*

9. Autonomy

Little by little, encourage children to become more independent and responsible for their learning and behavior in class. Provide them with simple age-appropriate strategies for everyday tasks, such as putting on their coats, and allow them to make their own choices wherever possible. As part of developing autonomy and metacognitive skills, encourage children to regularly reflect on their learning (see p18). Use the Review lessons in each unit to foster self-awareness and an ability to self-evaluate.

10. Making an effort

Encourage children to believe in their ability to master different skills through effort and persistence. Praise achievement while, at the same time, focusing on the underlying effort. If children find an activity challenging, encourage them not to give up by singing the Level 2 song: *I can do it if I try* (CD1 Track 41). Monitor children's response to their learning in each unit using the self-evaluation in the Review lesson and emphasize that increased effort will lead to more progress.

11. Free play

Child-led play is one of the key ways in which children naturally develop SEL skills, such as relating to friends, managing emotions, solving problems, resolving conflict, developing autonomy and making decisions. An English Language Area (ELA) (see p25) can be a great way to provide opportunities for free play.

Activities Bank: Life skills

Life skills

Pre-school may be children's first experience of extended separation from their family. By teaching basic life skills, you help children adapt to the new social context of life at school. Teaching life skills also enriches children's exposure to English and allows them to acquire new language in a natural and meaningful way.

1. Clean up

Allow time for children to clean up materials. Ensure everyone knows where each kind of material belongs and have children work together in teams to get the classroom clean and neat. Use the *Clean up song* (see p17) to signal when it's time to clean up.

2. Little helpers

Nominate helpers to give out or collect classroom materials. Rotate the helpers on a daily or weekly basis so everyone gets a turn. This will make children feel valued and help them see the importance of their contribution.

3. Put it in the trash can

Encourage children to use the trash can when clearing up waste paper and snack wrappers. You could also show them how to sharpen their own pencils over the trash can.

4. Make a line or circle

To make a line, use gesture to show that children should stand one behind the other and place their hands on the shoulders or waist of the child in front of them. To make a circle, stand at the front of the line and ask everyone to hold hands. Lead children around to form a circle.

5. Put belongings in your backpack

Encourage children to take responsibility for their own possessions. Give time for children to take out and put away belongings in their backpacks. Praise children who do this independently.

6. Share materials

Encourage children to take turns and share materials. Show that you value a willingness to share materials and cooperate as much as completing the activity.

7. Say "please" and "thank you"

Teach these words early on. Consistently remind children to say *please* and *thank you* both to you and to each other. Make it clear that children are more likely to get a positive response when they use these words.

8. Motor skills and projects

Project work provides an opportunity for the integrated development of both language and fine motor skills, such as rolling modeling clay, tearing tissue paper and using finger paints. Demonstrate these skills before asking children to use them. Praise and value children's efforts.

9. Wash and dry your hands

Teach the procedure for washing hands (see Student's Book, p41). Establish when and why it is important for children to wash their hands, e.g. before and after meals, after going to the playground and bathroom, and encourage them to do this independently.

10. Be active

Teach children the importance of moving their bodies every day. Incorporate physical activity into your classroom routines by using action songs and games. This will help develop coordination and gross motor skills. Show children how to place a hand on their heart after physical activity to show that it's beating faster and explain why this is good for them.

11. Wait your turn

Gently insist that children wait their turn to speak, and listen to others without calling out or interrupting. Explain or elicit why this is important. During Circle time, it may help to have an object, e.g. a soft ball, to show whose turn it is to speak. Similarly, when playing classroom games, explain that everyone has equal right to participate and praise children who wait their turn.

12. Cover a cough or sneeze

Explain basic hygiene about spreading germs from coughs and colds. Train children to hold up their arms to cover their mouths when they cough or sneeze. This is preferable to using hands, which they may then use to touch classmates or shared materials.

13. Care with scissors

If children use scissors, make sure that they are holding the scissors correctly. When they get up to put any scraps of paper in the trash can, make sure they leave the scissors on the table.

14. Safe in the sun

Explain to children why it is important to wear a sunhat and sunscreen to protect them from the sun. Ask children to put on their hats before going outside and not to take them off until they come back inside.

15. Bathroom visits

Build in opportunities for children to go to the bathroom either before or after lessons and at recess. Make it clear, however, that if children need to go to the bathroom at any other time, they are free to do so. If the bathrooms are not in the classroom, children could wear a card around their necks to show that they have been authorized to leave the classroom.

16. Drink water

Explain to children why it is important to keep hydrated and drink water throughout the day. Make sure children know that they can ask for water if they feel thirsty.

17. Pleasure in participating

It is important not to force children to participate unless they are willing to do so. At the same time, it is crucial to create an environment in which children take pleasure in participating and learning with their peers. This will help children to develop other life and SEL skills, such as cooperation, tolerance, empathy and respect.

18. Trying new food

Ask children if they try new food like Harry and Zoe in the story on Student's Book, p50. Remind them that trying new food is the only way to find out if we like it or not. Make a wall chart with the children's names. Encourage them to draw a picture of every new food they try and add it to the chart. If possible, prepare a simple recipe with the children (e.g. pancakes – see Student's Book, p52) and encourage them to try the result.

19. Healthy eating

Make sure that children understand the importance of eating healthy food. Make healthy food minibooks by stapling together some blank sheets of paper. Ask children to draw healthy food they like eating and show their drawings to their friends.

20. Crossing the street

Crossing the street safely is an important life skill. If toy cars and dolls are available in the classroom, set up an area where children can role-play crossing the street. Remind them to say *Stop, look, listen* and follow the procedure on Student's Book, p61.

Activities Bank: Learning enrichment

Ferris Wheel provides everything you need to teach children English in an enjoyable and effective way. However, if you also have the time and opportunity to incorporate additional materials, resources and activities, this will enrich children's learning experience and ensure maximum appeal and motivation.

1. Picturebooks

Picturebooks are a great way to expose children to new language in a natural, motivating context. It is a good idea to focus on picturebooks that relate to the topic of the current unit, e.g. Meals, Town, Wild animals, and that contain simple and repetitive language. However, keep in mind that children don't need to understand every word to enjoy the story, and you can make use of the illustrations, intonation, facial expression, questions and repetition to support understanding. Once children become familiar with a picturebook, encourage them to join in with repeated phrases and, if appropriate, to act out the story.

You may also like to encourage children to bring English picturebooks from home to share with the class. Put children in small groups to look at their picturebooks together. Encourage them to talk about what they like and can see on each page.

2. Dressing up

Provide a selection of dress-up clothes. Encourage children to practice fine motor skills by putting on and removing the clothes independently, asking for help from their classmates if needed. Encourage children to give each other instructions as they get dressed, e.g. *Put on your shirt.* Allow them to play freely and imaginatively with the clothes, e.g. organizing a costume party or drawing pictures of themselves and each other wearing their costumes.

3. Posters and visual images

As well as using the *Ferris Wheel* posters (see Resource Bank) to decorate the classroom walls and reinforce key language, topics and concepts, collect and display other visuals that relate to the topic of the current unit. Make use of the posters to recycle language and play games, e.g. by asking children to run and touch something on the poster. You may also like to use children's artwork for recycling activities. This gives a specific purpose to the work children produce and raises self-esteem.

4. Toys and realia

Wherever the unit topic allows, try to provide real-life objects or toys that children can touch and interact with. This will help create a direct connection in children's minds between their language learning and the real world. It will also make children's learning feel less abstract and more meaningful. Use the toys and objects in place of, or as well as, flashcards when you present and practice vocabulary. You can also use them as props for role-plays, drama and "feely bag" games.

5. Mime and drama

Mime allows children to produce a non-verbal response to language and helps boost confidence and self-esteem. Children can mime what happens as you tell a familiar story about Mimi and Dylan, for example, or they can mime in response to a set of instructions you give. Drama enables you to create a realistic context for children to practice using English they know. For example: you can create simple role-plays using dress-up clothes and props; get children to act out a simplified version of the Mimi and Dylan stories; pretend to be the Meerkat family or the real children; or allow them to take on the role of teacher, as Mimi does in the Review lessons. Use the Mimi puppet to help you transition from the real world to fantasy, and vice versa.

6. Music, movement and dance

Music, movement and dance develop gross motor skills and rhythm, and provide an engaging context in which to respond to simple instructional language. You may like to use the karaoke version of a favorite song from the course as the basis for teaching children a simple dance. It is also beneficial to teach children simple movement sequences, in which you start with one or two instructions, e.g. *Put your arms in the air. Jump three times.*, and build additional actions cumulatively. You can then use these sequences at moments when you feel children's energy levels are getting low and they need to get up and move around.

7. Movies, TV and video clips

In addition to the *Ferris Wheel* animated stories, songs and real-life videos, you may like to select other short movies and video clips from online sources that relate to the current unit topic. You could also occasionally allow children to watch their favorite TV show in the original English language version. This will expose them to natural English being spoken in a familiar context by well-loved characters. You may also like to suggest that parents or carers show children the English version of their favorite TV shows at home.

8. Children's multilingual identities

The children in your class may have diverse cultural backgrounds and speak another language at home, in addition to the shared language of the classroom and English. It is important to show that you respect and value each child's culture and language. Encouraging children to talk about their culture in class will help reinforce a positive sense of identity and create an atmosphere of tolerance and mutual respect. For example, when learning a new word in English, you could ask children to tell you the word in the language they speak at home. Alternatively, you could ask *How many different words do we know for "lion"?* Show your own enthusiasm for learning words in different languages and ask *Do any of the words sound similar?* Similarly, you can ask questions that get children to compare aspects of their culture with North-American culture, e.g. *Do you have toast for breakfast? What do you have?*

9. Home-school link

Working in partnership with parents and carers can be a hugely beneficial way to enrich children's learning. Regular letters to parents (see Resource Bank) with information about your approach, content and expectations, along with specific guidance on how parents and carers can support their children's learning, will facilitate communication. It is also a good idea to hold regular meetings with parents and carers, and to ensure they know you are available whenever they have questions or concerns. Given that parents and carers are likely to have had a different experience of learning a foreign language, it may help them to understand your approach if they can informally observe a lesson. Alternatively, you could share video clips of your lessons during an explanatory talk. If parents have a good level of English, invite them to visit the class as a volunteer, either to assist children with individual work, read a story or give a short talk related to the current unit topic.

10. Out and about

Whenever appropriate and possible, it is beneficial to take children on trips outside the classroom in order to make the connection between their learning and the real world. This may involve visiting different places within the school, e.g. the playground or music room, or finding a window overlooking a street where children can identify different forms of transportation. If there is a school garden, children could visit the vegetable patch and identify food that is growing there. If possible, plant some seeds, water them regularly and monitor how they grow. Trips further afield might include a visit to a local park, farm, zoo or museum.

11. Learning stations

Learning stations provide meaningful, self-directed language practice and develop skills such as autonomy, responsible decision-making and cooperation.
When organized during lesson time, learning stations also provide you with an opportunity to give extra support to small groups of children. Start off with two or three learning stations, and add new stations gradually through the year. Ensure you use activities that children have already practiced with you before they use the station independently. Organize children in pairs or small groups and have them take turns visiting each station. Some ideas for learning stations include:

- **Feely bag:** Children take turns feeling and guessing the objects in a non-transparent bag.
- ***Ferris Wheel* mat games:** see p20.
- **Drawing station:** Children draw their favorite animal, toy, family member, etc.
- **Matching pairs:** Provide two copies of a selection of five to six flashcards, mix them up and place them face down. Children take turns turning over two cards. If they are a matching pair, they keep the cards. If not, they turn them back over in the same place and continue the game.
- **Watch and learn:** Play videos or animations from the current unit or previous units for children to watch and enjoy. For the songs, encourage them to sing along and join in with the actions.
- **Classification station:** Children work together to classify objects or flashcards using different criteria, e.g. colors, shapes, size, etc.

12. English Language Area (ELA)

In some educational contexts, it is usual practice to divide the pre-school classroom into different learning areas or activity centers. These provide opportunities for children to play and experiment with a range of resources and to interact with their peers in an autonomous, child-led way. Typical learning areas or activity centers include: a reading area (with soft cushions, books, audio devices and headphones); a communication and drama area (with props, e.g. store items or kitchen utensils, and dress-up clothes); a science area (with small slides, weights, balances, sand and water); and a modeling and construction area (with building blocks and modeling materials).
You can also create an English Language Area (ELA) using course materials, such as the *Ferris Wheel* mat, the Mimi puppet, a selection of flashcards and story cards, and a computer or tablet with headphones and access to the digital materials. Ensure that the activities and materials are familiar to the children so they can repeat, imitate, and create activities and games closely based on teacher-led activities using known language. For example, children may pretend to take on the role of teacher and use the *Ferris Wheel* mat and flashcards to play a well-known game, or use the Mimi puppet to test a friend on vocabulary, as Mimi does with Dylan in the Review lessons.
As the idea is for the teacher to monitor and observe, but not directly intervene, it is essential for each learning area to have clear rules, e.g. the reading area is strictly for quiet reading and only English can be spoken in the ELA. Observing children as they play in the ELA will also provide you with invaluable feedback on their learning and progress to date.

Hello
How are you?

Vocabulary and language

- **Main vocabulary:** Mommy, Daddy, Mimi, Dylan; Ferris Wheel; blue, green, orange, pink, red, yellow
- **Key language:** Hello. How are you? I'm fine, thank you.
- **Other language:** apple, hat, shoes, shorts, socks, T-shirt, water; late, sleepy; Goodbye; Where's number (one)? It's on (red). I'm (sleepy). Hurry up. Here's your (hat).

Unit objectives

- Activate familiar language
- Review colors and numbers
- Sing *Ferris Wheel*
- Ask and say how you are
- Understand and act out the story *Hurry up, Mommy*
- Name clothes

Story

CD1 Track 20

Picture 1

Narrator: It's morning.
Mommy: Oh, no! I'm late for my run!
Daddy: Hurry up!

Picture 2

Mommy: Hello, Mimi. How are you?
Mimi: Hello, Mommy. I'm sleepy. How are you?
Mommy: I'm late for my run!
Mimi: Oh, no! Here are your shorts and T-shirt. Hurry up, Mommy!

Picture 3

Mommy: Hello, Dylan. How are you?
Dylan: Hello, Mommy. I'm sleepy. How are you?
Mommy: I'm late for my run!
Dylan: Oh, no! Here are your shoes and socks. And here's your hat. Hurry up, Mommy!

Picture 4

Mimi: Here's your water, Mommy!
Dylan: And look. You're not late!
Mommy: Oh, great! Thank you, Mimi. Thank you, Dylan.
Mimi: Goodbye, Mommy!
Dylan: Goodbye, Mommy!
Mommy: Goodbye, Mimi! Goodbye, Dylan! See you soon!

Songs

Language song

Ferris Wheel CD1 Track 17

Ferris Wheel, Ferris Wheel (Make big circle with arms)
One, two, three (Hold up 1, 2 and then 3 fingers)
Ferris Wheel, Ferris Wheel (Make big circle with arms)
Mimi, Dylan and me. (Point to flashcards and then self)

Hello, hello Mimi (Wave to Mimi flashcard)
How are you today? (Shrug)
I'm fine, thank you. (Thumbs up and nod)
It's time to learn and play. (Tap watch three times)

(Chorus)

Hello, hello Dylan (Wave to Dylan flashcard)
How are you today? (Shrug)
I'm fine, thank you. (Thumbs up and nod)
It's time to learn and play. (Tap watch three times)

(Chorus)

Hello
How are you?

Vocabulary Lesson 1

1:17 1:19 hello

Listen and sing *Ferris Wheel*. Listen, point and say. Stick the number stickers. Circle your favorite number. Ask and say. Language: Mommy, Daddy, Mimi, Dylan; Ferris Wheel; blue, green, orange, pink, red, yellow; numbers 1–6; Hello. How are you? I'm fine, thank you. Where's number (one)? It's on (red).

3

Learning objectives

- Activate familiar language
- Review colors and numbers
- Sing *Ferris Wheel*
- Ask and say how you are

Materials

- Class CDs, flashcards, *Ferris Wheel* mat, Mimi puppet

Main vocabulary

- Mommy, Daddy, Mimi, Dylan; Ferris Wheel; blue, green, orange, pink, red, yellow; numbers 1–6

Key language

- Hello. How are you? I'm fine, thank you. Where's number (one)? It's on (red).

> **Teacher's tip: Circle time and Table time**
>
> If there isn't space for children to sit on the floor during Circle time, they can sit at their desks. For the *Circle time chant* (see p 17), when it says "hands together," have them hold hands with the children at their table.
>
> Table time is when children work with their books. When it's time to do so, ask them to stand up and form a train with the children at their table. All the trains then link up to make a whole-class train. Say the *Table time train chant* (see p 17) as you move around the room, dropping each team off at their table. When each team sits, they give each other a high five!

Circle time

Hello song and puppet (CD1 Track 2; see TB p 17 & 21)
Opening routines (see TB p 16)
Lesson aims (see TB p 18)

Introduce the Meerkat family.

- Use the flashcards and puppet to introduce or remind children of the characters.
- Say *Hello, I'm …* and name the characters (Mimi, Dylan, Mommy, Daddy). Children wave to them and say *Hello, (Mimi).*
- Use the puppet to say *Hello, I'm Mimi* to individual children. They respond *Hello, Mimi. I'm …*

Introduce the Ferris Wheel.

- Put the *Ferris Wheel* mat on the floor or board. Explain to, or remind, children that the Meerkat family live near the Ferris Wheel.
- Use the puppet to point and elicit or name the colors.
- Use the puppet to count the pods on the wheel.

Listen and sing *Ferris Wheel*.

CD1 Track 17

- Play the song. Hold up Mimi (puppet), Dylan (flashcard) in turn and point to the Ferris Wheel when it's mentioned in the song.
- Teach actions for the chorus (*Ferris Wheel*: make big circle with arms; *one, two, three*: hold up thumb and fingers to count; *Mimi, Dylan and me*: point to the characters and then to yourself). Wave to Mimi and Dylan for each verse. Children sing and do the actions.

Game: *Say hello to the Meerkats!*

- Put the character flashcards face down on different pods of the *Ferris Wheel* mat. Invite individual children to take a flashcard in turn and show it to the group. The group waves and says with you e.g. *Hello, Daddy. How are you today? I'm fine, thank you.*

Table time

Student's Book p 3

Listen, point and say.

- Hold up your book. Point to the numbers on the Ferris Wheel as Mimi and Dylan speak.
- Play the audio again. Children join in pointing to the numbers and colors on the pods in their books.

CD1 Track 19

Mimi: Where's number 1, Dylan?
Dylan: It's on red. Where's number 2, Mimi?
Mimi: It's on blue. Where's number 3, Dylan?
Dylan: It's on orange. Where's number 4, Mimi?
Mimi: It's on yellow. Where's number 5, Dylan?
Dylan: It's on pink. Where's number 6, Mimi?
Mimi: It's on green. Number 1 is on red. Number 2 is on blue. Number 3 is on orange. Number 4 is on yellow. Number 5 is on pink. Number 6 is on green.
Dylan: Very good, Mimi!
Mimi: Very good, Dylan!

Stick the number stickers.

- Children stick the number stickers.

Circle your favorite number.

- Children choose and circle their favorite number.

Ask and say.

- Children ask and say the numbers and colors. Ask if they recognize any of the characters (Grandpa, Zara the zebra). Explain that children will 'meet' the other characters in stories later in the book.

Activity Book p 3

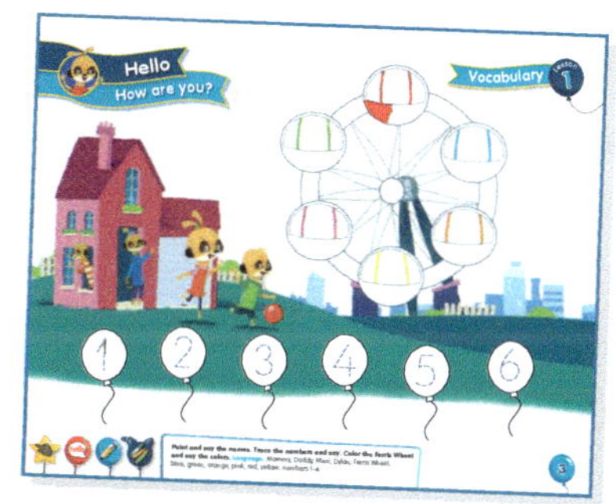

Point and say the names. Trace the numbers and say.

- Children point and say the characters' names.
- They trace and say the numbers.

Color the Ferris Wheel and say the colors.

- Children color the Ferris Wheel and say the colors.

Closing time

Learning review (see TB p 18)
Closing routines (see TB p 16)
Goodbye song and puppet (CD1 Track 3; see TB p 17 & 21)

Use the **Navio App** to play the vocabulary game, and encourage children to do the same at home.

Lesson 2 Story

Watch. Listen to the story *Hurry up, Mommy!* Circle and color the items Mimi and Dylan give Mommy. Ask and say. **Language:** apple, hat, shoes, shorts, socks, T-shirt, water; late, sleepy; Hello. How are you? I'm (sleepy). Hurry up. Here's your (hat). Goodbye.

4

Learning objectives

- Make a prediction about the story
- Understand and enjoy the story
- Identify items used in the story
- Say *Here's your (water).*

Materials

- Class CDs, printable story cards, flashcards, *Ferris Wheel* mat, Mimi puppet

Main vocabulary

- apple, hat, shoes, shorts, socks, T-shirt, water; late, sleepy

Key language

- Hello. How are you? I'm (sleepy.) Hurry up. Here's your (hat). Goodbye.

Teacher's tip: Story language and classroom routines

Distribute some familiar objects that belong to different children and encourage the children to give them to each other saying *Here's your (pencil)*, etc. Do this when you give things to individual children from now on.

Circle time

Hello song and puppet (CD1 Track 2; see TB p 17 & 21)
Opening routines (see TB p 16)
Recycling activity *(How are you? I'm fine, thank you)* (see TB p 19)
Lesson aims (see TB p 18)

Introduce the story *Hurry up, Mommy!*

- Say *It's story time!* Play the *Story rhyme* (CD1 Track 4; see TB p 17).
- Say *Alex and Lucy are listening to a story about Mimi, Dylan and Mommy. Guess who's late?* (tap watch/point to clock to show meaning). Listen to children's answers and respond.

Watch and listen to the story.

CD1 Track 20

- Watch the video, play the audio or read the story using the printable story cards. Pause, repeat words, point to the pictures, ask questions.
- Ask *Who's late?* and check the answer (Mommy).
- Ask children to name the items Mimi and Dylan give Mommy (shorts, T-shirt, shoes, socks, water, hat).
- Repeat and encourage children to join in with the words and phrases in the story. Ask *Do you like the story? Is it funny? Why? Is your Mommy or Daddy ever late? Do you help them not to be late?*

Game: *Help Mommy*

- Give flashcards of shorts, T-shirt, shoes, socks, hat and water to pairs or groups of children in the circle.
- Take the part of Mommy yourself. Say *I'm late for my run!* Encourage the children to hand you the flashcards and say e.g. *Here's your T-shirt! Hurry!*

Table time

Student's Book p 4

Watch. Listen to the story *Hurry up, Mommy!*

CD1 Track 20

- Read or play the audio of the story again. Children listen and point to the pictures in their books.
- Point to the pictures under the story and ask e.g. *Does Mimi say "Here's your apple"? (No). Does Mimi say "Here's your water"? (Yes).*

Story questions

Picture 1
Is it morning? *(Yes)*
Is Mommy late? *(Yes)*

Picture 2
Is Mimi sleepy? *(Yes)*
What does Mimi give to Mommy? *(Shorts/T-shirt)*

Picture 3
Is Dylan sleepy? *(Yes)*
What does Dylan give to Mommy? *(Shoes/socks)*

Picture 4
What does Mimi give to Mommy? *(Water)*
Is Mommy late now? *(No)*

Circle and color the items Mimi and Dylan give Mommy.

- Children circle the items Mimi and Dylan give Mommy in the story. Check answers and then give children time to color the items.

Ask and say.

- Point to each item and ask e.g. *What does Mimi say?* Children say e.g. *Here's your hat* as in the story.

Activity Book p 4

Trace, color and say.

- Children trace and color the clothing items, then point and say the words.

Find and circle six differences in the pictures. Point and say. Color the circle on the picture from the story.

- Children circle differences in the pictures.
- Children point and say the words in the pictures and color the circle on the picture from the story.

Closing time

Learning review (see TB p 18)
Closing routines (see TB p 16)
Goodbye song and puppet (CD1 Track 3; see TB p 17 & 21)

Use the **Navio App** to listen to the song, and encourage children to do the same at home.

School
A new friend

Vocabulary and language

- **Main vocabulary:** color, count, dance, draw, jump, paint, play, run, sing, think
- **Key language:** What do you do at school? I (draw) at school. Do you want to (paint)? Yes, I do. / No, I don't. I want to (play outside). I don't want to (draw).
- **Content language:** dance, play soccer, ride my bike, run, swim, walk (to school); What exercise do you do? I (play soccer).
- **Other language:** help, share, sit down; bag, banana, coat, crayons, friend, home, school; happy, sad; go, shake hands, stand; partner, window; chart, fantastic, great, picture; I like / don't like (school). I'm (happy). How many people (dance)? (Four). Our chart is (fantastic).

Unit objectives

- Identify and name school activities
- Sing the language song *What do you do at school?*
- Ask and say what you do at school
- Understand and act out the story *A new friend*
- Sing and act out the story song *Katy Kangaroo*
- Ask and say what you want to do
- Understand a story about being kind
- Recognize the value of being kind
- Identify and name activities we do to get exercise
- Sing and act out the traditional song *Go in and out the window*
- Review your learning and progress
- Participate in a collaborative project

Story

CD1 Track 27

Picture 1

Narrator:	It's time for school.
Mrs. Cat:	Good morning, children.
Children:	Good morning, Mrs. Cat.
Mrs. Cat:	This is Katy Kangaroo. Katy is a new girl.
Dylan:	Hello, Katy.
Mimi:	Welcome to our school!

Picture 2

Mrs. Cat:	This is Katy's first day at school. Please tell Katy: What do you do at school?
Mimi:	I draw, I color and I paint at school.
Mrs. Cat:	Very good, Mimi.
Leo:	I sing (tra,la,la) and I dance at school.
Mrs. Cat:	Very good, Leo.
Dylan:	I count (one, two, three) and I think at school.
Mrs. Cat:	Yes, you think a lot, don't you, Dylan?
Dylan:	Yes! I like school.
Katy:	Oh dear. I don't like school. I want to go home.

Picture 3

Narrator:	Katy sits at a table with Mimi.
Mimi:	Please don't be sad, Katy. I want to help you. Do you want to draw, Katy?
Katy:	No, I don't.
Mimi:	Do you want to color, Katy?
Katy:	No, I don't. I'm sad. I don't like school. I want to go home.
Mimi:	Oh, no. Poor Katy.

Picture 4

Mimi:	Please don't be sad, Katy. I want to help you. Do you want to paint, Katy?
Katy:	No, I don't.
Mimi:	Do you want to count, Katy?
Katy:	No, I don't. I'm sad. I don't like school. I want to go home.
Mimi:	Oh, no. Poor Katy. Listen! It's time for sports!
Mrs. Cat:	Let's go, children.
Leo:	I want to run.
Katy:	I want to jump.
Mimi:	Come on, Katy.

Picture 5

Narrator:	The children go outside.
Mimi:	I have an idea. Let's jump!
Leo:	Oh, yes!
Dylan:	Great idea! Look at me!
Mimi:	Very good, Dylan.
Leo:	Look at me!
Mimi:	Very good, Leo.
Katy:	And look at me! Yeah!
Leo:	Oh, wow!
Dylan:	Amazing!
Mimi:	Go, Katy, go! You're fantastic!

Picture 6

Narrator:	Katy jumps around the playground.
Katy:	Oh, thank you, Mimi. I'm happy. I like school now. I don't want to go home.
Mimi:	And I have a new friend! I'm happy, too.

Songs and story

Language song

What do you do at school? CD1 Track 25

What do you do at school, Alex? (Gesture around you)
I draw at school. I draw at school. (Mime drawing)
I paint at school. I paint at school. (Mime painting)
It's fun and it's cool! (Wave arms in the air)

What do you do at school, Lucy? (Gesture around you)
I sing at school. I sing at school. (Mime holding a microphone)
I dance at school. I dance at school. (Dance in place)
It's fun and it's cool! (Wave arms in the air)

What do you do at school, Alex? (Gesture around you)
I count at school. I count at school. (Count on fingers)
I think at school. I think at school. (Point to head and look thoughtful)
It's fun and it's cool! (Wave arms in the air)

What do you do at school, Lucy? (Gesture around you)
I run at school. I run at school. (Run in place)
I jump at school. I jump at school. (Jump in place)
It's fun and it's cool! (Wave arms in the air)

Story song

Katy Kangaroo CD1 Track 28

I'm Katy Kangaroo (Jump up and down)
Look at me! (Point to eyes and then self)
Boing, boing, boing. Hee! Hee! Hee! (Jump three times, then wiggle)

Do you want to draw? (Shrug and mime drawing)
No, I don't. Oh, no, no! I want to jump! (Shake head and waggle finger, then jump on the spot)
Go, Katy, go! (Punch both arms in the air)
(Chorus)

Do you want to color? (Shrug and mime coloring)
No, I don't. Oh, no, no! I want to jump!
Go, Katy, go!
(Chorus)

Do you want to paint? (Shrug and mime painting)
No, I don't. Oh, no, no! I want to jump!
Go, Katy, go!
(Chorus)

Do you want to count? (Shrug and count on fingers)
No, I don't. Oh, no, no! I want to jump!
Go, Katy, go!
(Chorus)

Values story

CD1 Track 31

Picture 1

Narrator: Jake is new at school.
Jake: I'm sad. I don't like school. I don't have any friends. I want to go home.
Harry: Poor Jake. Let's help.
Zoe: Good idea.

Picture 2

Harry: Don't be sad, Jake. I'm Harry.
Zoe: And I'm Zoe. We want to help you.
Harry: We want to be your friends.
Zoe: Put your coat and bag here!
Harry: Sit down here!
Zoe: Do you want to color, Jake?
Jake: Oh, yes, I do.
Zoe: Here are the crayons. Let's share.
Jake: Oh, thank you.

Picture 3

Narrator: It's playtime.
Harry: Do you want to play, Jake?
Jake: Oh, yes, please, Harry.
Zoe: Do you want to share my banana?
Jake: Oh, thank you, Zoe.

Picture 4

Narrator: It's time to go home.
Jake: I'm happy now. I like school. I have two new friends.
Harry: And we have a new friend, too.
Zoe: See you tomorrow, Jake!
Jake: Yes, bye!

Culture song

Go in and out the window CD1 Track 33

Go in and out the window, Go in and out the window (Children pass through the "windows")
Go in and out the window, As we all love to do. (Turn around)
Stand and face your partner, Stand and face your partner (Children face a partner)
Stand and face your partner, As we all love to do. (Turn around)
Dance around together, Dance around together (Children dance around each other)
Dance around together, As we all love to do. (Turn around)
Shake hands with your partner, Shake hands with your partner (Children shake hands)
Shake hands with your partner, As we all love to do. (Turn around)

School

A new friend

Vocabulary Lesson 1

Listen, point and repeat. Listen and stick the school activity stickers. Listen and play *Memory*. Circle the activities you like. Say. Language: color, count, draw, paint, play, sing; blue, green, orange, pink, red, yellow; Where's (draw)? It's on (red).

5

School

Lesson 1 Vocabulary

Learning objectives

- Identify and name school activities
- Listen and point to school activities
- Remember new school activities in a memory game

Materials

- Class CDs, flashcards, *Ferris Wheel* mat, Mimi puppet

Main vocabulary

- color, count, draw, paint, play, sing; blue, green, orange, pink, red, yellow

Teacher's tip: Associating actions, images and words

After presenting the new classroom action vocabulary, reinforce the association between the actions, images and words by hiding the flashcards in the pockets of the *Ferris Wheel* mat. Have the class predict which classroom action is inside each pocket by doing actions and saying the words. Remove correctly guessed items.

Circle time

Hello song and puppet (CD1 Track 2; see TB p 17 & 21)
Opening routines (see TB p 16)
Lesson aims (see TB p 18)

Introduce school activities.

- Use the puppet and real classroom items to introduce six school activities (*color, count, draw, paint, play, sing*). Say each word and children repeat it.
- Put the *Ferris Wheel* mat on the floor or board with the school activity flashcards face down (one on each color). Use the puppet to turn them over and name them. The children repeat the words.

Game: *Say the color!*

- Name the school activities and children say the color of the wheel. Then the reverse.

Game: *Mime and say!*

- Mime the school activities in turn. Children name the activities or point to them on the *Ferris Wheel* mat.
- Name the activities in random order. Children mime them and say the words.

Table time

Student's Book p 5

Listen, point and repeat.

- Play the audio. The children listen, point to each school activity as they hear it, and repeat the words.

CD1 Track 21

Mimi: Look, Dylan! Draw … color … sing … count … play. Repeat, Dylan!
Dylan: Yes, Mimi. Draw … color … sing … count … play.
Mimi: Very good, Dylan! Let's name the school activities together!
Both: Draw … color … sing … count … play. Fantastic!

- Draw children's attention to the question mark in their books. They identify the missing item (paint).

Listen and stick the school activity stickers.

- Play the audio. The children listen and point to the activities in their books.

CD1 Track 22

Where's "draw"? It's on … red.
Where's "color"? It's on … orange.
Where's "count"? It's on … pink.
Where's "sing"? It's on … yellow.
Where's "play"? It's on … green.
Where's "paint"? Can you guess? It's on … blue.
Yes, yes, yes! Paint is on blue. Yes, yes, yes!

- Ask questions about all the activities in the same way and children respond.
- Play the audio again. Children listen and stick the school activity stickers.

Listen and play *Memory*.

- Children cover their eyes with their hands.
- Play the audio. Children listen and try to remember the school activity on each color on the wheel.

CD1 Track 23

Close your eyes
One, two, three
Say the words
Play memory!
Blue … paint!
Red … draw!
Yellow … sing!
Green … play!
Pink … count!
Orange … color!

- Name the colors and children say the words.

Circle the activities you like. Say.

- Children circle, point to and say the activities they like.

Activity Book p 5

Look and match. Color, point and say.

- Children match the pictures. Then they color, point and say the words.

Closing time

Learning review (see TB p 18)
Closing routines (see TB p 16)
Goodbye song and puppet (CD1 Track 3; see TB p 17 & 21)

Use the **Navio App** to play the vocabulary game, and encourage children to do the same at home.

Lesson 2 Language

School

Listen and find the new school activities. Listen, point and sing *What do you do at school?* Match the activities to Lucy and Alex. Ask and say. Language: count, dance, draw, jump, paint, run, sing, think; What do you do at school? I (draw) at school.

6

Learning objectives

- Talk about school activities
- Identify and name four new school activities
- Sing the language song *What do you do at school?*
- Ask and say what you do at school

Materials

- Class CDs, flashcards, *Ferris Wheel* mat, Mimi puppet

Main vocabulary

- count, dance, draw, jump, paint, run, sing, think

Key language

- What do you do at school? I (draw) at school.

Teacher's tip: Singing in groups

Divide the class into eight groups. Each group sings and does one of the actions from the song. All the children join in with the first and last line of each verse. Make sure that in each group there are children with differing levels of confidence so that they can prompt each other.

Circle time

Hello song and puppet (CD1 Track 2; see TB p 17 & 21)

Opening routines (see TB p 16)

Recycling activity (six school activities from lesson 1) (see TB p 19)

Lesson aims (see TB p 18)

Introduce the new school activities.

- Put all ten flashcards of school activities on the floor or board.
- Children identify the four new school activities (*dance, think, run, jump*).
- Use the puppet to point to and say the words in turn. Children repeat the words in chorus.
- Children stand up. Name the activities in turn and children do actions in place (and point to the side of their head for *think*).
- Turn the four new flashcards face down. Mix them up. Point to one and ask *What's this? Dance? Think? Run? Jump?* Children guess. Repeat several times.

Introduce *What do you do at school? I draw, …*

- Children name all the school activity flashcards.
- Give a flashcard to the puppet. Ask the puppet e.g. *What do you do at school?* and model the response e.g. *I draw*.
- Repeat several times with different flashcards.
- Give individual children flashcards. Use the puppet to ask *What do you do at school?* and encourage children to respond e.g. *I paint*.
- Get the children to ask the puppet in chorus e.g. *What do you do at school?* and respond for the puppet in the same way.

Game: *Mime and guess!*

- Children ask you in chorus *What do you do at school?* Mime one of the activities and children guess. Repeat several times.
- Ask individual children in chorus and children take turns miming and guessing the activities in the same way.

***What do you do at school?* song**

CD1 Track 25

- Put the school activity flashcards face up on the board.
- Hold up the flashcards and introduce Alex and Lucy. Say *Let's listen and find out what Alex and Lucy do at school.*
- Hold up the flashcard of Alex for verses 1 and 2 and Lucy for verses 3 and 4. Children listen and point to the school activity flashcards in each verse. Play the audio again. Children mime each school activity and sing.
- Remember that you can use the karaoke version of the song when children are confident.

Table time

Student's Book p 6

Listen and find the new school activities.

- Children listen and find the four new school activities. Repeat and children say the words.

CD1 Track 24

One … two … Which words are new?

Run! Run! *Dance! Dance!*
Jump! Jump! *Think! Think!*

Listen, point and sing *What do you do at school?*

- Play the song. Children point to the school activities.

Match the activities to Lucy and Alex.

- Play the audio again. Pause after each verse. Children match the activities and characters.

Ask and say.

- The children ask and answer questions about what they do at school.

Activity Book p 6

Circle the activities you do at school.

- Children circle all the school activities they do.

Ask and say.

- Children ask and answer questions about what they do at school.

Closing time

Learning review (see TB p 18)

Closing routines (see TB p 16)

Goodbye song and puppet (CD1 Track 3; see TB p 17 & 21)

Use the **Navio App** to listen to the song, and encourage children to do the same at home.

Lesson 3 Story

Watch. Listen to the story *A new friend*. Circle who's new at school. Stick the story sticker.
Language: color, count, dance, draw, jump, paint, run, sing, think; What do you do at school? I (think) at school. Do you want to (color)? Yes, I do. / No, I don't. I want to (jump).

7

Learning objectives

- Watch, understand and enjoy the story *A new friend*
- Make a prediction about the story
- Identify who's new at school in the story

Materials

- Class CDs, printable story cards, flashcards, *Ferris Wheel* mat, Mimi puppet

Main vocabulary

- color, count, dance, draw, jump, paint, run, sing, think

Key language

- What do you do at school? I (think) at school. Do you want to (color)? Yes, I do. / No, I don't. I want to (jump).

Teacher's tip: Pausing audio to help comprehension

If your class finds it too challenging to answer the comprehension questions after listening to the story, play the story audio again, pausing in the corresponding parts so that the children can answer.

Circle time

Hello song and puppet (CD1 Track 2; see TB p 17 & 21)
Opening routines (see TB p 16)
Recycling activity (*What do you do at school?* and school activities) (see TB p 19)
Lesson aims (see TB p 18)

Introduce the story *A new friend*.

- Say *It's story time!* Play the *Story rhyme* (CD1 Track 4; see TB p 17)
- Say *Alex and Lucy are listening to a story about Mimi and Dylan's first day back at school. Which animal is Mimi's new friend? What does Mimi's new friend want to do?* Listen to children's ideas and respond.

Watch and listen to the story *A new friend*.

CD1 Track 27

- Watch the video, play the audio or read the story using the printable story cards. Pause, repeat words, point to the pictures, ask questions.
- Ask the pre-questions again and check the answers (a kangaroo, jump).
- Repeat the story. Encourage children to join in with the words and phrases in the story.
- Ask *Do you like the story? Is Katy happy or sad at the beginning / end of the story? How does Mimi help Katy?*

Game: ***Say the names***

- Ask e.g. *Who says "This is Katy Kangaroo. Katy is a new girl"?* (Mrs. Cat).
- Repeat with other sentences from the story.

Table time

Student's Book p 7

Watch. Listen to the story *A new friend*.

Story questions

Picture 1
Where are the children? *(At school)*
Who is a new girl? *(Katy Kangaroo)*

Picture 2
What does Mimi do at school? *(Draw/color/paint)*
Does Katy like school? *(No)*

Picture 3
Does Katy want to draw? *(No)*
Is Katy happy? *(No)*

Picture 4
Does Katy want to paint? *(No)*
Do the children like sports? *(Yes)*

Picture 5
What do the children do? *(Jump)*
Does Katy like jumping? *(Yes)*

Picture 6
Is Katy happy? *(Yes)*
Are Mimi and Katy friends now? *(Yes)*

CD1 Track 27

- Read or play the audio of the story again. Children listen and point to the pictures in their books.

Circle who's new at school. Stick the story sticker.

- Demonstrate circling the new character at school and sticking the story sticker.
- Ask *Who's kind to Katy in the story? (Mimi) Is it important to be kind to your friends?*

Activity Book p 7

Find and color Mimi, Dylan, Katy and Leo.

- Children find and color the characters.

Ask and say.

- Children ask and answer questions about what they do at school.

Closing time

Learning review (see TB p 18)
Closing routines (see TB p 16)
Goodbye song and puppet (CD1 Track 3; see TB p 17 & 21)

Use the **Navio App** to watch the video, and encourage children to do the same at home.

Lesson 4 Story Song

School

Watch. Listen, point and sing *Katy Kangaroo*. Trace ✔ or ✘ to show what Katy does and doesn't want to do. Trace and color Katy. Ask and say. Language: color, count, draw, jump, paint; Do you want to (draw)? Yes, I do. / No, I don't. I want to (jump).

8

Learning objectives

- Watch, sing and act out the story song *Katy Kangaroo*
- Listen to the story again and order the story cards
- Identify and say school activities
- Ask and say what you want to do

Materials

- Class CDs, printable story cards, flashcards, *Ferris Wheel* mat, Mimi puppet

Main vocabulary

- color, count, draw, jump, paint

Key language

- Do you want to (draw)? Yes, I do. / No, I don't. I want to (jump).

Teacher's tip: Learning a song in stages

Children need to listen to a song a number of times before being able to sing it confidently. You may need to play the song several times. Encourage children to join in first with the actions, then key words and repeated sections until they are confidently singing the whole song.

Circle time

Hello song and puppet (CD1 Track 2; see TB p 17 & 21)
Opening routines (see TB p 16)
Recycling activity (school activities) (see TB p 19)
Lesson aims (see TB p 18)

Retell the story *A new friend*.

- Watch the video, play the audio or read the story using the printable story cards.
- Demonstrate that children should wave their arms in the air every time they hear a school activity in the story.

Order the story cards.

- Put the printable story cards face up in jumbled order on the board. Invite children to take turns putting the cards in the correct order.
- Use the story cards to reconstruct a brief version of the story encouraging children to join in.

***Katy Kangaroo* song**

CD1 Track 28

- Play the video. Children watch and name the school activities in the song.
- Repeat. Pause after each verse and invite individual children to stick the activity flashcard on the board.
- Play the video again. Children listen, sing and act out the song (by miming the activities and pretending to jump like a kangaroo).

Pretend to be Katy Kangaroo.

- Children pretend to be Katy Kangaroo (knees bent, arms between legs ready to jump). Ask e.g. *Do you want to draw?* Children respond *No, I don't. I want to jump!* (and jump in place).
- Repeat asking questions about all the activities in the song.

Table time

Student's Book p 8

Watch. Listen, point and sing *Katy Kangaroo*.

CD1 Track 28

- Play the song (see TB p 33). Children listen, sing and point to the pictures.
- Remember that you can use the karaoke version of the song when children are confident.

Trace ✔ or ✘ to who what Katy does and doesn't want to do.

- Demonstrate that children should trace the ✔ under the picture of activities Katy wants to do and the ✘ under the picture of activities she doesn't want to do.

Trace and color Katy.

- The children trace and color the picture of Katy Kangaroo in the middle of the page.

Ask and say.

- Children pretend to be Katy and ask and answer questions about all the activities e.g. One child asks *Do you want to color?* and another child (as Katy) responds *No, I don't.*

Activity Book p 8

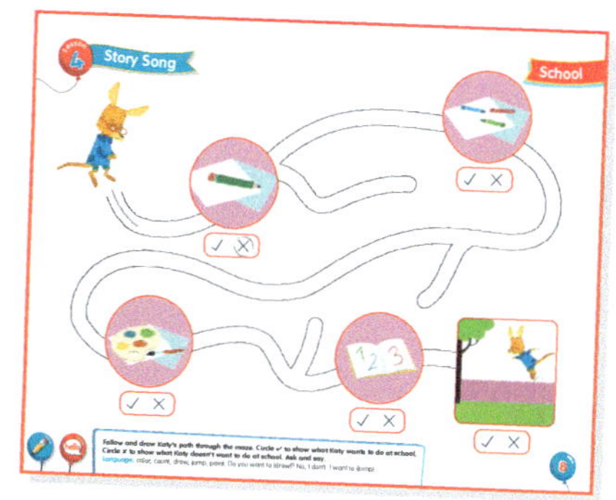

Follow and draw Katy's path through the maze.

- Children draw the path through the maze.

Circle ✔ to show what Katy wants to do at school. Circle ✘ to show what Katy doesn't want to do at school.

- Children circle the ✔ by each picture to show what Katy wants to do. They circle the ✘ to show what Katy doesn't want to do.

Ask and say.

- Children ask and answer questions about what they want to do.

Closing time

Learning review (see TB p 18)
Closing routines (see TB p 16)
Goodbye song and puppet (CD1 Track 3; see TB p 17 & 21)

Use the **Navio App** to watch the video, and encourage children to do the same at home.

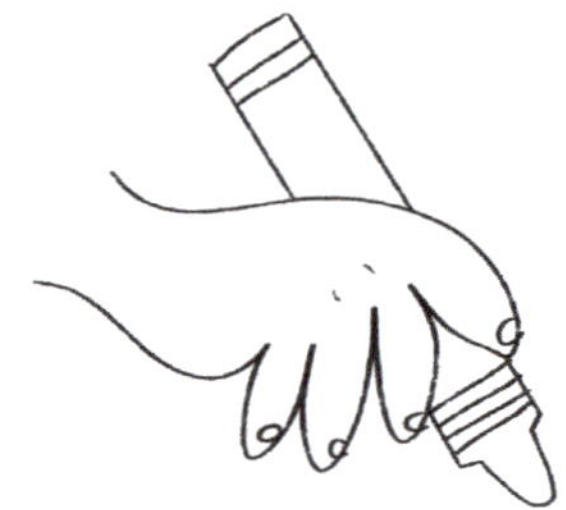

hello

Watch. Listen and point. Circle what Alex and Lucy want to do. Color what you want to do. Ask and say. Language: color, dance, draw, paint, play, sing; Do you want to (paint)? Yes, I do. / No, I don't. I want to (play outside). I don't want to (draw).

9

Learning objectives

- Ask and say what school activities you want to do
- Watch, understand and enjoy a video
- Identify school activities in the video

Materials

- Class CDs, flashcards, *Ferris Wheel* mat, Mimi puppet

Main vocabulary

- color, dance, draw, paint, play, sing

Key language

- Do you want to (paint)? Yes, I do. / No, I don't. I want to (play outside). I don't want to (draw).

Teacher's tip: Giving time to speak

Life skills

As this is the first lesson of the year with a focus on speaking, you may find children are quiet or reluctant to speak on their own. This is completely normal. It is important not to force any child to speak if he/she is not ready. Ask the questions yourself and encourage any children not yet ready to speak to use non-verbal responses.

Circle time

Hello song and puppet (CD1 Track 2; see TB p 17 & 21)
Opening routines (see TB p 16)
Recycling activity (story song) (CD1 Track 28; see TB p 19)
Lesson aims (see TB p 18)

Game: ***Stand up if you want to …***

- Give out the flashcards to individual children.
- Say e.g. *Stand up if you want to dance!* Demonstrate this.
- The child with the flashcard stands up, shows the flashcard to the class and says *I want to run.*
- Repeat with the other flashcards.

Game: ***Do you want to … ?***

- Give out the flashcards face down to individual children or pairs. Children look at their flashcard but don't show anyone.
- Get the class to ask one child or pair with you in chorus, e.g. *Do you want to paint?*
- Encourage children to answer *Yes, I do. / No, I don't.* depending on the flashcard they have.
- Repeat with different children.

Watch the video.

- Explain that Alex and Lucy are talking to their Auntie Vicky. It's raining and Auntie Vicky is asking them what they want to do.
- Ask *What do Alex and Lucy want to do?* Children guess.
- Play the video and check the answer (sing and dance).
- Watch again. Pause and children repeat the questions and answers.

Table time

Student's Book p 9 Life skills

Watch. Listen and point.

- Children identify Alex, Lucy and Auntie Vicky and the activities around the photo.
- Play the audio or video. Use the pause button. Children listen and point to the pictures.

Circle what Alex and Lucy want to do.

- Children circle the picture that shows what Alex and Lucy want to do.

CD1 Track 30

Auntie Vicky: Oh, no. It's raining. We can't play outside. Do you want to draw?
Lucy: No, I don't. I want to play outside.
Auntie Vicky: Do you want to color?
Alex: No, I don't.
Auntie Vicky: Do you want to paint?
Lucy: No, I don't.
Auntie Vicky: Umm. Do you want to play a game?
Alex: No, I don't.
Auntie Vicky: Aha. I have an idea. Do you want to sing and dance?
Lucy and Alex: No, I don't. Oh, yes, please, Auntie Vicky!
Lucy: Woohoo! This is great! I don't want to color. I don't want to play a game.
Alex: I don't want to draw. I don't want to paint. And I don't want to play outside!
Alex: I want to sing and dance!
Lucy: Me, too!

Color what you want to do.

- Children color the activities they want to do.

Ask and say.

- Children ask and answer questions about what they want to do.

Activity Book p 9

Imagine it's raining. Draw a picture to show what you want to do.

- Tell children to imagine it is raining so they can't go outside. Children draw a picture of an activity they want to do inside.

Ask and say.

- Children ask and answer questions about what they want to do when it's raining.

Closing time

Learning review (see TB p 18)
Closing routines (see TB p 16)
Goodbye song and puppet (CD1 Track 3; see TB p 17 & 21)

Use the **Navio App** to watch the video, and encourage children to do the same at home.

Lesson 6 Values Being kind

Listen and point to the story. Say. Color the child being kind at school.
Language: color, help, play, share, sit down; bag, banana, coat, crayons, friend, home, school; happy, sad; Do you want to (play)? I like/don't like (school). I'm (happy). I want to (go home).

SOCIAL AND EMOTIONAL LEARNING

10

Learning objectives

- Recognize the value of being kind
- Understand and enjoy a story about being kind
- Identify who's being kind
- Say how you are kind

Materials

- Class CDs, flashcards, *Ferris Wheel* mat, Mimi puppet

Main vocabulary

- color, help, play, share, sit down; bag, banana, coat, crayons, friend, home, school; happy, sad

Key language

- Do you want to (play)? I like/don't like school. I'm (happy). I want to (go home).

Teacher's tip: Building social awareness

Emphasize the importance of being nice to any new children. Do a mini role-play with some children pretending to be new at school. Encourage the others to include them in different school activities asking e.g. *Do you want to paint? Do you want to sing?* Use the activity flashcards and scaffold the questions.

Circle time

Hello song and puppet (CD1 Track 2; see TB p 17 & 21)

Opening routines (see TB p 16)

Recycling activity *(Do you want to...? Yes, I do. / No, I don't.)* (see TB p 19)

Lesson aims (see TB p 18)

Watch the *A new friend* story video.

- Play the story video.
- Take the part of Mrs. Cat yourself. Encourage children to join in acting out the story in three groups (Mimi, Katy, Dylan/Leo).
- Ask e.g. *Is Katy sad at school? (Yes) Is Mimi kind to Katy? (Yes). Are you kind to friends at school? Is it important to be kind? How are you kind?*

Story about being kind from *Little Book of Values.*

CD1 Track 31

- Use the Mimi puppet to explain that Mimi and Dylan have a book called *Little Book of Values* with stories about a brother and sister called Harry and Zoe. In this story, Jake is a new boy at school.
- Say *Listen and find out. Are Harry and Zoe kind to Jake? (Yes) How are they kind? (Zoe shows Jake where to put his coat and bag, Harry invites Jake to sit with him, Zoe shares her crayons with Jake, Harry asks Jake to play at playtime, Zoe shares her banana with Jake)*
- Play the audio. Check the answers.
- Play the audio again. Use the pause button to review the ways Harry and Zoe are kind to Jake.

Table time

Student's Book p 10

Listen and point to the story. Say.

CD1 Track 31

- Play the audio of the story. Children listen and point to the pictures.
- Ask *Is Jake happy or sad at the beginning of the story? (Sad) Is Jake happy or sad at the end of the story? (Happy) What do Harry and Zoe do to make Jake happy? What do you do to be kind to your friends at school?*

Color the child being kind at school.

- Children draw a picture to show how they're kind to friends at school.

Activity Book p 10

Circle the pictures of children being kind at school.

- Children circle the pictures of children being kind.

Say how you are kind at school.

- Children talk about how they are kind.

Closing time

Learning review (see TB p 18)

Closing routines (see TB p 16)

Goodbye song and puppet (CD1 Track 3; see TB p 17 & 21)

Use the **Navio App** to listen to the story, and encourage children to do the same at home.

Lesson 7 Content

1:32

Listen and point. Match the activities to Auntie Vicky, Alex and Lucy. Circle the exercise you do. Ask and say. **Language:** dance, play soccer, ride my bike, run, swim, walk (to school); What exercise do you do? I (play soccer).

11

Learning objectives

- Identify and name activities we do to get exercise
- Listen and identify the activities
- Ask and say activities you do to get exercise

Materials

- Class CDs, printable content flashcards, *Ferris Wheel* mat, Mimi puppet

Main vocabulary

- dance, play soccer, ride my bike, run, swim, walk (to school)

Key language

- What exercise do you do? I (play soccer).

Teacher's tip: Being active

Life skills

It's important to encourage young children to enjoy doing exercise. Once the children are familiar with the new vocabulary, ask them which activities they do regularly. Set up a wall chart to record the different types of exercise the children do.

Circle time

Hello song and puppet (CD1 Track 2; see TB p 17 & 21)
Opening routines (see TB p 16)
Recycling activity (see TB p 19)
Lesson aims (see TB p 18)

Introduce content vocabulary.

- Use the printable flashcards and the puppet to introduce the new activities (dance, play soccer, swim, ride my bike, run, walk). Children repeat the words.
- Say the words and demonstrate miming the activities. Repeat several times. Reverse the procedure, mime the activities yourself and children say the words.
- Explain that all these activities give us exercise and are good for us.

Sort the flashcards.

- Put all the school activity flashcards on the board. Children identify the activities.
- Ask children to help you sort the activities into two sets: activities which give you exercise e.g. *run*, *dance* and activities which don't give you exercise e.g. *paint*.
- Collect the seven flashcards that give you exercise and challenge children to recall them. Prompt with mime as necessary.

Game: *Freeze!*

- Children stand up. Name an activity that gives you exercise. Children mime or do the activity in place. Say *Freeze!* Children stay as still as they can and name the activity. Repeat with different activities.

Table time

Student's Book p 11

Listen and point. Match the activities to Auntie Vicky, Alex and Lucy.

- Say *Alex and Lucy are talking to Auntie Vicky about what they do to get exercise.*
- Play the audio. Children listen and match the characters and activities with their fingers.

CD1 Track 32

Auntie Vicky: When you run, you get exercise. Exercise is good for you. What exercise do you do, Lucy?
Lucy: Umm. I dance. I play soccer. Oh, yes, and I walk to school.
Auntie Vicky: What exercise do you do, Alex?
Alex: I swim. Umm. I ride my bike. And I walk to school too.
Auntie Vicky: Great!
Lucy: And what exercise do you do, Auntie Vicky?
Auntie Vicky: Well, I run. I swim. And I ride my bike too.
Lucy: I like exercise!
Alex: Me, too!

- Play the audio again. Children listen and draw a line to match the characters and activities. Use the pause button as necessary.
- Play the audio again and check the answers. (Lucy: dance, play soccer, walk. Alex: swim, ride my bike, walk. Auntie Vicky: run, swim, ride my bike)

Circle the exercise you do.

- Children circle the activities they do to get exercise.

Ask and say.

- Children take turns asking and saying what they do.

Activity Book p 11

Circle the activities you do. Draw and color a picture of you doing exercise.

- Children circle all the pictures of activities they like to do. They draw and color a picture of themselves doing exercise.

Ask and say.

- Children ask and answer questions about what they do to exercise.

Closing time

Learning review (see TB p 18)
Closing routines (see TB p 16)
Goodbye song and puppet (CD1 Track 3; see TB p 17 & 21)

Use the **Navio App** to play the vocabulary and language games, and encourage children to do the same at home.

Lesson 8 Culture

1 2 3 4

Watch. Listen, point and sing *Go in and out the window*. Match and number the photos in order.
Language: dance, go, shake hands, stand; partner, window; numbers 1–4

12

Learning objectives

- Watch, sing and act out the traditional song *Go in and out the window*
- Play an action game
- Order and name the actions in the song

Materials

- Class CDs, flashcards, *Ferris Wheel* mat, Mimi puppet

Main vocabulary

- dance, go, shake hands, stand, partner, window; numbers 1–4

Teacher's tip: Videoing children's performance

Encourage the children to give their best performance of the song by videoing them*. Allow the children to watch the video. You could also show it to the parents or upload it to the school blog.

*Check first to make sure parents or carers have granted permission for you to do this.

Circle time

Hello song and puppet (CD1 Track 2; see TB p 17 & 21)
Opening routines (see TB p 16)
Recycling activity (see TB p 19)
Lesson aims (see TB p 18)

Game: *Mimi says ...*

- Explain that children are going to learn a traditional song and dance that also gives them exercise.
- Children stand in a circle and hold hands at shoulder height leaving space between. Say *These are the "windows."*
- Choose a child and say *Go in and out the windows.* Demonstrate that the child moves around the circle weaving in and out of the "windows." Repeat several times with different children.
- Give instructions for other lines of the song in turn: *Stand and face your partner. / Dance around together. / Shake hands with your partner.* Demonstrate the actions and children respond.
- Use the puppet to give instructions in random order e.g. *Mimi says shake hands with your partner!* Speed up as children get more confident in responding.

Go in and out the window song

CD1 Track 33

- Children stay standing in a circle. Say *Now let's learn the song "Go in and out the window."*
- Demonstrate the actions for the song (as above).
- Play the audio. Children listen and do the actions for the song with you. Choose two children on opposite sides of the circle to "go in and out the windows."
- Repeat. Children join in singing and dancing the song.

Watch the *Go in and out the window* song video.

- Children watch the video and join in singing the song and doing the actions with Alex and Lucy.

Table time

Student's Book p 12

Watch. Listen, point and sing *Go in and out the window.*

CD1 Track 33

- Play the audio. Children listen and point to the photos.

Match and number the photos in order.

- Children match and number the photos in order.

Activity Book p 12

Match the children doing the same actions.

- Children match the pictures that show the same actions.

Point and say.

- Children point and say the actions.

Closing time

Learning review (see TB p 18)
Closing routines (see TB p 16)
Goodbye song and puppet (CD1 Track 3; see TB p 17 & 21)

Use the **Navio App** to watch the video, and encourage children to do the same at home.

Review

I can ...

Vocabulary

Story

Speaking

Content

Circle the school activities you know. Listen, point and say. Listen and answer. Ask and say. Complete the faces to show what you can do. Language: color, count, dance, draw, jump, paint, play, run, sing, think; What do you do at school? I (draw) at school. Do you want to (sing)? Yes. / No. I want/don't want to (color).

13

Learning objectives

- Review what you have learned in this unit
- Complete a self-evaluation
- Point to and say the school activities you want to do

Materials

- Class CDs, flashcards, *Ferris Wheel* mat, Mimi puppet

Main vocabulary

- color, count, dance, draw, jump, paint, play, run, sing, think

Key language

- What do you do at school? I (draw) at school. Do you want to (sing)? Yes. / No. I want/don't want to (color).

Teacher's tip: Familiarizing children with self-evaluation

If the children are new to *Ferris Wheel*, they may not yet have been exposed to the idea of self-evaluation. Give plenty of praise and encouragement as they complete the review and point out everything that they have learned during the unit.

Circle time

Hello song and puppet (CD1 Track 2; see TB p 17 & 21)
Opening routines (see TB p 16)
Recycling activity (see TB p 19)
Lesson aims (see TB p 18)

School activity flashcard games

- Choose one or two flashcard games with the *Ferris Wheel* mat and/or the puppet to review main vocabulary (see TB p 20 & 21).

Sing *What do you do at school?*

CD1 Track 25

- Play the audio. Children sing and do the actions.
- Children ask and answer questions about what they do at school.

Game: *Guess the action.*

- Hide one of the action flashcards behind your back. Children guess which action by asking *Do you want to (sing)?* and you respond.

Game: *What do you do at school?*

- Put the children into pairs. Show one of the action flashcards and use the puppet to ask e.g. *What do you do at school?* One child repeats the question and the other answers e.g. *I draw*. Change roles and repeat for all the actions.

Watch the story video.

- Children watch the story video. Ask *Who is Mimi's new friend? How is Mimi kind to her new friend?*

Table time

Student's Book p 13

Circle the school activities you know.

- Explain and demonstrate the activity.

Listen, point and say.

- Play the audio. Children check the words they know, point to the pictures and repeat the words.

CD1 Track 34

Mimi: I'm the teacher! Can you remember the school activities, Dylan?
Dylan: Yes, I can. Draw.
Mimi: Draw.
Dylan: Color.
Mimi: Color.
Dylan: Paint.
Mimi: Paint.
Dylan: Sing.
Mimi: Sing.
Dylan: Play.
Mimi: Play.
Dylan: Dance.
Mimi: Dance.
Dylan: Count
Mimi: Count.
Dylan: Run.
Mimi: Run.
Dylan: Jump.
Mimi: Jump.
Dylan: Think.
Mimi: Think. Well done, Dylan!
Both: Fantastic!

Listen and answer. Ask and say.

- Play the audio. Children listen to the questions.

CD1 Track 35

Mimi: What do you do at school?
Do you want to draw?
Do you want to color?
Do you want to sing?
Do you want to run?
Do you want to play?

- Play the audio again. Children listen, repeat and answer the questions.
- Children ask and answer questions about what they want to do.

Complete the faces to show what you can do.

- Explain the four pictures: *I can name school activities; I can understand the story; I can ask and answer questions about school activities; I can identify activities which give me exercise.*
- Demonstrate that children should complete the face with a smile or downturned mouth depending on how well they think they have done in the unit.
- Monitor and encourage children to think positively about their progress.

Activity Book p 13

Complete the faces to show what you do at school. Ask and say.

- Children complete the faces with a smile if they do the action at school.
- Children ask and answer questions about what they do at school and what they want to do.

Think and circle the number to show your progress.

- Children think about their progress in the unit and circle the number.

Closing time

Learning review (see TB p 18)
Closing routines (see TB p 16)
Goodbye song and puppet (CD1 Track 3; see TB p 17 & 21)

Use the **Navio App** to review what children have learned in this unit, and encourage them to do the same at home.

Project

COOPERATIVE LEARNING

Choose and paint your favorite school activity. Glue your picture on the chart. Ask and say. **Language:** dance, paint, play, sing; colors; numbers; chart; What do you do at school? I (dance) at school. How many people (dance)? (Four). Do you want to (paint)? Yes, I do. / No, I don't. I want to (play). I don't want to (sing). I like the (blue) pictures.

14

Learning objectives

- Work together to do a collaborative project
- Paint a picture of your favorite school activity
- Ask and answer questions about the project

Materials

- Class CDs, Mimi puppet, photocopiable templates, colored card, finger paints, glue
- optional: crayons

Main vocabulary

- dance, paint, play, sing; colors; numbers; chart, fantastic, great, picture

Key language

- What do you do at school? I (dance) at school. How many people (dance)? (Four). Do you want to (paint)? Yes, I do. / No, I don't. I want to (play). I don't want to (sing). I like the (blue) pictures.

Teacher's tip: Using a quiet signal

COOPERATIVE LEARNING

Before starting to give the instructions for the project, make sure you have everyone's full attention. Using a "quiet signal" is very effective. You can ring a small bell to signal children should stop what they are doing and listen to you, or you can simply raise your hand or count down from five. Wait until everyone is quiet and looking at you before beginning to give the instructions.

Circle time

Hello song and puppet (CD1 Track 2; see TB p 17 & 21)
Opening routines (see TB p 16)
Recycling activity (see TB p 19)
Lesson aims (see TB p 18)

Prepare for your project.

- Say *Let's do a project and make a chart of our favorite school activities!*
- Explain the color code for the chart by sticking the flashcards of *paint / pink*; *sing / green*; *play / blue*; *dance / yellow*; in pairs on the board.
- Show children the activity template. Explain that children should choose their favorite school activity from the selection of templates and paint it, then stick it on the appropriate colored card.
- Explain and demonstrate that children will then use their pictures to make a chart of their favorite activities.

Table time

COOPERATIVE LEARNING

Student's Book p 14

Choose and paint your favorite school activity.

- Say e.g. *We're going to make our activity chart like this. Look at what we need for our project: colored cards for our pictures, finger paints, glue.* Children listen and point to the pictures.
- Give a copy of the project template to each child. Make sure children have finger paints available.
- Children paint their favorite school activity.

Glue your picture on the chart.

- Following the flashcard color key on the board, children stick their activity to the correct colored card. They then stick their cards in the correct place on the chart you have prepared.

Ask and say.

- Explain how the chart works to show how many children like each activity. Talk about the pictures and chart using language of the unit and other language children know.
- Ask children *Do you like our activity chart?* Make the point that everyone has helped make the activity chart and that they couldn't have made such a beautiful chart on their own.

Alternative version of project

- Children could use crayons instead of finger paints to color their activity template.

Activity Book p 14

Find and glue a photo of you doing an activity.

- Children find a photo of themselves doing an activity from the unit and glue it on the page.

Circle the picture of the activity. Ask and say.

- Children circle the activity they are doing in the photo, then ask and answer questions about it.

Closing time

Learning review (see TB p 18)
Closing routines (see TB p 16)
Goodbye song and puppet (CD1 Track 3; see TB p 17 & 21)

The park
Mimi's kite

Vocabulary and language

- **Main vocabulary:** bench, flowers, grass, merry-go-round, path, pond, seesaw, slide, swings, trees
- **Key language:** There's a (pond). There are (trees). Is there (grass)? Are there (trees)?
- **Content language:** flower, leaves, plant, roots, seed, sun, water; There's (a seed). There are (leaves).
- **Other language:** kite, windy; clean, park, trash, trash can; apples, cake, cookies, ears, eyes; house, teeth, wolf; It's (windy). Where's (Mommy)? Under the (tree). On the (bench). Put your (trash) in the (trash can). I put my trash in the trash can. What's in the park? How many (trees)? (Six). My (seesaw) is (red). I like the (slide). Do you like the (slide)? Yes. / No.

Unit objectives

- Identify and name things in the park
- Sing the language song *There's a pond in the park*
- Say what there is in the park
- Understand and act out the story *Mimi's kite*
- Sing and act out the story song *Fly the kite*
- Ask and say what there is in the park
- Sing the values song *Put your trash in the trash can*
- Recognize the value of looking after the environment
- Learn about the life cycle of a plant
- Understand the traditional story *Little Red Riding Hood*
- Review your learning and progress
- Participate in a collaborative project

Story

CD1 Track 42

Picture 1

Narrator: Mimi and Dylan are in the park with Mommy and Daddy. Mimi has her kite.
Mimi: Look at my kite, Dylan. It's in the air.
Dylan: Where?
Mimi: Look, up there!
Dylan: Oh, wow! There's the kite!
Mimi: It's beautiful.

Picture 2

Narrator: Suddenly, it's very windy.
Mimi: Quick! Help me, Dylan!
Dylan: Yes, Mimi.
Narrator: Mimi and Dylan pull and pull, but the kite is strong.

Picture 3

Mimi: Oh, look! We're in the air. There's the path and there's the pond.
Dylan: Oh, yes. And look, Mimi. There are the trees and flowers. Where's Mommy?
Mimi: She's on the bench.
Dylan: Oh, yes. And where's Daddy?
Mimi: He's under the tree. Watch out Dylan! There's a tree.

Picture 4

Dylan: Oh, no.
Mimi: Mommy! Daddy! Help us please!
Mommy: Don't worry!

Picture 5

Narrator: Mommy and Daddy talk to the gardener.
Mommy: Look! Mimi and Dylan are in the tree.
Daddy: Can you help us, please?
Gardener: Yes, of course.
Daddy: Oh, thank you.

Picture 6

Mommy: Phew, what an adventure!
Daddy: You're safe now!
Mimi & Dylan: Yippee! Thank you.
Dylan: Are there swings in the park?
Gardener: Yes.
Mimi: Is there a slide in the park?
Gardener: Yes. Look. Over there.
Mimi: Oh, great. Can we play on the swings and slide now, please?
Dylan: We don't want to fly the kite!
Mommy & Daddy: Yes, of course!

Songs and story

Language song

There's a pond in the park CD1 Track 40

There's a pond in the park (Make a circular motion with hands)
There are trees and flowers too (Bring hands upward and separate)
And there's a bench to sit on (Mime sitting)
A bench for me and you! (Point to self then hold out both arms)

There's a pond in the park
There are trees and flowers too
And there's a path to walk on (Make walking motion with fingers)
A path for me and you!

There's a pond in the park
There are trees and flowers too
And there's grass to lie on (Mime lying down)
Grass for me and you!

There's a pond in the park
There are trees and flowers too
And there are swings to play on (Move arms back and forth)
Swings for me and you!

Story song

Fly the kite CD1 Track 43

Fly, fly, fly the kite. Look! It's in the air. (Mime flying a kite, then look up in the air)
There's the kite. There's the kite. (Point excitedly)
Where? Look over there! (Shrug, then point)

Fly, fly, fly the kite. Now we're in the air. (Mime flying a kite, then lift your arms and turn around)
There's the pond. There's the pond. (Make a circular motion with hands)
Where? Look over there!

Fly, fly, fly the kite. Now we're in the air.
There are the trees. There are the trees. (Bring hands upward and separate)
Where? Look over there!

Fly, fly, fly the kite. Now we're in the air.
There are the flowers. There are the flowers. (Mime smelling a flower)
Where? Look over there!

Fly, fly, fly the kite. Oh dear! We're in the tree. (Place hand on forehead)
Help us please! Help us please! (Place hands together)
Now we're safe! Yippee! (Punch both fists in the air)

Values song

Put your trash in the trash can, in the trash can CD1 Track 46

Put your trash in the trash can, in the trash can (mime putting trash in the trash can)
Put your trash in the trash can, in the trash can (repeat)
Play in the park, Have a lot of fun (skip in place, then wave arms)
Keep it clean
For everyone, everyone (open arms wide)
(Repeat)

Culture story

Little Red Riding Hood CD1 Track 48

Picture 1

Narrator: Little Red Riding Hood is going to visit Grandma.
Mommy: Here's a basket of food for Grandma: cookies, cake and apples.
LRRH: Thank you, Mommy.
Mommy: Now remember, Little Red Riding Hood. Stay on the path. Don't talk to strangers.
LRRH: Yes, Mommy. Goodbye!
Mommy: Goodbye.

Picture 2

Narrator: In the forest there are trees and flowers. Little Red Riding Hood stops to pick flowers for Grandma. Suddenly a wolf appears.
Wolf: Hello, little one.
LRRH: Oh, hello.
Wolf: Where are you going?
LRRH: To see my Grandma. She lives in the house over there.
Wolf: Ahhaa.
Narrator: The wolf runs to Grandma's house.

Picture 3

Narrator: Little Red Riding Hood arrives at Grandma's house. She looks at the wolf.
LRRH: Grandma, what big eyes you have!
Wolf: To see you, little one!
LRRH: Grandma, what big ears you have!
Wolf: To hear you, little one!
LRRH: Grandma, what big teeth you have!
Wolf: To eat you, little one!

Picture 4

Narrator: Suddenly, Daddy appears. The wolf runs away.
Daddy: You're safe now, Little Red Riding Hood.
LRRH: You're safe now, Grandma.
Grandma: Oh, thank you!

The park
Mimi's kite

Vocabulary Lesson 1

Listen, point and repeat. Listen and stick the park stickers. Listen and play *Memory*. Circle the things in your park. Say. **Language:** bench, merry-go-round, pond, seesaw, slide, swing; blue, green, orange, pink, red, yellow; Where's (the seesaw)? It's on (pink).

15

Learning objectives

- Identify and name things in the park
- Listen and point to things in the park
- Remember things in a park in a memory game

Materials

- Class CDs, flashcards, *Ferris Wheel* mat, Mimi puppet

Main vocabulary

- bench, merry-go-round, pond, seesaw, slide, swing; blue, green, orange, pink, red, yellow

Teacher's tip: Safety at the park

Life skills

After introducing the park vocabulary, remind the children that safety is important at the park. Ask them if they go up or down the slide. Ask if they sit down or stand up on the swings and seesaw and if they hold on with one or two hands. Use the children's responses to establish essential safety rules.

Circle time

Hello song and puppet (CD1 Track 2; see TB p 17 & 21)
Opening routines (see TB p 16)
Lesson aims (see TB p 18)

Introduce things in the park.

- Ask children if they go to the park. Ask them what they see there. As they respond in their shared language, show the flashcards and children repeat the words in English.
- Put the *Ferris Wheel* mat on the floor or board with the park flashcards face down (one on each color). Use the puppet to turn them over and name them. The children repeat the words.

Game: ***Say the color!***

- Name the things in the park on the Ferris Wheel and children name the color. Then the reverse.

Game: ***Sort the flashcards!***

- Put the flashcards on the board in jumbled order. Say e.g. *Can you find things to play on in the park? (swing, slide, seesaw, merry-go-round).* Children name the flashcards and group them together.
- Ask children e.g. *Do you go on the swing in the park? Do you like the swing?*

Table time

Student's Book p 15

Listen, point and repeat.

- Play the audio. The children listen, point to each item as they hear it, and repeat the words.

CD1 Track 36

Mimi: Look Dylan! Slide …pond … swing … seesaw … merry-go-round. Repeat, Dylan!
Dylan: Yes, Mimi. Slide …pond … swing … seesaw … merry-go-round.
Mimi: Very good, Dylan! Let's name the park words together!
Both: Slide …pond … swing … seesaw … merry-go-round. Fantastic!

- Draw children's attention to the question mark in their books. They identify the missing item (bench).

Listen and stick the park stickers.

- Play the audio. The children listen and point to the items in their books.

CD1 Track 37

Where's the pond? It's on … orange.
Where's the slide? It's on … blue.
Where's the seesaw? It's on … pink.
Where's the swing? It's on … yellow.
Where's the merry-go-round? It's on … green.
Where's the bench? Can you guess? It's on … red.
Yes, yes, yes! The bench is on red. Yes, yes, yes!

- Ask questions about all the things in the park in the same way and children respond.
- Play the audio again. Children listen and stick the park stickers.

Listen and play *Memory*.

- Children copy you covering your eyes with your hands. Play the audio. Children listen and remember the park item on each color on the wheel.

CD1 Track 38

Close your eyes
One, two, three
Say the words
Play memory!
Blue … slide!
Red … bench!
Yellow … swing!
Green … merry-go-round!
Pink … seesaw!
Orange … pond!

- Play the game.

Circle the things in your park. Say.

- Children circle things they see in their park, then point and say the words.

Activity Book p 15

Look and match.

- Children match the things in the park.

Color, point and say.

- They color the pictures and point and say the words.

Closing time

Learning review (see TB p 18)
Closing routines (see TB p 16)
Goodbye song and puppet (CD1 Track 3; see TB p 17 & 21)

Use the **Navio App** to play the vocabulary game, and encourage children to do the same at home.

Lesson 2 Language

The park

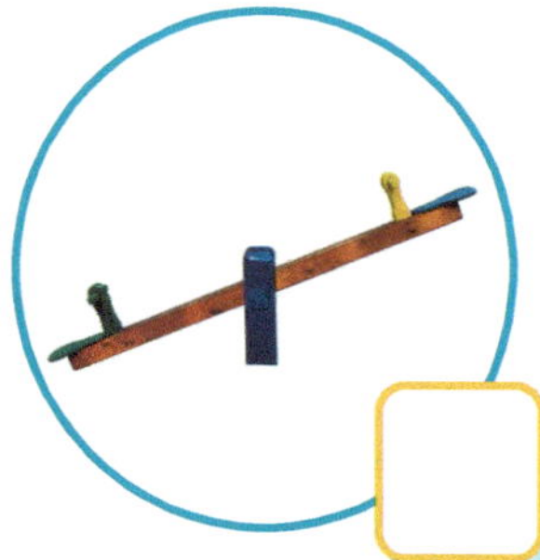

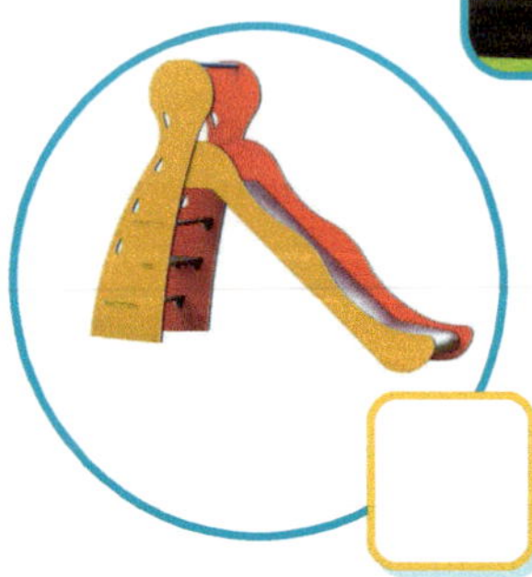

Listen and find the new park words. Listen, point and sing *There's a pond in the park.* Check (✓) the park objects in the song. Say. Language: bench, flowers, grass, merry-go-round, path, pond, seesaw, slide, swings, trees; There's (a pond). There are (trees).

16

Learning objectives

- Talk about things in the park
- Identify and name four new things in the park
- Sing the language song *There's a pond in the park*
- Say what there is in the park

Materials

- Class CDs, flashcards, *Ferris Wheel* mat, Mimi puppet

Main vocabulary

- bench, flowers, grass, merry-go-round, path, pond, seesaw, slide, swing, trees

Key language

- There's (a pond). There are (trees).

Teacher's tip: Making a vocabulary wall

Make a vocabulary wall on one of the classroom walls. Stick pictures of the vocabulary items from the topic you are working on. Encourage the children to draw the vocabulary items and add them to the display.

Circle time

Hello song and puppet (CD1 Track 2; see TB p 17 & 21)
Opening routines (see TB p 16)
Recycling activity (six park words from lesson 1) (see TB p 19)
Lesson aims (see TB p 18)

Introduce the new things in the park.

- Put the park flashcards on the floor or board.
- Children identify the four new words (*trees, flowers, path, grass*).
- Use the puppet to point to and say the words in turn. Children repeat the words in chorus.
- Stick the four new flashcards on different walls in the classroom. Say e.g. *Point to the trees!* and children respond.
- Repeat with actions and pairs or small groups of children e.g. *Jump to the flowers!*

Introduce *There's a ... / There are ...*

- Tell the children about a park near your house. Show a real photo or use the flashcards to describe it e.g. *There's a pond. / There's a path. / There are trees. / There are flowers.* Children repeat.
- Encourage children to point to a flashcard and say a sentence about a park they know. Be ready to recast the sentences, but do not attempt any kind of grammatical explanation.

Game: ***Guess what's in the park!***

- Choose four of the flashcards e.g. *trees, flowers, path* and *bench*, and children say the words.
- Use the puppet to turn the flashcards face down and mix them up.
- Point to one flashcard and say *Guess what's in the park!* Children respond e.g. *There's a bench. / There are trees.* The child who guesses correctly mixes up the flashcards and points to another one. Children guess in the same way. Repeat several times.

***There's a pond in the park* song**

CD1 Track 40

- Put the park flashcards face up on the floor or board.
- Hold up the flashcards of Alex and Lucy. Say *Let's listen and find out about the park near Alex and Lucy. What is there in the park?*
- Play the audio. Children listen and point to the flashcards with you as they hear them in the song.
- Children say sentences about what's in the park (pond, trees, flowers, bench, path, grass, swings).
- Play the audio again. Children join in singing the song. They point to themselves and hold out both arms in the last line of each verse.
- Remember that you can use the karaoke version of the song when children are confident.

Table time

Student's Book p 16

Listen and find the new park words.

- Children listen and find the four new park words. Repeat and children say the words.

CD1 Track 39

One ... two ... Which words are new?
Trees! Trees! *Path! Path!*
Flowers! Flowers! *Grass! Grass!*

Listen, point and sing *There's a pond in the park.*

- Play the song. Children listen and point to the photos.

Check (✔) the park objects in the song. Say.

- Play the song again with pauses. Children should choose the photos if they are in the song.
- Children look at the photos they have chosen and say what's in the park e.g. *There are trees.*

Activity Book p 16

Find and circle five differences.

- Children find and circle five differences.

Point and say.

- Children point and describe the differences e.g. *(In 1) there's a pond. / (In 2) there are trees.*

Closing time

Learning review (see TB p 18)
Closing routines (see TB p 16)
Goodbye song and puppet (CD1 Track 3; see TB p 17 & 21)

Use the **Navio App** to listen to the song, and encourage children to do the same at home.

Lesson 3

Story

Watch. Listen to the story *Mimi's kite*. Circle the weather in the story. Stick the story sticker.
Language: bench, flowers, kite, path, pond, slide, swings, trees; windy; It's (windy). There's (the pond). There are (the flowers). Is there (a slide)? Are there (swings)? Where's (Mommy)? Under (the tree). On (the bench).

17

Learning objectives

- Watch, understand and enjoy the story *Mimi's kite*
- Make a prediction about the story
- Identify the weather in the story

Materials

- Class CDs, printable story cards, flashcards, *Ferris Wheel* mat, Mimi puppet

Main vocabulary

- bench, flowers, kite, path, pond, slide, swings, trees, windy

Key language

- It's (windy). There's the (pond). There are (the flowers). Is there (a slide)? Are there (swings)? Where's (Mommy)? Under the (tree). On the (bench).

Teacher's tip: Identifying emotions

Ask the children how they think Mimi and Dylan feel when they are up in the air with the kite (scared). Ask how they feel after the adventure is over (happy). Ask how they think Mommy and Daddy feel. Ask them to think about when they feel scared, happy etc.

Circle time

Hello song and puppet (CD1 Track 2; see TB p 17 & 21)
Opening routines (see TB p 16)
Recycling activity (*There's a ... / There are ...* and things in the park) (see TB p 19)
Lesson aims (see TB p 18)

Introduce the story *Mimi's kite*.

- Say *It's story time!* Play the *Story rhyme* (CD1 Track 4; see TB p 17)
- Say *Alex and Lucy are listening to a story about Mimi and Dylan in the park. Mimi has her kite.* (Show or draw a picture or explain what this is.) *What's the weather like? What happens to Mimi and Dylan?* Encourage children to guess.

Watch and listen to the story *Mimi's kite*.

CD1 Track 42

- Watch the video, play the audio or read the story using the printable story cards. Pause, repeat words, point to the pictures, ask questions.
- Ask the pre-questions again and check answers. (It's windy; Mimi, Dylan and the kite are in a tree.)
- Repeat the story. Encourage children to join in with words and phrases in the story.
- Ask e.g. *What can Mimi and Dylan see from the tree? (path, pond, trees, flowers, bench, Mommy, Daddy) Who rescues them? (the gardener) Do you like the story? Do you have a kite?*

Look and find.

- Say *Find the pond!* Children look at the story and point to the pond as fast as they can.
- Repeat with other things in the park.

Table time

Student's Book p 17

Watch. Listen to the story *Mimi's kite*.

Story questions

Picture 1
Where are Mimi and Dylan? *(The park)*
What does Mimi have? *(A kite)*

Picture 2
What's the weather like? *(Windy)*
Does Mimi need help? *(Yes)*

Picture 3
Is Mommy under the tree? *(No)*
Where is Daddy? *(Under the tree)*

Picture 4
Where are Mimi and Dylan? *(In the air)*
Do Mimi and Dylan need help? *(Yes)*

Picture 5
Who do Mommy and Daddy talk to? *(The gardener)*
Where are Mimi and Dylan now? *(In the tree)*

Picture 6
Are there swings in the park? *(Yes)*
Do Mimi and Dylan want to fly the kite? *(No)*

CD1 Track 42

- Read or play the audio of the story again. Children listen and point to the pictures in their books.

Circle the weather in the story. Stick the story sticker.

- Demonstrate circling the weather in the story (it's windy) and sticking the story sticker.
- Ask *What do Mimi and Dylan want to play on at the end of the story? (the swings and slide)*

Activity Book p 17

Trace and color what Mimi and Dylan can see in the park.

- Children trace and color the things in the park.

Point and say.

- Children point to the things in the park and say the words.

Closing time

Learning review (see TB p 18)
Closing routines (see TB p 16)
Goodbye song and puppet (CD1 Track 3; see TB p 17 & 21)

Use the **Navio App** to watch the video, and encourage children to do the same at home.

Lesson 4 Story Song

The park

1 2 3 4 5

Watch. Listen, point and sing *Fly the kite*. Trace the numbers. Match the numbers and pictures in order. Say. **Language:** flowers, kite, pond, trees; numbers 1–4; There's (the pond). There are (the trees).

18

Learning objectives
- Watch, sing and act out the story song *Fly the kite*
- Listen to the story again and act it out
- Identify and say things in the park
- Talk about what there is in the park

Materials
- Class CDs, printable story cards, flashcards, *Ferris Wheel* mat, Mimi puppet

Main vocabulary
- flowers, kite, pond, trees; numbers 1–4

Key language
- There's (the pond). There are (the trees).

Teacher's tip: Checking in pairs
COOPERATIVE LEARNING

Encourage children to start working cooperatively by having them check each other's work once they have finished. With a partner, they can take turns checking that the frames from the story song are correctly matched to the numbers.

Circle time

Hello song and puppet (CD1 Track 2; see TB p 17 & 21)
Opening routines (see TB p 16)
Recycling activity (things in the park) (see TB p 19)
Lesson aims (see TB p 18)

Retell the story *Mimi's kite*.
- Watch the video, play the audio or read the story using the printable story cards.
- Demonstrate that children should wave their arms in the air every time they hear a word for something in the park in the story.

Play with an imaginary kite and mime the story.
- Mime holding the string of a kite and looking up at the sky. Get children to do the same.
- Use language from the story song (see TB p 55) as you mime a version of the story. Children listen and copy your actions.
- Repeat, encouraging children to join in saying phrases with you e.g. *It's very windy. / There's the pond. / Help us, please!*

***Fly the kite* song**

CD1 Track 43
- Watch the video. Children listen and do actions as per the song.
- Watch the video again. Children listen, do actions and sing the song.
- Ask questions e.g. *Is it windy? Is the kite strong?* and children respond.

Say the missing words.
- Hold up the puppet. Use the puppet to mime the story song as previously. Use language from the song and encourage children to say the missing words e.g. *Fly, fly, fly the … (kite). / Look! It's in the … (air) / There's the … (pond).*

Table time

Student's Book p 18

Watch. Listen, point and sing *Fly the kite*.

CD1 Track 43
- Play the song (see TB p 55). Children listen, sing and point to the pictures.
- Remember that you can use the karaoke version of the song when children are confident.

Trace the numbers. Match the numbers and pictures in order. Say.
- They point and say *There's the (pond).* Children trace the numbers and match the numbers and pictures to show the sequence of the objects in the song.

Activity Book p 18

Follow and draw Mimi and Dylan's path through the park maze.
- Children draw the path through the maze.

Point and say what Mimi and Dylan see in the park.
- Children point to the things in the park and say the words.

Closing time

Learning review (see TB p 18)
Closing routines (see TB p 16)
Goodbye song and puppet (CD1 Track 3; see TB p 17 & 21)

Use the **Navio App** to watch the video, and encourage children to do the same at home.

Lesson 5

Speaking

Life skills

The park

Watch. Listen and point. Circle what's in the park. Ask and say. Language: bench, flowers, grass, merry-go-round, path, pond, seesaw, slide, swings, trees; Is there (grass)? Are there (trees)? Yes. / No. There's (a merry-go-round). There are (swings).

19

The park

Lesson 5 Speaking

Learning objectives
- Ask and say what there is in the park
- Watch, understand and enjoy a video
- Identify things in the park in the video

Materials
- Class CDs, flashcards, *Ferris Wheel* mat, Mimi puppet

Main vocabulary
- bench, flowers, grass, merry-go-round, path, pond, seesaw, slide, swing, trees

Key language
- Is there (grass)? Are there (trees)? Yes. / No. There's (a merry-go-round). There are (swings).

Teacher's tip: Scaffolding words to sentences

Life skills

Initially, children may just answer with single words to describe what's in the park. Scaffold their sentences by recasting and adding to what they say so that they gradually gain the confidence to start producing the full sentence: *There's a (slide). There are (trees).*

Circle time

Hello song and puppet (CD1 Track 2; see TB p 17 & 21)
Opening routines (see TB p 16)
Recycling activity (story song) (CD1 Track 43; see TB p 19)
Lesson aims (see TB p 18)

Game: *Take a photo!*
- Stick the park flashcards in different places around the classroom.
- Ask children to imagine the classroom is a park and that they have a camera. Demonstrate what you mean.
- Divide children into pairs. Say e.g. *There's a bench in the park. Take a photo of the bench!* The pair you ask walk to the flashcard and mime taking a photo.
- Repeat with other flashcards and pairs of children.

Watch the video.
- Explain that Auntie Vicky is telling Alex and Lucy about a new park near her house.
- Ask *What is there in the park?* Children guess.
- Play the video.
- Ask the question again and children respond *(trees, grass, path, bench, swings, (big) merry-go-round).*
- Watch again. Pause after sentences with *There's … / There are …* and children repeat.
- Ask *Do you want to go to the park near Auntie Vicky's house?*

Table time

Student's Book p 19 Life skills

Watch. Listen and point.
- Children identify Alex, Lucy and Auntie Vicky. Point to the pictures around the photo and children say the words.
- Play the audio or video. Children listen and point to the pictures.

Circle what's in the park.
- Play the audio again. Use the pause button. Children circle the things that are in the park.

CD1 Track 45

Auntie Vicky:	There's a new park near my house.
Alex:	Are there trees?
Auntie Vicky:	Yes. There are trees in the park. Look!
Alex:	Wow!
Lucy:	Is there grass?
Auntie Vicky:	Yes. There's grass in the park. There's a path. There's a bench.
Lucy:	Are there swings?
Auntie Vicky:	Yes. There are swings.
Lucy:	Oh, fantastic. Is there a merry-go-round?
Auntie Vicky:	Yes. There's a big merry-go-round.
Lucy:	Oh, amazing. I love merry-go-rounds!
Alex:	Me, too.
Auntie Vicky:	Come on. Put your coats on. Let's go!

Ask and say.
- Children ask and answer questions about what's in the park. e.g. One child asks *Are there trees?* and another child responds *Yes, (there are trees in the park).*

Activity Book p 19

Trace and color what's in the park.
- Children trace and color the things in the park.

Ask and say.
- They ask and answer questions about what's in the park.

Closing time

Learning review (see TB p 18)
Closing routines (see TB p 16)
Goodbye song and puppet (CD1 Track 3; see TB p 17 & 21)

Use the **Navio App** to watch the video, and encourage children to do the same at home.

Lesson 6 Values Looking after the environment

The park

Listen, point and sing *Put your trash in the trash can*. Trace and color the trash can black. Find and match the trash to the trash can. Say. Language: park, trash, trash can; clean; Put your (trash) in (the trash can). I put my trash in the trash can.

20

Learning objectives

- Recognize the value of looking after the environment
- Sing the values song *Put your trash in the trash can*
- Identify and say when you can put trash in a trash can

Materials

- Class CDs, flashcards, *Ferris Wheel* mat, Mimi puppet

Main vocabulary

- park, trash, trash can; clean

Key language

- Put your (trash) in (the trash can). I put my trash in the trashcan

Teacher's tip: Looking after the environment

If possible, take the children outside the classroom into the playground to see if there is any trash lying around. Encourage them to pick it up and put it in the trash can. Compare the playground before and after picking up the trash and encourage the children to always put their wrappers and other trash in the trash can.

Circle time

Hello song and puppet (CD1 Track 2; see TB p 17 & 21)
Opening routines (see TB p 16)
Recycling activity (*There's ... / There are ...*) (see TB p 19)
Lesson aims (see TB p 18)

Watch the *Mimi's kite* story video.

- Play the story video.
- Take the parts of the narrator, Mommy, Daddy and the gardener yourself. Encourage children to join in acting out the story in two groups (Mimi, Dylan).
- Ask *What can Mimi and Dylan see from the tree? Is the park clean?* (explain what you mean) *Is there trash in the park?* (show children trash in a trash can to demonstrate what you mean). *Is it important to keep the park clean? Is it important to put trash in the trash can?* and demonstrate this.

***Put your trash in the trash can* song**

CD1 Track 46

- Use the Mimi puppet to say *Listen to the song and put your trash in the trash can!*
- Play the audio. Children listen and do actions (see song lyrics for suggested actions on TB p 55).
- Play the audio again. Children sing the song and do the actions.

Table time

Student's Book p 20

Listen, point and sing *Put your trash in the trash can.*

CD1 Track 46

- Play the song. Children sing and point to the trash and trash can and children playing.

Trace and color the trash can black. Find and match the trash to the trash can.

- Children look at the picture. They color the trash can black and find and match all the trash to the trash can.
- Check children have done this correctly by getting the children to count the pieces of trash with you (there are nine pieces of trash).

Say.

- Children say sentences about where they put trash in the trash can e.g. *I put trash in the trash can in the park / in the classroom / in my bedroom / in the playground.*

Activity Book p 20

Color the pictures of children looking after the environment.

- Children color the pictures of children looking after the environment.

Say where you put your trash.

- They say where they put their trash.

Closing time

Learning review (see TB p 18)
Closing routines (see TB p 16)
Goodbye song and puppet (CD1 Track 3; see TB p 17 & 21)

Use the **Navio App** to listen to the song, and encourage children to do the same at home.

Lesson 7 Content

The park

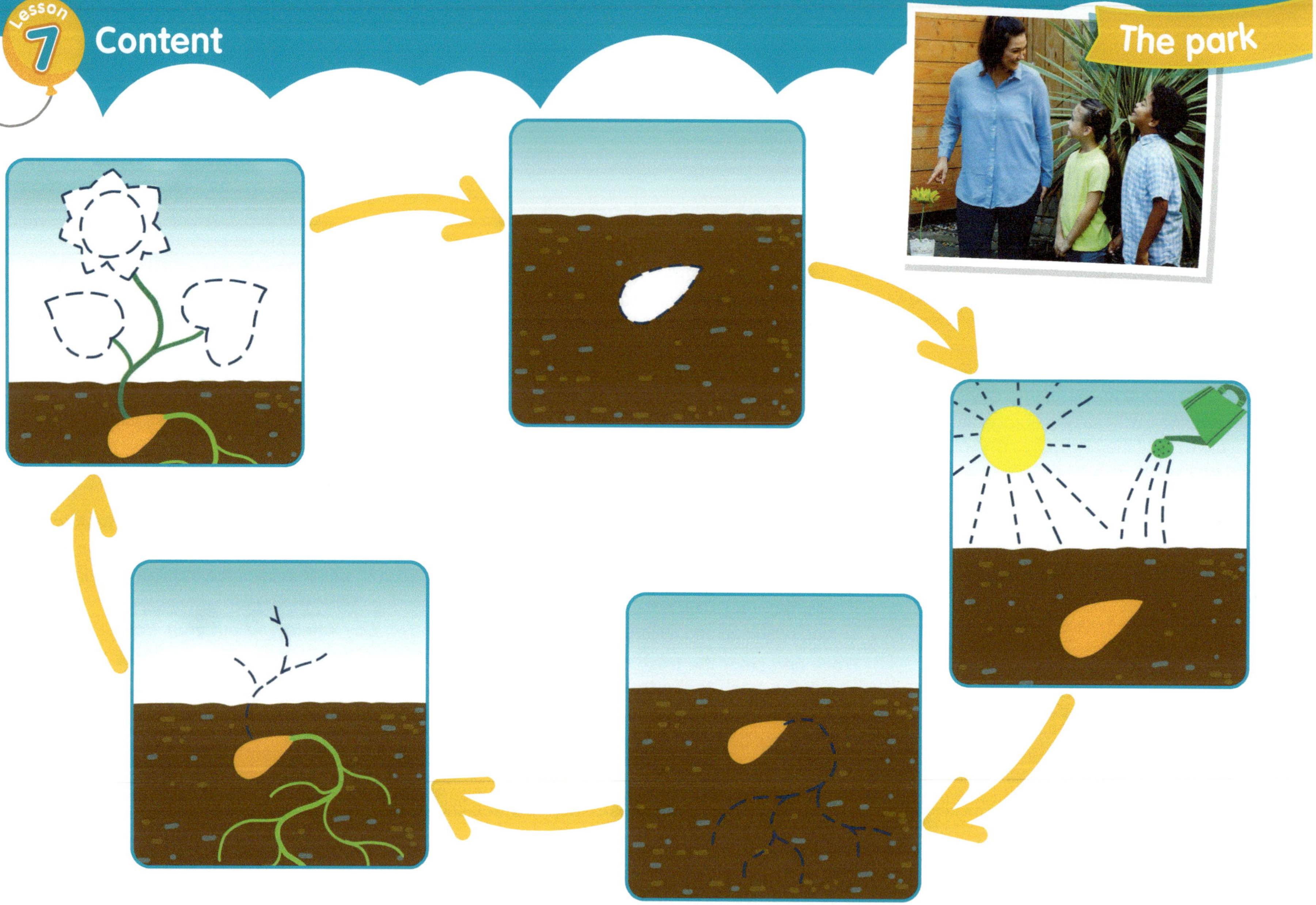

Listen and point. Trace and color the pictures to show the life cycle of a plant.
Language: flower, leaves, plant, roots, seed, sun, water; There's (a seed). There are (leaves).

21

Learning objectives

- Learn about the life cycle of a plant
- Listen and identify parts of a plant
- Act out and order the life cycle of a plant

Materials

- Class CDs, printable content flashcards, *Ferris Wheel* mat, Mimi puppet

Main vocabulary

- flower, leaves, plant, roots, seed, sun, water

Key language

- There's (a seed). There are (leaves).

Teacher's tip: Planting seeds

Life skills

Looking after plants helps children understand how nature works. It also gives them responsibility for caring for something and pride in the results. Plant some seeds in pots in the classroom and involve children in observing their growth and helping water and care for them.

Circle time

Hello song and puppet (CD1 Track 2; see TB p 17 & 21)
Opening routines (see TB p 16)
Recycling activity (see TB p 19)
Lesson aims (see TB p 18)

Introduce content vocabulary.

- Show children a real plant or a photo of a plant with a flower.
- Use the printable flashcards to introduce the new words (*seed*, *plant*, *roots*, *leaves*). Children repeat the words.
- Explain that children are going to learn how a plant grows. Elicit their ideas. Use the flashcards of *water*, *sun* and *flower* as prompts for this.

Game: ***Guess the flashcard.***

- Use the puppet to turn the seven flashcards face down on the board and mix them up.
- The puppet points to one flashcard and children guess what it is. The child who guesses correctly has the next turn at mixing up the flashcards. Repeat several times.
- At the end, collect the flashcards in turn by asking individual children *Can you give me the plant, please?*

Mime the life cycle of a plant.

- Stick the flashcards on the board in the following order: *seed*, *roots*, *plant*, *leaves*, *flower*.
- Children stand up. Say *Imagine you're a tiny seed and you're going to grow into a beautiful flower!* Point to the flashcards in turn, use language from the audio below, and get children to mime growing from a seed into a flower with you. Repeat once or twice.

Table time

Student's Book p 21

Listen and point.

- Say *Lucy and Alex are asking Auntie Vicky about the life cycle of a plant.*
- Play the audio. Children listen and point to the pictures in the life cycle.
- Play the audio again. Use the pause button. Check children are pointing to the correct pictures.

CD1 Track 47

Alex:	How do flowers grow, Auntie Vicky?
Auntie Vicky:	A tiny seed is in the earth. The seed needs sun and water. Little roots grow. A tiny plant grows. The plant grows big. There are leaves and a flower.
Lucy:	Amazing!
Alex:	The flower is beautiful!
Lucy:	Can we grow a flower, Auntie Vicky?
Auntie Vicky:	Yes, of course.

Trace and color the pictures to show the life cycle of a plant.

- Children trace and color the pictures to show the life cycle of a plant.
- Play the audio again. Use the pause button. Children point to the pictures and repeat the sentences that describe the life cycle.
- Children point to the pictures in turn and say e.g. *There's a seed.* / *There are roots.*

Activity Book p 21

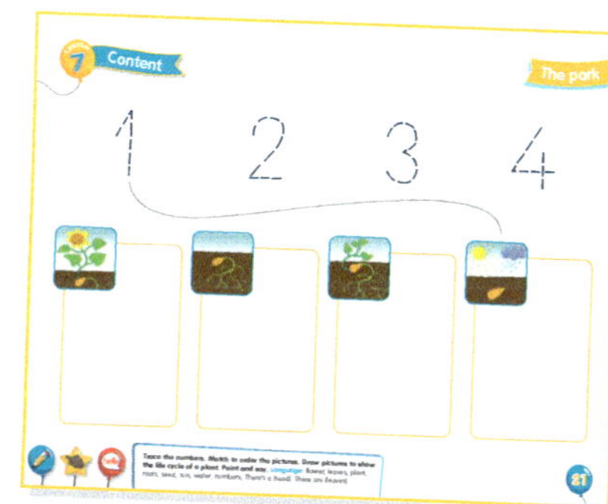

Trace the numbers. Match to order the pictures.

- Children trace the numbers. Then they match the numbers to the pictures to order them.

Draw pictures to show the life cycle of a plant.

- Children draw the stages of the plant's life cycle.

Point and say.

- They point and say the parts of the plant.

Closing time

Learning review (see TB p 18)
Closing routines (see TB p 16)
Goodbye song and puppet (CD1 Track 3; see TB p 17 & 21)

Use the **Navio App** to play the vocabulary and language games, and encourage children to do the same at home.

Lesson 8

Culture

Watch. Listen and point to the story *Little Red Riding Hood*. Circle the words you hear in the story. Say. **Language:** apples, cake, cookies, ears, eyes, flowers, house, path, teeth, trees, wolf; There are (trees).

22

Learning objectives

- Watch, understand and enjoy the traditional story *Little Red Riding Hood*
- Act out the story
- Identify items from the story

Materials

- Class CDs, printable story cards, flashcards, *Ferris Wheel* mat, Mimi puppet

Main vocabulary

- apples, cake, cookies, ears, eyes, flowers, house, path, teeth, trees, wolf

Key language

- There are (trees).

Teacher's tip: Enjoying traditional stories

Listening to traditional stories is a great way to engage children, especially if they are already familiar with the story in their own language. If this is the case, ask children to tell you what the characters in the story are called in their language, whether the same characters are "good" and "bad," and whether the story they know has the same or a different ending.

Circle time

Hello song and puppet (CD1 Track 2; see TB p 17 & 21)
Opening routines (see TB p 16)
Recycling activity (see TB p 19)
Lesson aims (see TB p 18)

Introduce the story *Little Red Riding Hood*.

- Explain that children are going to watch and listen to one of Alex and Lucy's favorite traditional stories: *Little Red Riding Hood*.
- Ask if children know who Little Red Riding Hood is. Give clues e.g. *Little Red Riding Hood has a red cape with a hood. Grandma lives in a house in a forest. Little Red Riding Hood visits Grandma with a basket of food and meets a wolf* (mime or explain meaning).
- If children know the story, ask *Do you want to watch and listen to the story in English?*

Watch and listen to the story.

CD1 Track 48

- Ask *What's in the basket of food for Grandma?* (cookies, cake, apples) *What happens to the wolf at the end of the story?* (the wolf runs away).
- Play the video. Children watch and listen to the story.
- Ask the pre-questions again and children respond.
- Play the video again. Use the pause button. Ask questions and clarify as necessary.
- Ask *Is Little Red Riding Hood safe at the end of the story? Is Grandma safe? Who is your favorite character in the story?*

Mime and act out the story.

- Divide the children into two groups: Little Red Riding Hood / wolf. Take the parts of Mommy, Daddy and the narrator yourself.
- Play the video or audio or tell the story yourself. Children mime being Little Red Riding Hood or the wolf in their groups.

Table time

Student's Book p 22

Watch. Listen and point to the story *Little Red Riding Hood*.

Story questions

Picture 1
Who is Little Red Riding Hood going to visit? *(Grandma)*
What food does Little Red Riding Hood have for Grandma? *(Cookies/cake/apples)*

Picture 2
Are there trees and flowers in the forest? *(Yes)*
Who does Little Red Riding Hood talk to in the forest? *(Wolf)*

Picture 3
Where does Little Red Riding Hood go now? *(Grandma's house)*
Who has big teeth? *(Grandma/Wolf)*

Picture 4
Who comes to Grandma's house now? *(Daddy)*
Are Little Red Riding Hood and Grandma safe? *(Yes)*

CD1 Track 48

- Play the audio of the story. Children listen and point to the pictures.
- Say e.g. *Find Grandma / the wolf / flowers!* etc. and children respond.

Circle the words you hear in the story. Say.

- Play the audio again. Use the pause button. Children circle the words they hear in the story.
- Children point to the pictures they have circled and say the words.
- Ask the children if they enjoyed learning a traditional story in English and listen to their responses.

Activity Book p 22

Draw the path from Little Red Riding Hood to Grandma's house.

- Children draw the path to Grandma's house.

Trace and color. Point and say.

- They trace and color the things from the story. Then they point and say the words.

Closing time

Learning review (see TB p 18)
Closing routines (see TB p 16)
Goodbye song and puppet (CD1 Track 3; see TB p 17 & 21)

Use the **Navio App** to watch the video, and encourage children to do the same at home.

Review

The park

I can …

Vocabulary

Story

Speaking

Content

Circle the park words you know. Listen, point and say. Listen and answer. Ask and say. Complete the faces to show what you can do. Language: bench, flowers, grass, merry-go-round, path, pond, seesaw, slide, swing, trees; What's in the park? There's (a pond). There are (flowers). Is there (a slide)? Are there (swings)?

23

The park

Learning objectives
- Review what you have learned in this unit
- Complete a self-evaluation
- Ask and say what there is in the park

Materials
- Class CDs, flashcards, *Ferris Wheel* mat, Mimi puppet

Main vocabulary
- bench, flowers, grass, merry-go-round, path, pond, seesaw, slide, swing, trees

Key language
- What's in the park? There's (a pond). There are (flowers). Is there (a slide)? Are there (swings)?

Teacher's tip: Thinking time

Giving children adequate thinking time can help them focus their ideas and concentrate. Show children how to put their fingers on their head and think quietly before raising their hand to answer the question. Remind them that nobody should say the answer during thinking time.

Circle time

Hello song and puppet (CD1 Track 2; see TB p 17 & 21)
Opening routines (see TB p 16)
Recycling activity (see TB p 19)
Lesson aims (see TB p 18)

Park flashcard games

- Choose one or two flashcard games with the *Ferris Wheel* mat and/or the puppet to review main vocabulary (see TB p 20 & 21).

Sing *There's a pond in the park.*

CD1 Track 40

- Play the audio. Children sing and do the actions.

Game: ***What's in the park?***

- Hide one of the flashcards behind a book. Ask children to guess by saying e.g. *There's a bench.* Slowly reveal the flashcard.

Game: ***Memory chain***

- Say e.g. *There's a slide.* The child next to you repeats your item and adds another e.g. *There's a slide and a seesaw.* Continue with other children.

Watch the story video.

- Children watch the story video. Ask *Where are Mimi and Dylan in the story? What can they see?*

Table time

Student's Book p 23

Circle the park words you know.

- Demonstrate that children should circle the park words they know. Children say the words.

Listen, point and say.

- Explain and demonstrate the activity.

CD1 Track 49

Mimi: I'm the teacher! Can you remember what's in the park, Dylan?
Dylan: Yes, I can. Trees.
Mimi: Trees.
Dylan: Flowers.
Mimi: Flowers.
Dylan: Path.
Mimi: Path.
Dylan: Grass.
Mimi: Grass
Dylan: Pond.
Mimi: Pond.
Dylan: Bench.
Mimi: Bench.
Dylan: Swing.
Mimi: Swing
Dylan: Slide.
Mimi: Slide.
Dylan: Seesaw.
Mimi: Seesaw.
Dylan: Merry-go-round.
Mimi: Merry-go-round. Well done, Dylan!
Both: Fantastic!

Listen and answer. Ask and say.

CD1 Track 50

- Play the audio. Children listen to the questions.
  Mimi: What's in the park near you? Is there a path?
  Is there a bench?
  Are there trees?
  Are there flowers?
  Are there swings?
  Is there a slide?
  Is there a seesaw?
- Play the audio again. Children listen, repeat and answer the questions.
- Children ask and answer questions about what's in the park near them.

Complete the faces to show what you can do.

- Explain the four pictures: *I can name things in the park; I can understand the story; I can say what's in the park; I can identify stages in the life cycle of a plant.*
- Remind children they should complete each face with a smile or frown depending on how well they think they have done.

Activity Book p 23

Complete the faces to show what you see in the park. Ask and say.

- Children complete the faces with a smile to show what they see in the park.
- Children ask and answer questions about what's in the park.

Think and circle the number to show your progress.

- Children think about their progress in the unit and circle the number.

Closing time

Learning review (see TB p 18)
Closing routines (see TB p 16)
Goodbye song and puppet (CD1 Track 3; see TB p 17 & 21)

Use the **Navio App** to review what children have learned in this unit, and encourage them to do the same at home.

Project

COOPERATIVE LEARNING

The park

Choose and paint an object for the park. Glue your picture on the model of a park. Ask and say. **Language:** bench, merry-go-round, seesaw, slide; colors; numbers; There's (a slide). There are (seesaws). Is there (a bench)? Are there (flowers)? How many (trees)? (Six.) My (slide) is (red). I like (the merry-go-round). Do you like (the slide)? Yes. / No.

24

The park

Learning objectives

- Work together to do a collaborative project
- Choose and make something for the park
- Ask and answer questions about the project
- Draw and paint your favorite park

Materials

- Class CDs, Mimi puppet, photocopiable templates, colored card, finger paints, glue
- optional: crayons

Main vocabulary

- bench, merry-go-round, seesaw, slide; colors; numbers

Key language

- There's a (slide). There are (seesaws). Is there (a bench)? Are there (flowers)? How many (trees)? (Six). My (slide) is (red). I like (the merry-go-round). Do you like (the slide)? Yes. / No.

Teacher's tip: Engaging children individually

While the children are working on the project, use the opportunity to circulate around the class and ask children questions individually e.g. *Do you like the slide? What's your favorite thing at the park?* etc. Get down to the children's level, make eye contact and show interest when listening to their responses to ensure that they feel comfortable.

Circle time

Hello song and puppet (CD1 Track 2; see TB p 17 & 21)
Opening routines (see TB p 16)
Recycling activity (see TB p 19)
Lesson aims (see TB p 18)

Prepare for your project.

- Say *Let's do a project and make a model of a park with a children's playground!*
- Show children the template of things to play on in the park. Explain that children should choose and paint their favorite thing to play on in the park.
- Explain and demonstrate that children will then use their pictures to make a model of the park.

Table time

COOPERATIVE LEARNING

Student's Book p 24

Choose and paint an object for the park. Glue your picture on the model of a park.

- Say e.g. *We're going to make a model of a park like this. Look at what we need for our project: a picture of our favorite thing to go on in the park, finger paints, colored card, and glue.* Children listen and point to the pictures.
- Children choose the template they want to paint. Make sure children have finger paints available.
- Children paint the picture.
- When they are ready, invite children to come and stick their pictures on to the model of the park you have prepared. To make the objects stand up, glue a folded piece of card to the back of each object. Glue the top part of the folded card to the back of the object and the bottom part to the green background to form an L-shape.

Ask and say.

- Talk about the pictures and model using language of the unit and other language children know. Count how many of each item there are in the model and find out the class's favorite.
- Ask children *Do you like our model of the park?* Make the point that everyone has helped make the model and that they couldn't have made such a beautiful model of the park on their own.

Alternative version of project

- Children could use crayons instead of finger paints to color their park picture. They then stick their pictures on a flat poster, rather than a 3D model.

Activity Book p 24

Imagine your favorite park. Draw and paint.

- Children draw and paint their ideal park.

Ask and say.

- They ask and answer questions about what's in their park.

Closing time

Learning review (see TB p 18)
Closing routines (see TB p 16)
Goodbye song and puppet (CD1 Track 3; see TB p 17 & 21)

Wild animals
The surprise

Vocabulary and language

- **Main vocabulary:** crocodile, elephant, giraffe, hippo, lion, monkey, parrot, snake, tiger, zebra
- **Key language:** What's that? It's (a snake). It's (black and white). It has (big teeth). What are those? They're (monkeys).
- **Content language:** claws, ears, eyes, fur, legs, nose, tail, whiskers; big, small; brown; What's that? It's (a meerkat). It has (big eyes).
- **Other language:** binoculars; mouse; head, teeth; I'm a (crocodile). I'm hungry. I can help you! Thank you. (Five) little monkeys sitting in a tree. You can't catch me! Along comes Mr. Crocodile. How many (elephants)? (Four). I like the (giraffe). Do you like the (crocodile)? Yes. / No.

Unit objectives

- Identify and name wild animals
- Sing the language song *What's that?*
- Ask about and describe wild animals
- Understand and act out the story *The surprise*
- Sing and act out the story song *The party surprise*
- Understand a story about expressing thanks
- Recognize the value of saying *"thank you"*
- Learn about real meerkats
- Sing and act out the traditional song *Five little monkeys*
- Review your learning and progress
- Participate in a collaborative project

Story

CD2 Track 7

Picture 1

Narrator: It's Dylan's birthday.
Mimi: Here's a present for you, Dylan.
Dylan: Ooh. Yippee! What's this?
Mimi: Open it and see!
Dylan: Binoculars! Oh, great. Thank you, Mimi!

Picture 2

Narrator: Later …
Mimi: Let's go to the yard and play with your binoculars, Dylan.
Dylan: Yes, great idea!
Mimi: What can you see, Dylan?

Picture 3

Mimi: Look. What's that?
Dylan: It's orange and black. It's a tiger!
Mimi: And what's that?
Dylan: It's green and yellow. It's a snake!

Picture 4

Mimi: And look, Dylan. What's that?
Dylan: It's red, yellow and blue. I think it's a … Yes, it's a parrot! Oh wow.
Mimi: And look. What's that?
Dylan: It's yellow and it has big eyes. It's a lion! Amazing!
Mimi: Yes! Close your eyes now, Dylan!

Picture 5

Mimi: Open your eyes! Look, Dylan! It's your friends! It's a surprise birthday party!
Katy: Hello, Dylan.
Leo: Happy birthday, Dylan!
Zara: I'm a tiger! Grrrr!
Leo: I'm a snake! Hiss!
Katy: I'm a parrot! Squawk!
Harry: I'm a lion! Roar!
Mimi: And I'm a monkey! Ooo-ooo!
Daddy: And here's a present for you, Dylan!
Dylan: What's this?
Daddy: Open it and see!
Dylan: It's a crocodile costume. Oh, fantastic! Thank you, Daddy! Thank you, Mommy!

Picture 6

Dylan: What's this?
Mommy: It's your birthday cake!
Dylan: Oh, hurray! Yummy!
Everyone: Happy birthday, Dylan!
Dylan: Oh, thank you! I'm a crocodile. Snap snap. And this is the best birthday ever!

Songs and story

Language song

What's that? CD2 Track 5

What's that? Look over there! (Shrug, then point to zebra flashcard)
It's black and white. (Gesture stripes with your hand)
It's a … zebra. (Mime zebra's tail with one hand)
A zebra! Oh, oh, oh! Amazing! (Wave arms in the air)

What's that? Look over there! (Shrug, then point to snake flashcard)
It's green and yellow.
It's a … snake.
A snake! Oh, oh, oh! Amazing! (Wave arms in the air)

What's that? Look over there! (Shrug, then point to tiger flashcard)
It has big teeth. (Bare your teeth and point to them)
It's a … tiger. (Mime claws with your fingers)
A tiger! Oh, oh, oh! Amazing! (Wave arms in the air)

What's that? Look over there! (Shrug, then point to giraffe flashcard)
It has long legs. (Point to your neck)
It's a … giraffe. (Walk majestically like a giraffe)
A giraffe! Oh, oh, oh! Amazing! (Wave arms in the air)

Story song

The party surprise CD2 Track 8

Open your eyes (Cover and uncover eyes with hands)
For the party surprise! (Wave arms in air)

I'm a tiger. Grrrr! Grrr! (Mime claws with your fingers)
I'm a tiger. Let's play! Let's play! (Skip in place)
I'm a snake. Hiss! Hiss! (Wiggle one arm like a snake)
I'm a snake. Hurray! Hurray! (Wave arms in air)

(Chorus)

I'm a parrot. Squawk! Squawk! (Flap arms like wings)
I'm a parrot. Let's play! Let's play! (Skip in place)
I'm a lion. Roar! Roar! (Mime claws with your fingers)
I'm a lion. Hurray! Hurray! (Wave arms in air)

(Chorus)

I'm a monkey. Ooo-ooo! Ooo-ooo! (Mime being a monkey)
I'm a monkey. Let's play! Let's play! (Skip in place)
I'm a crocodile. Snap! Snap! (Clap your arms together in front of you)
I'm a crocodile. Hurray! Hurray! (Wave arms in air)

(Chorus)

Values story

CD2 Track 11

Picture 1

Narrator: Harry and Zoe are doing a puppet show.
Harry as narrator: One day Lion is sleeping. A little mouse is on his head.
Zoe as lion: What's that?
Harry as mouse: It's me. I'm a little mouse.
Zoe as lion: Ha, ha. Delicious! I'm hungry.

Picture 2

Harry as mouse: Oh, please don't eat me, Lion.
Zoe as lion: Ha, ha. You're too little to eat. You can go free.
Harry as mouse: Fantastic! Bye bye, Lion!
Zoe as lion: And what do you say?
Harry as mouse: Oh, thank you, Lion. Thank you!

Picture 3

Harry as narrator: The next day, the lion is in a net. The little mouse sees the lion.
Zoe as lion: Roar! Roar! Help me.
Harry as mouse: Don't roar, Lion. I can help you.

Picture 4

Harry as narrator: The little mouse bites the net with his teeth. The lion is free.
Zoe as lion: Fantastic! Bye bye, little mouse!
Harry as mouse: And what do you say?
Zoe as lion: Oh, thank you, little mouse. Thank you!
Harry as mouse: Ha, ha! You see. We both know when to say "thank you"!

Culture song

Five little monkeys CD2 Track 13

Five little monkeys sitting in a tree (Hold up five fingers, mime sitting)
Shout to Mr. Crocodile: "You can't catch me!" (Cup hands around mouth)
Along comes Mr. Crocodile (Move arms back and forth as if creeping)
Hungry as can be, and SNAP! (Rub your tummy, then clap with arms outstretched)
Four little monkeys … (Hold up four fingers)
Three little monkeys … (Hold up three fingers)
Two little monkeys … (Hold up two fingers)
One little monkey … (Hold up one finger)

No little monkeys sitting in a tree (Shake head)
Along comes Mr. Crocodile (Move arms back and forth as if creeping)
Sleepy as can be (Put hands together on one side of head)
And YAWN! (Mime a big yawn)
Five little monkeys are free! (Hold up five fingers and spread arms wide)

Wild animals

The surprise

Vocabulary Lesson 1

2:01 · hello · 2:02 · 2:03

Listen, point and repeat. Listen and stick the wild animal stickers. Listen and play *Memory*. Circle the animals you like. Say. Language: crocodile, elephant, hippo, lion, monkey, parrot; blue, green, orange, pink, red, yellow; Where's (the crocodile)? It's on (green).

25

Learning objectives

- Identify and name wild animals
- Listen and point to wild animals
- Remember wild animals in a memory game

Materials

- Class CDs, flashcards, *Ferris Wheel* mat, Mimi puppet

Main vocabulary

- crocodile, elephant, hippo, lion, monkey, parrot; blue, green, orange, pink, red, yellow

Teacher's tip: Using toy animals

As well as playing vocabulary games with the flashcards, you can also play them using plastic or stuffed toy animals from the children's toy box. Place them in a feely bag or box and encourage children to identify the animals by touch.

Circle time

Hello song and puppet (CD1 Track 2; see TB p 17 & 21)
Opening routines (see TB p 16)
Lesson aims (see TB p 18)

Introduce wild animals.

- Use the puppet and flashcards to introduce the wild animals. Say the words and children repeat them.
- Put the *Ferris Wheel* mat on the floor or board with the wild animal flashcards face down (one on each color). Use the puppet to turn them over and name them. The children repeat the words.

Game: ***Say the color!***

- Name the wild animals on the Ferris Wheel and children name the color. Then the reverse.

Game: ***Freeze!***

- Children stand up. Teach them a mime for each animal in turn.
- Name the animals in random order and children respond by doing the mimes. When you say *Stop!* they freeze in position. Comment on these e.g. *What a lovely lion!* before continuing. Repeat several times.

Table time

Student's Book p 25

Listen, point and repeat.

- Play the audio. Children listen, point and repeat.

CD2 Track 1

Mimi: Look Dylan! Elephant … parrot … lion … hippo … crocodile. Repeat, Dylan!
Dylan: Yes, Mimi. Elephant … parrot … lion … hippo … crocodile.
Mimi: Very good, Dylan! Let's name the wild animals together!
Both: Elephant … parrot … lion … hippo … crocodile. Fantastic!

- Draw attention to the question mark in their books. They identify the missing wild animal (monkey).

Listen and stick the wild animal stickers.

- Play the audio. Children listen and point.

CD2 Track 2

Where's the elephant? It's on … red.
Where's the lion? It's on … yellow.
Where's the hippo? It's on … pink.
Where's the parrot? It's on … blue.
Where's the crocodile? It's on … green.
Where's the monkey? Can you guess? It's on … orange. Yes, yes, yes!
The monkey is on orange. Yes, yes, yes!

- Repeat the questions and children respond.
- Play the audio again. Children listen and stick the wild animal stickers.

Listen and play *Memory*.

- Children cover their eyes. Play the audio. Children listen and remember which animal is on each color.

CD2 Track 3

Close your eyes
One, two, three
Say the words
Play memory!
Blue … parrot!
Red … elephant!
Yellow … lion!
Green … crocodile!
Pink … hippo!
Orange … monkey!

- Play the game.

Circle the animals you like. Say.

- Children circle, point and say the animals they like.

Activity Book p 25

Look and match.

- Children look and match the missing body parts to the animals.

Draw and color the missing body parts. Point and say.

- Children draw and color what's missing from each animal. They point and say the animals.

Closing time

Learning review (see TB p 18)
Closing routines (see TB p 16)
Goodbye song and puppet (CD1 Track 3; see TB p 17 & 21)

Use the **Navio App** to play the vocabulary game, and encourage children to do the same at home.

Language

Wild animals

2:04 2:05 hello

Listen and find the new wild animals. Listen, point and sing *What's that?* Check (✓) the animals Alex and Lucy see. Ask and say. Language: elephant, giraffe, hippo, monkey, parrot, snake, tiger, zebra; colors; What's that? It's (a snake). It's (black and white). It has (big teeth).

26

Learning objectives

- Talk about wild animals
- Identify and name four new wild animals
- Sing the language song *What's that?*
- Ask about and describe wild animals

Materials

- Class CDs, flashcards, *Ferris Wheel* mat, Mimi puppet

Main vocabulary

- crocodile, elephant, giraffe, hippo, lion, monkey, parrot, snake, tiger, zebra, colors

Key language

- What's that? It's (a snake). It's (black and white). It has (big teeth).

Teacher's tip: Pre-reading: identifying initial sounds

Begin to lay the foundations for early reading by encouraging the children to focus on sounds that make up words. The animals in the unit each begin with a different sound. Say the initial sound and have the children say the name of the animal and point to the flashcard. As children gain confidence listening for individual sounds, say the animal name and have the children produce the initial sound.

Circle time

Hello song and puppet (CD1 Track 2; see TB p 17 & 21)

Opening routines (see TB p 16)

Recycling activity (six wild animals from lesson 1) (see TB p 19)

Lesson aims (see TB p 18)

Introduce the new wild animals.

- Put the wild animals flashcards on the floor or board.
- Children identify the four new wild animals. Use the puppet to point to and say the words in turn. Children repeat in chorus.
- Turn the four new flashcards face down. Mix them up. Point to one and ask *Is it a zebra, giraffe, tiger or snake?* Children guess. Repeat several times.
- Children stand up. Teach a mime for each new animal. Say a word and children do the mime.

Introduce *What's that? It's a … / It has …*

- Stick the wild animal flashcards on different walls of the classroom away from the children.
- Mime that you have a pair of binoculars. Get children to do the same. Pretend to look through your imaginary binoculars at the flashcard of the elephant and ask *What's that? (It's an elephant.)*
- Repeat with all the animals. Children join in pretending to look at the animals through their imaginary binoculars and asking and answering the questions with you.

Game: *Name the animal!*

- Keep the flashcards on the classroom walls.
- Say e.g. *It's black and white.* Children mime looking through their binoculars at the flashcards and name the animal: *It's a zebra!*
- Repeat with other sentences and animals e.g. *It's gray. / It has a big nose (elephant) / It's blue, red and yellow (parrot)* and as in the song (see TB p 77).

***What's that?* song**

CD2 Track 5

- Put the flashcards face up on the board. Play the audio. The children listen and point to the flashcards of the animals in each verse of the song.
- Play the audio again. Children mime the animals in each verse and join in singing the song. They wave their arms in the air for *Amazing!* at the end of each verse.
- Remember that you can use the karaoke version of the song when children are confident.

Table time

Student's Book p 26

Listen and find the new wild animals.

- Children listen and find the four new wild animals. Repeat and children say the words.

CD2 Track 4

One … two … Which words are new?
Zebra! Zebra! *Tiger! Tiger!*
Giraffe! Giraffe! *Snake! Snake!*

Listen, point and sing *What's that?*

- Play the song. Children listen and point to the photos of animals named in each verse of the song.

Check (✔) the animals Alex and Lucy see. Ask and say.

- Demonstrate that children should choose the animals that are in the song and that Lucy and Alex see.
- Children take turns pointing, asking and saying e.g. *What's that? It's a zebra. It's black and white.*

Activity Book p 26

Find and circle the wild animals in the picture.

- Children find and circle all ten wild animals.

Point, ask and say.

- Children point to the pictures and take turns asking and saying sentences about all the animals.

Closing time

Learning review (see TB p 18)

Closing routines (see TB p 16)

Goodbye song and puppet (CD1 Track 3; see TB p 17 & 21)

Use the **Navio App** to listen to the song, and encourage children to do the same at home.

Lesson 3 Story

2:07

Watch. Listen to the story *The surprise*. Circle Mimi's birthday present to Dylan. Stick the story sticker. Language: binoculars; crocodile, lion, monkey, parrot, snake, tiger; colors; What's that? It's (a tiger). It's (orange and black). It has (big eyes). I'm (a crocodile).

27

Learning objectives

- Watch, understand and enjoy the story *The surprise*
- Make a prediction about the story
- Identify Mimi's present to Dylan in the story

Materials

- Class CDs, printable story cards, flashcards, *Ferris Wheel* mat, Mimi puppet

Main vocabulary

- binoculars; crocodile, lion, monkey, parrot, snake, tiger; colors

Key language

- What's that? It's a (tiger). It's (orange and black). It has (big eyes). I'm a (crocodile).

Teacher's tip: Presenting the story in different ways

Present the story in different ways to sustain children's interest. You may first use the printable story cards, either with the audio or telling the story yourself, and then show the video, or vice versa. Pause the video or audio to ask questions, or alternatively, invite children to come up and point to different things on the story cards or screen.

Circle time

Hello song and puppet (CD1 Track 2; see TB p 17 & 21)
Opening routines (see TB p 16)
Recycling activity (*It's a ... It has ...* and wild animals) (see TB p 19)
Lesson aims (see TB p 18)

Introduce the story *The surprise*.

- Say *It's story time!* Play the *Story rhyme* (CD1 Track 4; see TB p 17)
- Say *Alex and Lucy are listening to a story about Mimi and Dylan. It's Dylan's birthday. There's a surprise. What's the surprise? Can you guess?*

Watch and listen to the story *The surprise*.

CD2 Track 7

- Watch the video, play the audio or read the story using the printable story cards. Pause, repeat words, point to the pictures, ask questions.
- Ask *What's the surprise? (a birthday party) What's Katy? (a parrot) What's Leo? (a snake), What's Zara? (a tiger), What's Harry? (a lion) What's Dylan? (a crocodile) What's Mimi? (a monkey).*
- Repeat the story. Encourage children to join in with the words and phrases in the story.
- Ask *Do you like the story? Do you like costume parties?*

Look, find and say.

- Say e.g. *It's orange and black!* Children look and say *It's a tiger*. Repeat with other animals.
- Ask *What does Leo say?* Children find Leo and say *I'm a snake! Hiss!* Repeat with other characters.

Table time

Student's Book p 27

Watch. Listen to the story *The surprise*.

Story questions

Picture 1
Whose birthday is it? *(Dylan's)*
Does Dylan like his present? *(Yes)*

Picture 2
Where do Mimi and Dylan go? *(The yard)*
What do Mimi and Dylan play with? *(Binoculars)*

Picture 3
What animals can Mimi and Dylan see? *(Tiger/snake)*
What animal is green and yellow? *(Snake)*

Picture 4
What colors can Dylan see now? *(Red/yellow/blue)*
What animal is red, yellow and blue? *(Parrot)*

Picture 5
What animal is Mimi at the party? *(Monkey)*
What costume does Dylan have? *(Crocodile)*

Picture 6
What do they eat at the party? *(Cake)*
Is Dylan happy? *(Yes)*

CD2 Track 7

- Read or play the audio of the story again (see TB p 76). Children listen and point to the pictures in their books.

Circle Mimi's birthday present to Dylan. Stick the story sticker.

- Demonstrate circling Mimi's birthday present to Dylan and sticking the story sticker.
- Ask *Who's a crocodile at the party? (Dylan) Who's a monkey at the party? (Mimi).*

Activity Book p 27

Number the pictures in order. Circle your favorite picture.

- Children number the story pictures in order and circle their favorite picture.

Ask and say.

- They ask and answer about the animals.

Closing time

Learning review (see TB p 18)
Closing routines (see TB p 16)
Goodbye song and puppet (CD1 Track 3; see TB p 17 & 21)

Use the **Navio App** to watch the video, and encourage children to do the same at home.

Lesson 4

Story Song

Watch. Listen, point and sing *The party surprise*. Match the animals to the characters. Circle your favorite animal and character. Ask and say. Language: crocodile, lion, monkey, parrot, snake, tiger; What's that? It's (a snake). I'm (a tiger).

28

Learning objectives

- Watch, sing and act out the story song *The party surprise*
- Listen to the story again and mime the animals
- Identify and say wild animals
- Ask and answer questions about wild animals

Materials

- Class CDs, printable story cards, flashcards, *Ferris Wheel* mat, Mimi puppet

Main vocabulary

- crocodile, lion, monkey, parrot, snake, tiger

Key language

- What's that? It's (a snake). I'm (a tiger).

Teacher's tip: Using slow actions to calm children down

If the children become over-excited when miming the wild animals, ask them to do the actions very slowly. Slowing everything down can have a calming effect on the class and increase the level of concentration. Vary the speed so that the children can release energy doing the actions quickly again.

Circle time

Hello song and puppet (CD1 Track 2; see TB p 17 & 21)
Opening routines (see TB p 16)
Recycling activity (wild animals) (see TB p 19)
Lesson aims (see TB p 18)

Retell the story *The surprise*.

- Play the audio or video, or read the story using the printable story cards.
- Demonstrate that children should wave their arms in the air every time they hear the name of a wild animal in the story.

Game: ***Mime, guess and say.***

- Ask pairs or small groups of children to stand up in turn. Whisper to them the name of an animal at the birthday party without the rest of the class hearing.
- Children mime the animal to the class who guess the animal. When they guess correctly, children say e.g. *Yes! I'm a tiger. Grrr!*
- Repeat with other pairs or groups of children and wild animals at the party.

***The party surprise* song**

CD2 Track 8

- Ask *How many animals are in the song?* (six) *What are they?* (tiger, snake, parrot, lion, monkey, crocodile) Children watch the video and respond.
- Play the video again. Children act out being the animals in each verse, hold their index fingers and thumbs around their eyes and open them very wide in the chorus, and join in singing the song.
- Ask e.g. *Which animal do you want to be?* and children respond.

Name and mime the wild animal.

- Say e.g. *Squawk!* Children respond by saying *I'm a parrot.* and mime flying.
- Repeat with all the sounds and animals in the song.

Table time

Student's Book p 28

Watch. Listen, point and sing *The party surprise*.

CD2 Track 8

- Play the song (see TB p 77). Children listen, sing and point to the characters at the party in the picture.
- Remember that you can use the karaoke version of the song when children are confident.

Match the animals to the characters.

- Children draw a line to match the animals and characters at the party.

Circle your favorite animal and character.

- Children circle their favorite animal and character and say e.g. *I'm a crocodile.*

Ask and say.

- Children ask and answer questions about all the pictures e.g. *What's that? It's a snake.*

Activity Book p 28

Choose a wild animal costume. Draw and color a picture of you in your costume.

- Children choose one the costumes and draw and color themselves wearing it.

Say.

- Children say what animal they are.

Closing time

Learning review (see TB p 18)
Closing routines (see TB p 16)
Goodbye song and puppet (CD1 Track 3; see TB p 17 & 21)

Use the **Navio App** to watch the video, and encourage children to do the same at home.

Lesson 5 Speaking

Life skills

Watch. Listen and point. Check (✔) the wild animals Auntie Vicky, Alex and Lucy see at the safari park. Draw a wild animal you want to see. Ask and say. **Language:** crocodile, elephant, hippo, monkey, parrot; What's that? It's (an elephant). It has (big ears). What are those? They're (monkeys).

Learning objectives

- Ask and answer questions about wild animals
- Watch, understand and enjoy a video
- Identify wild animals in the video
- Identify different quantities of animals

Materials

- Class CDs, flashcards, *Ferris Wheel* mat, Mimi puppet

Main vocabulary

- crocodile, elephant, hippo, monkey, parrot

Key language

- What's that? It's (an elephant). It has (big ears). What are those? They're (monkeys).

Teacher's tip: Speaking in pairs

Life skills

Working in pairs can greatly maximize speaking time in class. It also gives children an opportunity to work responsibly with a partner and to rehearse speaking in a safe way. Have the children ask and answer about the animal they draw in pairs. Move around the classroom encouraging children as appropriate and monitoring carefully to make sure all the children are on task.

Circle time

Hello song and puppet (CD1 Track 2; see TB p 17 & 21)
Opening routines (see TB p 16)
Recycling activity (story song) (CD2 Track 8; see TB p 19)
Lesson aims (see TB p 18)

Game: ***Guess the animal***

- Use the puppet to put the wild animal flashcards face up on the board. Children name the animals as you do this.
- Say sentences e.g. *It has a big nose. / It's long and green.* Use mime and gesture to support understanding as necessary. Children guess the animals

Watch the video.

- Explain that Lucy and Alex are with Auntie Vicky at a safari park. They're looking at the wild animals through binoculars.
- Ask *What animals do they see?* Children guess.
- Play the video of Lucy, Alex and Auntie Vicky.
- Ask the question again and check the answer (elephant, crocodile).
- Watch again. Pause and children repeat the sentences about the animals.
- Ask e.g. *Which animal has a big nose?*

Table time

Student's Book p 29

Life skills

Watch. Listen and point.

- Children identify Lucy, Alex and Auntie Vicky and the animals in the photos.
- Play the audio or video. Children listen and point to the photos of the animals Lucy, Alex and Auntie Vicky see.

Check (✔) the wild animals Auntie Vicky, Alex and Lucy see at the safari park.

- Children choose the animals they see at the park.
- Play the audio again. Use the pause button and children repeat the sentences about the animals. Check they have checked the correct boxes.

CD2 Track 10

Auntie Vicky:	Let's go to the safari park!
Lucy and Alex:	Oh, yes. Fantastic!
Lucy:	Oh, look, Auntie Vicky. What's that? It's gray. And it's enormous!
Auntie Vicky:	It's an elephant.
Alex:	Oh, yes! Look. It has big ears!
Lucy:	And it has a big nose! Oh, wow!
Alex:	And what's that … in the water?
Auntie Vicky:	I think it's a crocodile.
Alex:	Yes, it is a crocodile!
Lucy:	It has big teeth.
Auntie Vicky:	Be careful, children. It's dangerous. Don't go too close!
Alex and Lucy:	No way! Don't worry, Auntie Vicky. We won't.
Lucy:	And look … in the trees. What are those?
Auntie Vicky:	They're parrots. They're beautiful.

Draw a wild animal you want to see. Ask and say.

- Children draw a wild animal they want to see. They ask and say sentences about their pictures e.g. *What's that? It's a lion. It's yellow. It has big teeth.*

Activity Book p 29

Circle the pictures with one wild animal red. Circle the pictures with two or more wild animals green.

- Children circle the pictures with only one animal in red. They circle the pictures with more than one animal in green.

Ask and say.

- They ask and answer questions about the animals.

Closing time

Learning review (see TB p 18)
Closing routines (see TB p 16)
Goodbye song and puppet (CD1 Track 3; see TB p 17 & 21)

Use the **Navio App** to watch the video, and encourage children to do the same at home.

Lesson 6 Values Saying 'thank you'

2:11

Listen and point to the story. Say. Color the children saying 'thank you'.
Language: lion, mouse; head, teeth; I'm hungry. I can help you! Thank you.

SOCIAL AND EMOTIONAL LEARNING

30

Learning objectives

- Recognize the value of saying "thank you"
- Understand and enjoy a story about expressing thanks
- Identify when we can say "thank you"

Materials

- Class CDs, flashcards, *Ferris Wheel* mat, Mimi puppet

Main vocabulary

- lion, mouse, head, teeth

Key language

- I'm hungry. I can help you! Thank you.

Teacher's tip: Saying 'thank you'

Bring *thank you* into the classroom routines. Always say *thank you* yourself when children give you their work or books etc. Encourage them to say *thank you* when something is given to them. If they forget, give them a gentle reminder.

Circle time

Hello song and puppet (CD1 Track 2; see TB p 17 & 21)

Opening routines (see TB p 16)

Recycling activity *(What's that? It's a ... It has ...)* (see TB p 19)

Lesson aims (see TB p 18)

Watch *The surprise* story video.

- Play the story video.
- Take the parts of the narrator, Mommy and Daddy yourself. Encourage children to join in acting out the story in two groups (Mimi, Dylan) and get everyone to act out being the animals at the surprise birthday party in picture 5.
- Ask e.g. *What does Dylan say to Mimi for his birthday present? (Thank you) What does he say to Mommy and Daddy for his birthday present? (Thank you) What does he say for his birthday cake and surprise birthday party? (Thank you).*
- Ask e.g. *Is it important to say "thank you" when people give you a present or do something nice for you? Why?*

Story about expressing thanks from *Little Book of Values*

CD2 Track 11

- Use the Mimi puppet to remind children of the *Little Book of Values* with stories about a brother and sister called Harry and Zoe. In this story, Harry and Zoe use a puppet of a lion and a mouse to tell a story about saying *thank you.*
- Say *Listen and find out. Why does the mouse say "thank you" to the lion? (because the lion doesn't eat the mouse) Why does the lion say "thank you" to the mouse? (because the mouse frees the lion from the net).* Children guess.
- Play the audio. Check the answers.
- Play the audio again. Use the pause button and ask questions e.g. *Who's hungry? (the lion) Who's little? (the mouse).*

Table time

Student's Book p 30

Listen and point to the story. Say.

CD2 Track 11

- Play the audio of the story. Children listen and point to the pictures.
- Ask questions e.g. *Is the lion hungry? (Yes) Does the lion eat the mouse? (No) Is the mouse free? (Yes) What does the mouse say? (Thank you) Is the lion free? (Yes) What does the lion say? (Thank you)*
- Ask *Do you say "thank you"? When do you say "thank you"? Who do you say "thank you" to?* Listen to the children's answers.

Color the children saying 'thank you'.

- Children color the children saying "thank you."

Activity Book p 30

Check (✓) the pictures to show when you say 'thank you'.

- Children check the pictures that show when they say "thank you."

Say.

- They talk about when they say "thank you."

Closing time

Learning review (see TB p 18)

Closing routines (see TB p 16)

Goodbye song and puppet (CD1 Track 3; see TB p 17 & 21)

Use the **Navio App** to listen to the story, and encourage children to do the same at home.

Lesson 7 Content

Wild animals

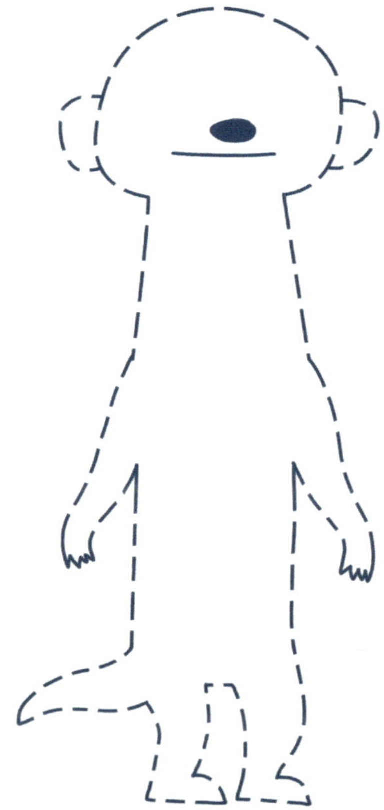

Listen and point. Match the parts of the body to the photo of a meerkat. Trace and complete the picture of a meerkat. Point and say. Language: claws, ears, eyes, fur, legs, nose, tail, whiskers; big, small; brown; What's that? It's (a meerkat). It has (big eyes).

Learning objectives

- Learn about real meerkats
- Listen and identify parts of a meerkat's body
- Ask about and describe meerkats

Materials

- Class CDs, printable content flashcards, *Ferris Wheel* mat, Mimi puppet

Main vocabulary

- claws, ears, eyes, fur, legs, nose, tail, whiskers; big, small, brown

Key language

- What's that? It's (a meerkat). It has (big eyes).

Teacher's tip: Applying new vocabulary to other animals

Once the children are familiar with the new language, extend it to talk about other animals that have a tail, fur, whiskers or claws. Show the other flashcards one by one and encourage the children to say if they have the same features e.g. tiger: *It has claws. It has fur. It has a tail. It has whiskers.*

Circle time

Hello song and puppet (CD1 Track 2; see TB p 17 & 21)
Opening routines (see TB p 16)
Recycling activity (see TB p 19)
Lesson aims (see TB p 18)

Introduce content vocabulary.

- Use the puppet and the printable flashcards to introduce the new words (*tail, fur, whiskers* and *claws*).
- Say the words and use gesture to show each one. Children repeat the words and copy your gestures.
- Say *We're going to learn about real meerkats.* Use the puppet to show how excited Mimi is about this. Project an image of a real meerkat, or show the children a photo if you have one available.

Game: ***Show me your tail!***

- Children stand up. Say *You're a meerkat! Show me your tail!* Children respond by making a gesture to show their imaginary tail.
- Repeat with other parts of the body.

Game: ***Repeat if it's true!***

- Hold up the photo or point to the projected image of a meerkat. Use the puppet to say a sentences e.g. *It has big eyes!* Children repeat the sentence if it's true and fold their arms and stay silent if it isn't true.
- Repeat with other true and false sentences about the physical features of meerkats (see audio text below) and children respond.

Table time

Student's Book p 31

Listen and point.

- Say *Lucy, Alex and Auntie Vicky are looking at a web page about meerkats.*
- Children identify the parts of the body in the pictures and on the meerkat in the photo.
- Play the audio. Children listen and point to the parts of the body.

CD2 Track 12

Alex: Look, Auntie Vicky! What's that?
Auntie Vicky: It's a meerkat. It has brown fur and whiskers. It has a tail and claws. It has small ears, a small nose and big eyes. It stands on two legs.
Lucy: Oh wow! It's very cute!
Auntie Vicky: Yes, but a meerkat is a wild animal. A meerkat lives in a big family. Meerkats are friendly and help each other.
Alex: Like Mimi and Dylan in our favorite meerkat stories … ?
Auntie Vicky: Ha, ha. Well, something like that …

- Play the audio again. Use the pause button. Children repeat the sentences to describe a meerkat.

Match the parts of the body to the photo of a meerkat.

- Children draw a line to match the parts of the body to the photo of the meerkat.

Trace and complete the picture of a meerkat.

- Children trace, complete and color the picture of a meerkat. Monitor and make sure they have included all the key features (fur, whiskers, tail, claws) as well as ears and eyes.

Point and say.

- Children point to their pictures and say sentences, e.g. *It has (brown) fur. It has a tail.*

Activity Book p 31

Match the meerkats. Draw the missing body parts.

- Children match the meerkats that are the same. Then they draw the missing body parts.

Color the meerkats.

- Children color the meerkats.

Point and say.

- They point and say what the meerkats have.

Closing time

Learning review (see TB p 18)
Closing routines (see TB p 16)
Goodbye song and puppet (CD1 Track 3; see TB p 17 & 21)

Use the **Navio App** to play the vocabulary and language games, and encourage children to do the same at home.

Lesson 8

Culture

Wild animals

2:13

hello

Watch. Listen, point and sing *Five little monkeys*. Trace the numbers. Trace and color the monkeys. Say. **Language:** crocodile, monkey; numbers 1–5; (Five) little monkeys sitting in a tree. You can't catch me! Along comes Mr. Crocodile.

32

Learning objectives

- Watch, sing and act out the traditional song *Five little monkeys*
- Play an action game
- Count the monkeys and circle the correct number

Materials

- Class CDs, flashcards, *Ferris Wheel* mat, Mimi puppet

Main vocabulary

- crocodile, monkey; numbers 1–5

Key language

- (Five) little monkeys sitting in a tree. You can't catch me! Along comes Mr. Crocodile.

Teacher's tip: Acting out the song in groups

Once the children are familiar with the song *Five little monkeys*, have them act it out in groups of six. One child is the crocodile in each group. Number the remaining children 1–5. They should stand in a line as if on a branch. Each time a monkey falls, one of the children sits down while the "crocodile" walks back and forth menacingly, opening and closing their outstretched arms to be jaws. If space is limited, have the groups take turns coming to the front and acting out the song. The rest of the class sings along.

Circle time

Hello song and puppet (CD1 Track 2; see TB p 17 & 21)
Opening routines (see TB p 16)
Recycling activity (see TB p 19)
Lesson aims (see TB p 18)

Game: *Little monkeys!*

- Show children the flashcard of the monkey and children say the word.
- Children stand up and mime being little monkeys sitting in a tree. Put your arms out straight and open and close them as a crocodile. Say *I'm Mr. Crocodile. I'm hungry!* pretend to catch one of the little monkeys and say *Snap!*
- Invite that child to join you as a crocodile and repeat. Count the little monkeys you and the children catch as you play the game.

Five little monkeys song

CD2 Track 13

- Ask *How many monkeys in the song? Does the crocodile eat them?* Children guess.
- Play the audio and children listen to the song. Check the answers (five, no).
- Play the audio again. Children act out being the monkeys and the crocodile and join in singing the song.

Watch the *Five little monkeys* song video.

- Children watch the video and join in acting out and singing the song with Alex and Lucy.

Table time

Student's Book p 32

Watch. Listen, point and sing *Five little monkeys*.

CD2 Track 13

- Play the audio. Children listen and point to the monkeys and crocodile as they join in singing the song.

Trace the numbers. Trace and color the monkeys. Say.

- Children trace the numbers and trace and color the monkeys. They point to the monkeys and say *Five little monkeys*.
- Play the audio again. Children cover the monkeys in turn with their fingers for each verse and sing the song.

Activity Book p 32

Find and color the monkeys in the picture.

- Children find the five monkeys in the picture and color them.

Count the monkeys and circle the correct number.

- They count the monkeys and circle the correct number.

Closing time

Learning review (see TB p 18)
Closing routines (see TB p 16)
Goodbye song and puppet (CD1 Track 3; see TB p 17 & 21)

Use the **Navio App** to watch the video, and encourage children to do the same at home.

Review

Wild animals

I can ...

Vocabulary

Story

Speaking

Content

Color the circles of the animals you know. Listen, point and say. Listen and answer. Ask and say. Complete the faces to show what you can do. Language: crocodile, elephant, giraffe, hippo, lion, monkey, parrot, snake, tiger, zebra; What's that? It's (an elephant). It has (big ears). What are those? They're (monkeys).

Wild animals

Learning objectives

- Review what you have learned in this unit
- Complete a self-evaluation
- Ask and answer questions about wild animals

Materials

- Class CDs, flashcards, *Ferris Wheel* mat, Mimi puppet

Main vocabulary

- crocodile, elephant, giraffe, hippo, lion, monkey, parrot, snake, tiger, zebra

Key language

- What's that? It's (an elephant). It has (big ears). What are those? They're (monkeys).

Teacher's tip: Comparing animals

Encourage children to use the unit language to compare the animals in the safari park. e.g. an elephant and a hippo: *It has big / small ears.* This will help consolidate the meaning of vocabulary and reinforce working memory.

Circle time

Hello song and puppet (CD1 Track 2; see TB p 17 & 21)
Opening routines (see TB p 16)
Recycling activity (see TB p 19)
Lesson aims (see TB p 18)

Wild animal flashcard games

- Choose one or two flashcard games with the *Ferris Wheel* mat and/or the puppet to review main vocabulary (see TB p 20 & 21).

Sing *What's that?*

CD2 Track 5

- Stick the flashcards on the board. Play the audio. Children sing and do the actions.
- Children ask and answer questions about the animals.

Photo safari

- Stick the flashcards at children's height around the classroom. Have children walk around with a pretend camera ready to spot the animals on the "safari."
- Say *It's green. It has big teeth.* Children go and take a photo of the crocodile. Repeat with the other animals.

Guessing game

- Stick the animal flashcards on the board. Organize the class into pairs. One child describes an animal, e.g. *It has big ears.* The other child names it, e.g. *It's an elephant.*

Watch the story video.

- Children watch the story video. Ask *Which animals come to Dylan's birthday party? (tiger, snake, parrot, lion, monkey, and Dylan as a crocodile)*

Table time

Student's Book p 33

Color the circles of the wild animals you know.

- Explain and demonstrate the activity.

Listen, point and say.

- Play the audio. Children check the words they know, point to the pictures and repeat the words.

CD2 Track 14

Mimi: I'm the teacher! Can you remember the wild animals, Dylan?
Dylan: Yes, I can. Lion.
Mimi: Lion.
Dylan: Tiger.
Mimi: Tiger.
Dylan: Elephant.
Mimi: Elephant.
Dylan: Hippo.
Mimi: Hippo.
Dylan: Monkey.
Mimi: Monkey.
Dylan: Parrot.
Mimi: Parrot.
Dylan: Snake.
Mimi: Snake.
Dylan: Crocodile.
Mimi: Crocodile.
Dylan: Zebra.
Mimi: Zebra.
Dylan: Giraffe.
Mimi: Giraffe. Well done, Dylan!
Both: Fantastic!

Listen and answer. Ask and say.

- Play the audio. Children listen to the questions.

CD2 Track 15

Mimi: What's that? It has big ears.
What's that? It's orange and black.
What's that? It has big teeth.
What's that? It's red, yellow and blue.
What's that? It's yellow and it has big eyes.
What's that? It has long legs.

- Play the audio again. Children listen, repeat and answer the questions.
- Children ask and answer about wild animals.

Complete the faces to show what you can do.

- Explain the four pictures: *I can name wild animals; I can understand the story; I can identify and describe wild animals; I can describe meerkats.*
- Remind children they should complete each face with a smile or frown depending on how well they think they have done.

Activity Book p 33

Complete the faces to show the wild animals you like. Ask and say.

- Children complete the faces with a smile if they like the animal.
- Children ask and answer about the animals.

Think and circle the number to show your progress.

- Children circle the number.

Closing time

Learning review (see TB p 18)
Closing routines (see TB p 16)
Goodbye song and puppet (CD1 Track 3; see TB p 17 & 21)

Use the **Navio App** to review what children have learned in this unit, and encourage them to do the same at home.

Project

COOPERATIVE LEARNING

Wild animals

1

2

3

Choose, color and decorate a wild animal. Put your animals together to make a safari park mobile. Ask and say.
Language: crocodile, elephant, lion, zebra; numbers; colors; What's that? It's (a zebra). It's (black and white). It has (a tail). What are those? They're (lions). How many (elephants)? (Four). I like (the zebra). Do you like (the crocodile)? Yes. / No.

34

Wild animals

Learning objectives

- Work together to do a collaborative project
- Make an animal
- Ask and answer questions about the animals
- Make a collage of wild animals

Materials

- Class CDs, Mimi puppet, photocopiable templates, crayons, pieces of colored yarn and tissue paper, glue, string, a hanger
- optional: modeling clay

Main vocabulary

- crocodile, elephant, lion, zebra; numbers; colors

Key language

- What's that? It's (a zebra). It's (black and white). It has (a tail). What are those? They're (lions). How many (elephants)? (Four). I like (the zebra). Do you like (the crocodile)? Yes. / No.

Teacher's tip: Giving simple instructions

COOPERATIVE LEARNING

The most effective way of making sure children follow instructions correctly is to give one instruction at a time and to keep them short and simple. Use your fingers and add stages to help children complete the instructions in the right order, e.g. *Number 1, choose an animal; number 2, build the animal's body; number 3, add the animal's head,* etc.

Circle time

Hello song and puppet (CD1 Track 2; see TB p 17 & 21)
Opening routines (see TB p 16)
Recycling activity (see TB p 19)
Lesson aims (see TB p 18)

Prepare for your project.

- Say *Let's do a project. Let's make a safari park mobile!*
- Show children the templates for this unit. Explain that children should choose their favorite wild animal and color and decorate it using tissue paper and yarn.
- Explain and demonstrate that children will then use their pictures of their animals to make safari park mobiles. Depending on the size of your class, you can make one large mobile or one mobile per group of 6–10 children.

Table time

Student's Book p 34

COOPERATIVE LEARNING

Choose, color and decorate a wild animal. Put your animals together to make a safari park mobile.

- Say e.g. *We're going to make a safari park mobile like this. Look at what we need for our project: the animal templates, crayons, colored yarn and tissue paper, glue, string and a hanger.* Children listen and point to the pictures.
- Children choose their favorite animal template. Make sure children have crayons, tissue paper, pieces of yarn and glue available.
- Children color their animal. They can glue pieces of tissue paper and yarn to their animal to give it skin and fur.
- When they are ready, invite children to come and hang their animal on the hanger you have prepared to make the mobile.

Ask and say.

- Talk about the animals in the safari park mobile using language of the unit and other language children know. Count how many of each animal there are with the children to find out the class's favorite.
- Ask children *Do you like our safari park mobile(s)?* Make the point that everyone has helped make the safari park mobile and that they couldn't have made such a beautiful mobile on their own.

Alternative version of project

- Children could use modeling clay to make their favorite wild animal and put them together to make a model of a safari park.

Activity Book p 34

Find photos and make a collage of wild animals. Circle the wild animals that are in your collage.

- Children find photos of wild animals and glue them on the page to make a collage. Then they circle the animals in the frame that are in their collage.

Ask and say.

- Children ask and answer questions about the animals in their collage.

Closing time

Learning review (see TB p 18)
Closing routines (see TB p 16)
Goodbye song and puppet (CD1 Track 3; see TB p 17 & 21)

Daily routines

Giant Joe

Unit objectives

- Identify and name daily routines
- Sing the language song *What do you do every day?*
- Say what you do every day
- Understand and act out the story *Giant Joe*
- Sing and act out the story song *Giant Joe's day*
- Ask and say where you do things
- Sing the values song *I sleep, I eat, I learn, I play*
- Recognize the value of having a daily routine
- Learn about how and when to wash your hands
- Understand the traditional story *Goldilocks and the three bears*
- Review your learning and progress
- Participate in a collaborative project

Vocabulary and language

- **Main vocabulary:** brush my hair, brush my teeth, get dressed, get up, have breakfast, have lunch, have dinner, take a shower, wash my face, wash my hands
- **Key language:** What do you do every day? I (have lunch). Do you (wash your hands)? What do you do at (home)? I (have breakfast) at (home). Do you (have lunch) at (school)? Yes, I do. / No, I don't. I don't (have dinner) at (school).
- **Content language:** clean, faucet, soap, towel, wash my hands, water; I wash my hands with soap.
- **Other language:** home, school, drink water, eat, learn, play, sleep; bed, bowl, chair; big, small, tiny; Mommy, Daddy, Baby Bear; It's time to (get dressed). This (bowl) is (small).

Story

CD2 Track 22

Picture 1

Narrator: Mimi and Dylan are going to stay with Grandma and Grandpa. They're excited.
Mimi: Oh, fantastic! I love Grandma and Grandpa.
Dylan: I love Grandpa's stories!
Mimi: Me too!
Dylan: Hello, Grandma.
Mimi: Hello, Grandpa.
Grandpa & Grandma: Hello, Mimi. Hello, Dylan.
Grandpa: Come in. You're just in time to have dinner!

Picture 2

Narrator: The next morning Mimi and Dylan get up early and go to Grandma and Grandpa's bedroom.
Mimi: Good morning, Grandma.
Dylan: Good morning, Grandpa.
Grandma: Hello, Mimi.
Grandpa: Hello, Dylan. You get up early!
Mimi: Oops, sorry. Can we have a story please, Grandpa?
Dylan: Oh, yes! Can we have a story, please, Grandpa?
Grandpa: Oh, no. Not now. It's time to err… get dressed.
Mimi & Dylan: Oh alright.

Picture 3

Mimi: Look. We're ready. Can we have a story now, please, Grandpa?
Dylan: Oh, yes! Can we have a story now, please, Grandpa?
Grandpa: Oh, no. Not now. It's time to err … have breakfast.
Mimi & Dylan: Oh, alright.

Picture 4

Mimi: Mmm. Delicious breakfast. Thank you, Grandma.
Dylan: Can we have a story now, please, Grandpa?
Mimi: Oh, yes! Can we have a story now, please, Grandpa?
Grandpa: A story?! Mmm, alright. I'm Giant Joe and I'm hungry …

Picture 5

Grandpa: I get up. I get dressed.
Mimi: Do you wash your face?
Grandpa: Yes, I do.
Dylan: Do you wash your hands?
Grandpa: Yes, I do. I wash my face and my hands. I brush my hair. And now … it's time for breakfast!

Picture 6

Grandpa: Ha, ha! Got you! Mmm. Delicious breakfast. Yummy!
Mimi: Tee, hee, hee. It's time to brush your teeth now, Giant Joe!
Grandpa: Ha, ha, ha, ha. You're right, Mimi!
Mimi: Can we have the story again, please, Grandpa?
Dylan: Oh, yes! Can we have the story again, please, Grandpa?
Grandpa: Err umm … no, not now. I'm tired.
Mimi: But Giant Joe isn't tired!
Grandpa: Oh, alright. Here I come!

Songs and story

Language song

What do you do every day? CD2 Track 20

What do you do every day? (Shrug)
I get up. I get up. (Mime getting out of bed)
I get dressed. I get dressed. (Mime putting on a T-shirt)
And I play! (Jump up and down in place)

What do you do every day? (Shrug)
I wash my face. I wash my face. (Mime washing your face)
I brush my hair. I brush my hair. (Mime brushing your hair)
And I play! (Jump up and down in place)

What do you do every day? (Shrug)
I have breakfast. I have breakfast. (Mime eating cereal)
I brush my teeth. I brush my teeth. (Mime brushing your teeth)
And I play! (Jump up and down in place)

What do you do every day? (Shrug)
I wash my hands. I wash my hands. (Mime washing your hands)
I have lunch. I have lunch. (Mime cutting food and eating it)
And I play! (Jump up and down in place)

What do you do every day? (Shrug)
I have dinner. I have dinner. (Mime cutting food and eating it)
I have a shower. I have a shower. (Mime washing your arms)
And I play! (Jump up and down in place)

Story song

Giant Joe CD2 Track 23

Fee, fi, fum, fo (March in place)
I'm a giant. My name is Joe. (Point to self)
Fee, fi, fo, fum (March in place)
Now I'm hungry, yum, yum, yum! (Rub tummy)

I get up. I get dressed. (Mime getting out of bed and putting on a T-shirt)
I do this every day. (Point around you)
I wash my face. I wash my hands. (Mime washing face and hands)
And this is what I say: (Cup hands around mouth)

(Chorus)

I brush my hair. I brush my teeth. (Mime brushing hair and teeth)
I do this every day. (Point around you)
I have breakfast. I have dinner. (Mime eating)
And this is what I say: (Cup hands around mouth)

(Chorus)

Values song

I sleep, I eat, I learn, I play CD2 Track 26

I sleep, I eat. (mime sleeping and eating)
I learn, I play. (point to your head with a finger and skip in place)
I take a shower every day. (mime washing your arms)
(Chorus)
I drink water every day. (mime drinking water)
(Chorus)
I brush my teeth every day. (mime brushing teeth)
(Chorus)
I wash my hands every day. (mime washing your hands)
I have a routine. I do it every day. (point to self)
It's good for me in every way. (thumbs up, then open arms wide)

Culture story

Goldilocks and the three bears CD2 Track 28

Picture 1

Narrator:	Daddy Bear, Mommy Bear and Baby Bear have porridge for breakfast every day. One day the porridge is very hot.
Mommy bear:	Come on, bears! Let's go for a walk.
Daddy bear:	Great idea!
Baby bear:	Hurray!

Picture 2

Narrator:	Goldilocks comes to the Bears' house. Goldilocks tries the porridge.
Goldilocks:	This bowl is big. No! This bowl is small. No! This bowl is tiny. Mmm. Delicious!
Narrator:	Goldilocks tries the chairs.
Goldilocks:	This chair is big. No! This chair is small. No! This chair is tiny. Mmm. Perfect!

Picture 3

Narrator:	Now Goldilocks is sleepy. Goldilocks tries the beds.
Goldilocks:	This bed is big. No! This bed is small. No! This bed is tiny. Mmm. Perfect!
Narrator:	Goldilocks goes to sleep.

Picture 4

Narrator:	The bears come back to their house.
Baby bear:	Look! Who's in my bed?
Mommy bear:	It's Goldilocks!
Baby bear:	Oh, hello, Goldilocks ... Let's play.

Vocabulary Lesson 1

Daily routines

Giant Joe

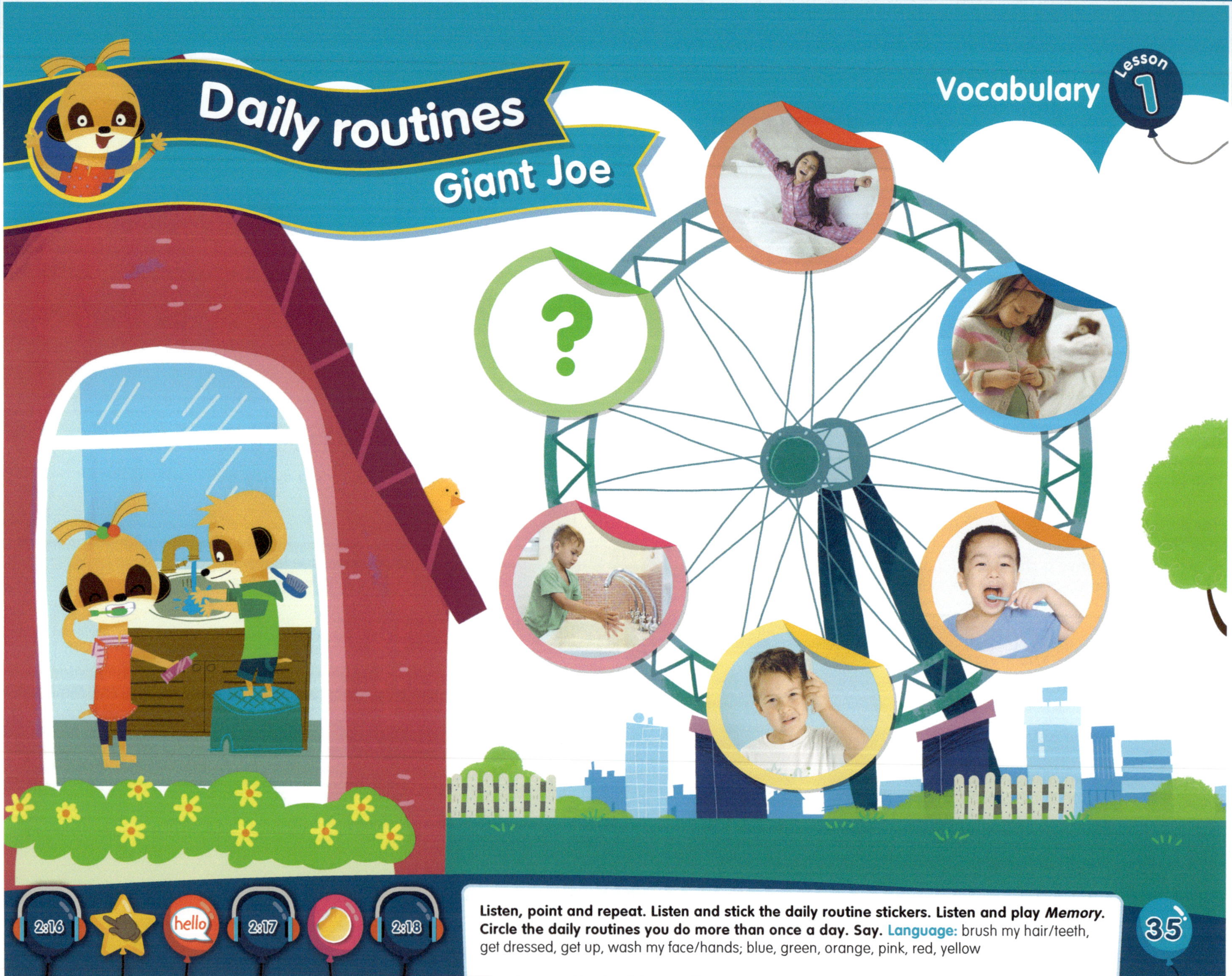

Listen, point and repeat. Listen and stick the daily routine stickers. Listen and play *Memory*. Circle the daily routines you do more than once a day. Say. **Language:** brush my hair/teeth, get dressed, get up, wash my face/hands; blue, green, orange, pink, red, yellow

Daily routines

Learning objectives

- Identify and name daily routines
- Listen and point to daily routines
- Remember daily routines in a memory game

Materials

- Class CDs, flashcards, *Ferris Wheel* mat, Mimi puppet

Main vocabulary

- brush my hair/teeth, get dressed, get up, wash my face/hands; blue, green, orange, pink, red, yellow

Teacher's tip: Using props

If possible, bring in some props related to each of the daily routines, e.g. a toothbrush, hairbrush, towel, plastic bowl and spoon, etc. These help young children form a closer connection with the new vocabulary. In addition, fast finishers can use them for role-play.

Circle time

Hello song and puppet (CD1 Track 2; see TB p 17 & 21)
Opening routines (see TB p 16)
Lesson aims (see TB p 18)

Introduce daily routines.

- Use the puppet and flashcards to introduce six daily routines. Children mime the routines with you and repeat the words.
- Put the *Ferris Wheel* mat on the floor or board with the daily routine flashcards face down (one on each color). Use the puppet to turn them over and name them. The children repeat the daily routines.

Game: *Say the color!*

- Name the daily routines on the Ferris Wheel and children name the color. Then the reverse.

Game: *Mimi says!*

- Use the puppet to say e.g. *Wash your hands!* or *Wash your hands, please!* Children mime the action when Mimi says please and fold their arms and stay silent when she doesn't.
- Repeat with all the routines in random order.

Table time

Student's Book p 35

Listen, point and repeat.

- Play the audio. Children listen, point and repeat.

CD2 Track 16

Mimi: Look Dylan! I … get up … get dressed … brush my teeth … brush my hair … and wash my hands! Repeat, Dylan!
Dylan: Yes, Mimi. I … get up … get dressed … brush my teeth … brush my hair … and wash my hands!
Mimi: Very good, Dylan! Let's name the daily routines together!
Both: I get up … get dressed … brush my teeth … brush my hair … and wash my hands! Fantastic!

- Draw children's attention to the question mark. They identify the missing daily routine (wash my face).

Listen and stick the daily routine stickers.

- Play the audio. The children listen and point to the daily routines in their books.

CD2 Track 17

Where's "get up"? It's on … red.
Where's "brush my teeth"? It's on … orange.
Where's "wash my hands"? It's on … pink.
Where's "get dressed"? It's on … blue.
Where's "brush my hair"? It's on … yellow.
Where's "wash my face"? Can you guess? It's on … green. Yes, yes, yes!
"Wash my face" is on green. Yes, yes, yes!

- Ask questions about all the daily routines in the same way and children respond.
- Play the audio again. Children listen and stick the daily routine stickers.

Listen and play *Memory*.

- Children cover their eyes with their hands. Play the audio. Children listen and remember the daily routine on each color on the wheel.

CD2 Track 18

Close your eyes
One, two, three
Say the words
Play memory!
Yellow … brush my hair!
Red … get up!
Orange … brush my teeth!
Green … wash my face!
Pink … wash my hands!
Blue … get dressed!

- Play the game.

Circle the daily routines you do more than once a day. Say.

- Children circle the daily routines they do more than once a day. They point and say the words.

Activity Book p 35

Look and match. Trace and color the pictures.

- Children match the objects to the characters. Then they trace and color the pictures.

Point and say.

- Name characters and children point and say the routine e.g. *Grandpa!* / *Get dressed!*

Closing time

Learning review (see TB p 18)
Closing routines (see TB p 16)
Goodbye song and puppet (CD1 Track 3; see TB p 17 & 21)

Use the **Navio App** to play the vocabulary game, and encourage children to do the same at home.

Lesson 2 Language

Daily routines

2:19 2:20 hello

Listen and find the new daily routines. Listen, point and sing *What do you do every day?* Check (✓) the routines in the song. Draw a routine. Ask and say. **Language:** brush my hair/teeth, get dressed, get up, have breakfast/lunch/dinner, take a shower, wash my face/hands; I (have lunch).

36

Learning objectives

- Talk about daily routines
- Identify and name four new routine activities
- Sing the language song *What do you do every day?*
- Say what you do every day

Materials

- Class CDs, flashcards, *Ferris Wheel* mat, Mimi puppet

Main vocabulary

- brush my hair/teeth, get dressed, get up, have breakfast/lunch/dinner, take a shower, wash my face/hands

Key language

- I (have lunch).

Teacher's tip: Backchaining

If your class finds the pronunciation of the vocabulary challenging, give them plenty of encouragement and break down the phrases into single words so that they can practice each word separately before attempting the whole phrase e.g. *hands / my hands / wash my hands.*

Circle time

Hello song and puppet (CD1 Track 2; see TB p 17 & 21)
Opening routines (see TB p 16)
Recycling activity (six daily routines from lesson 1) (see TB p 19)
Lesson aims (see TB p 18)

Introduce the new daily routines.

- Put the daily routines flashcards on the floor or board.
- Children identify the four new daily routines.
- Use the puppet to point to and name the routines in turn. Children repeat in chorus.
- Turn the four new daily routine flashcards face down. Mix them up. Point to one and ask *Is this have breakfast, have lunch, have dinner or have a shower?* Children guess. Repeat several times.
- Children arrange the new flashcards in the order they do the routines every day and say the order.

Introduce *What do you do every day? I (get up).*

- Children name the daily routines flashcards.
- Point to the flashcards and tell children what you do every day e.g. *I get up. I get dressed*, etc.
- Ask children *What do you do every day?* Point to the flashcards. Children say sentences with you in chorus.

Game: *Mime your day!*

- Children stand up. Say *Let's mime our day!*
- Say sentences and mime all the daily routines starting with *I get up.*
- Children join in doing the mimes and saying the sentences with you. Repeat once or twice.

***What do you do every day?* song**

CD2 Track 20

- Put the daily routine flashcards face up on the board.
- Play the audio. Children listen and point to the daily routine flashcards as they hear them. Ask *What else do the children do every day in the song? (play)*
- Play the audio again. Children sing, mime the daily routines and jump up and down for "play."
- Remember that you can use the karaoke version of the song when children are confident.

Table time

Student's Book p 36

Listen and find the new daily routines.

- Play the audio. Children listen and find the four new daily routines. Repeat and children say the words.

CD2 Track 19

One … two … Which words are new?

Have breakfast!	*Have dinner!*
Have breakfast!	*Have dinner!*
Have lunch!	*Take a shower!*
Have lunch!	*Take a shower!*

Listen, point and sing *What do you do every day?*

- Play the song. The children listen and point to the daily routines as they hear them.

Check (✔) the routines in the song.

- Play the audio again with pauses. Show how children should check each box under the routines in the song.
- Children identify the routines that are in the song but not in the photos *(brush teeth, brush hair, wash hands, wash face).*

Draw a routine. Ask and say.

- Children draw a picture to show one of the missing routines. Children ask and say e.g. *What do you do every day? I get up.*

Activity Book p 36

Follow and draw the paths through the maze.

- Children follow the paths with their finger. They say the daily routine and number e.g. *I get up. One.* Then they draw the paths through the maze.

Ask and say.

- Say the numbers and children respond e.g. *Five / I have breakfast.* Children ask and answer about their routines.

Closing time

Learning review (see TB p 18)
Closing routines (see TB p 16)
Goodbye song and puppet (CD1 Track 3; see TB p 17 & 21)

Use the **Navio App** to listen to the song, and encourage children to do the same at home.

Lesson 3

Story

2:22

Watch. Listen to the story *Giant Joe*. Circle what Grandpa's story is about. Stick the story sticker. **Language:** brush my hair/teeth, get dressed, get up, have breakfast/dinner, wash my face/hands; Do you (wash your hands)? Yes, I do. I (get up). It's time to (get dressed).

Learning objectives

- Watch, understand and enjoy the story *Giant Joe*
- Make a prediction about the story
- Identify the subject of Grandpa's story

Materials

- Class CDs, printable story cards, flashcards, *Ferris Wheel* mat, Mimi puppet

Main vocabulary

- brush my hair/teeth, get dressed, get up, have breakfast/dinner, wash my face/hands

Key language

- Do you (wash your hands)? Yes, I do. I (get up). It's time to (get dressed).

Teacher's tip: Using actions and facial expressions

Make sure that the children realize it isn't important to understand every word in the story. Use actions or facial expressions when key words appear to help children focus on what they know, rather than what they don't.

Circle time

Hello song and puppet (CD1 Track 2; see TB p 17 & 21)

Opening routines (see TB p 16)

Recycling activity (*What do you do every day?* and daily routines) (see TB p 19)

Lesson aims (see TB p 18)

Introduce the story *Giant Joe*.

- Say *It's story time!* Play the *Story rhyme* (CD1 Track 4; see TB p 17)
- Say *Alex and Lucy are watching a story about Mimi and Dylan. Mimi and Dylan are going to stay at Grandma and Grandpa's house.* Ask *What do Mimi and Dylan want Grandpa to do?*

Watch and listen to the story *Giant Joe*.

CD2 Track 22

- Watch the video, play the audio or read the story using the printable story cards. Pause, repeat words, point to the pictures, ask questions.
- Ask the pre-question again and check the answer (Mimi and Dylan want Grandpa to tell a story). Ask *What's the story about? (Giant Joe).*
- Repeat and encourage children to join in with the words and phrases.
- Ask *Do you like the story? Do you like Grandpa's story? Does anyone in your family tell you stories?*

Game: ***It's time to … !***

- Say *It's time to* … and mime a daily routine. Children name the routine. Repeat several times with different routines.

Table time

Student's Book p 37

Watch. Listen to the story *Giant Joe*.

CD2 Track 22

- Read or play the audio of the story again (see TB p 98). Children listen and point to the pictures in their books.

Story questions

Picture 1
Are Mimi and Dylan excited to stay with Grandma and Grandpa? *(Yes)*
Is it time for breakfast now? *(No)*

Picture 2
Where are Grandma and Grandpa? *(In the bedroom)*
Do Mimi and Dylan get dressed? *(Yes)*

Picture 3
Does Grandpa tell them a story? *(No)*
Is it time for breakfast now? *(Yes)*

Picture 4
Does Mimi like her breakfast? *(Yes)*
Does Grandpa tell them a story? *(Yes)*

Picture 5
What does Giant Joe wash? *(Face/hands)*
Is it time for dinner? *(No)*

Picture 6
Who is tired? *(Grandpa)*
Who isn't tired? *(Giant Joe)*

Circle what Grandpa's story is about. Stick the story sticker.

- Demonstrate circling what Grandpa's story is about and sticking the story sticker.
- Ask *Do you think Grandpa likes telling the story?*

Activity Book p 37

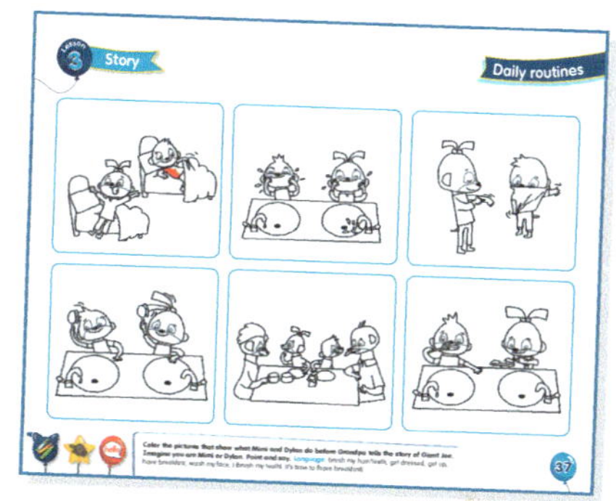

Color the pictures that show what Mimi and Dylan do before Grandpa tells the story of Giant Joe.

- Children color the pictures that show what Mimi and Dylan do before Grandpa tells the story.

Imagine you are Mimi or Dylan. Point and say.

- Children pretend to be Mimi and Dylan, point and say their routines.

Closing time

Learning review (see TB p 18)

Closing routines (see TB p 16)

Goodbye song and puppet (CD1 Track 3; see TB p 17 & 21)

Use the **Navio App** to watch the video, and encourage children to do the same at home.

Lesson 4

Story Song

Daily routines

Watch. Listen, point and sing *Giant Joe's day*. Circle the routines Giant Joe does every day. Ask and say.
Language: brush my hair/teeth, get dressed, get up, have breakfast/lunch/dinner, take a shower, wash my face/hands; I (brush my hair). Do you (wash your face)? Yes, I do. / No, I don't.

38

Learning objectives

- Watch, sing and act out the story song *Giant Joe's day*
- Listen to the story again and act it out
- Identify and say daily routines
- Ask and answer questions about your daily routine

Materials

- Class CDs, printable story cards, flashcards, *Ferris Wheel* mat, Mimi puppet

Main vocabulary

- brush my hair/teeth, get dressed, get up, have breakfast/lunch/ dinner, take a shower, wash my face/hands

Key language

- I (brush my hair). Do you (wash your face)? Yes, I do. / No, I don't.

Teacher's tip: Using a breathing activity to calm children down

After the acting activity, children may benefit from learning a calming-down technique. Encourage them to breathe in slowly through their nose, hold for a count of three and then breathe out through their mouth. Repeat four or five times. Demonstrate and say *Breathe in … breathe out* while you do so.

Circle time

Hello song and puppet (CD1 Track 2; see TB p 17 & 21)
Opening routines (see TB p 16)
Recycling activity (daily routines) (see TB p 19)
Lesson aims (see TB p 18)

Retell the story *Giant Joe*.

- Play the audio, video or read the story using the printable story cards.
- Demonstrate that children should wave their arms in the air every time they hear a daily routine in the story.

Act out *Giant Joe*.

- Children stand up. Say *Let's pretend to be Giant Joe!* Children make themselves as big as a giant.
- Use a deep voice, say sentences from the story e.g. *I'm Giant Joe. I get up. I get dressed* and do the actions. Children do the actions and join in saying the sentences with you. Repeat once or twice.

***Giant Joe* song**

CD2 Track 23

- Ask *What does Giant Joe do every day?* Watch the video.
- Check the answers. (get up, get dressed, wash my face, wash my hands, brush my hair, brush my teeth, have breakfast, have dinner) Children say Giant Joe's daily routines.
- Watch the video again. Children do the actions and join in singing the song.
- Ask e.g. *Do you like Giant Joe?* and children respond.

Game: *Giant Joe says*

- Children stand up. Say *Giant Joe says take a shower.* Children mime taking a shower. Say *Take a shower* and children stand still with their hands on their heads.
- Explain that when children hear the words "Giant Joe says" they should mime the action, but if they only hear the action, they should stand still. If children make a mistake, they have to sit down.
- Play the game until all the actions have been practiced at least once or until all the children are sitting down.

Table time

Student's Book p 38

Watch. Listen, point and sing *Giant Joe's day*.

CD2 Track 23

- Play the song (see TB p 99). Children listen, sing and point to the pictures of daily routines.
- Remember that you can use the karaoke version of the song when children are confident.

Circle the routines Giant Joe does every day. Ask and say.

- Children circle the pictures to show what Giant Joe does every day.
- Children pretend to be Giant Joe and ask and say e.g. *Do you wash your hands? Yes, I do. / No, I don't.*

Activity Book p 38

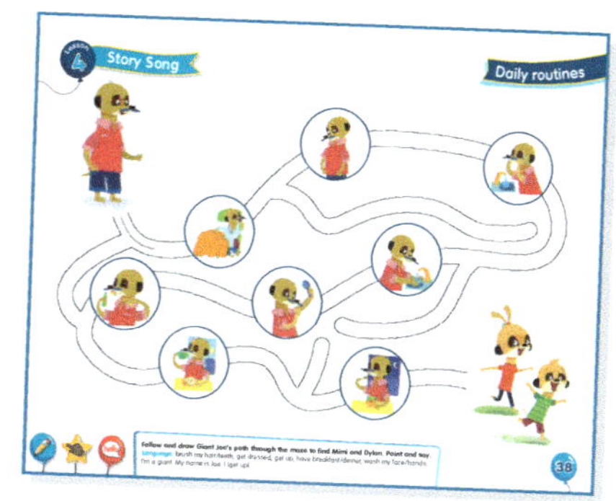

Follow and draw Giant Joe's path through the maze to find Mimi and Dylan.

- Children follow and then draw a path through the maze that shows Giant Joe's routine.

Point and say.

- Children point and say the routines.

Closing time

Learning review (see TB p 18)
Closing routines (see TB p 16)
Goodbye song and puppet (CD1 Track 3; see TB p 17 & 21)

Use the **Navio App** to watch the video, and encourage children to do the same at home.

Lesson 5

Speaking

Life skills

Daily routines

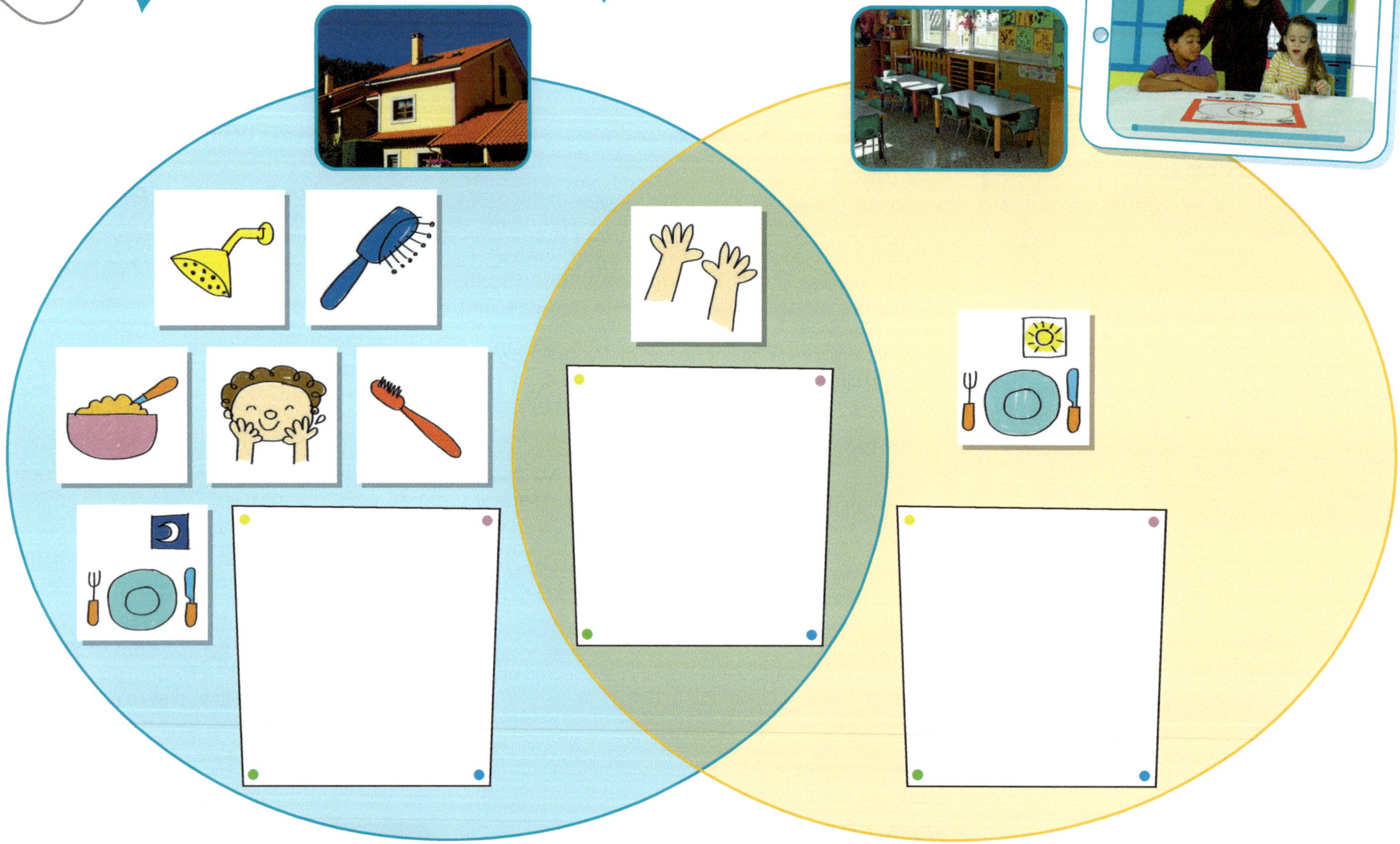

2:25

Watch. Listen and point. Draw three of your routines in the diagram. Ask and say. Language: brush my hair/teeth, have breakfast/lunch/dinner, take a shower, wash my face/hands; home, school; What do you do at (home)? I (have breakfast) at (home). I don't (have dinner) at (school). Do you (have lunch) at (school)? Yes. / No.

39

Daily routines

Lesson 5 Speaking

Learning objectives

- Ask and say where you do things
- Watch, understand and enjoy a video
- Identify home or school routines

Materials

- Class CDs, flashcards, *Ferris Wheel* mat, Mimi puppet

Main vocabulary

- brush my hair/teeth, have breakfast/ lunch/dinner, take a shower, wash my face/hands; home, school

Key language

- What do you do at (home)? I (have breakfast) at (home). I don't (have dinner) at (school). Do you (have lunch) at (school)? Yes. / No.

Teacher's tip: Visual support

Life skills

If you have hoops available, place them on the floor so that they cross over in the center creating a Venn diagram, or draw two large overlapping circles on the board. Tell children to put the flashcards of actions they do at home on one side, actions they do at school on the other, and actions they do at home and school in the middle.

Circle time

Hello song and puppet (CD1 Track 2; see TB p 17 & 21)
Opening routines (see TB p 16)
Recycling activity (story song) (CD2 Track 23; see TB p 19)
Lesson aims (see TB p 18)

Game: *Place the flashcard!*

- Put the daily routine flashcards face up on the floor or board. Children name the routines as you do this.
- Explain that one side of the circle is for daily routines children do at home, the other side is for daily routines they do at school, and the middle is for daily routines they do at home and at school. Alternatively, draw two large overlapping circles on the board.
- Hold up the *have breakfast* flashcard and ask children *Do you have breakfast at school?* Encourage them to respond *Yes, I do. / No, I don't.* Put the flashcard in the correct place in the circle or on the board.
- Ask about other daily routines and continue placing the flashcards until they are arranged in three groups: *home*, *school*, *home* and *school*.

Watch the video.

- Explain that Auntie Vicky and Alex are asking Lucy about daily routines she does at home and at school. Ask *What does Lucy do (at home)?* and encourage children to guess.
- Play the video of Alex, Lucy and Auntie Vicky. Ask the questions again and children respond. Put the flashcards in groups as previously and be ready to prompt or help as they do this.
- Watch again. Pause and children repeat the questions and answers. Ask *Are Lucy's daily routines the same or different to yours?* and listen to children's responses.

Table time

Student's Book p 39 Life skills

Watch. Listen and point.

- Children identify home and school in the photos and name the daily routines.
- Explain that one side of the circle is for routines Lucy does at home and the other side is for routines Lucy does at school. Demonstrate that the middle, where the circles overlap, is for routines Lucy does at home and at school.
- Play the audio or video. Children listen and point to the daily routines and where they go in the diagram.

CD2 Track 25

Alex: Let's play the game. What do you at school? What do you do at home?
Lucy: Yeah!
Alex: Do you wash your hands at school?
Lucy: Yes, I do. I wash my hands at school. And I wash my hands at home.
Alex: Do you wash your face at school?
Lucy: No, I don't. I wash my face at home.
Alex: Do you brush your teeth at school?
Lucy: No, I don't. I brush my teeth at home.
Alex: What about your hair?
Lucy: I brush my hair at home. I take a shower at home too.
Alex: Do you have breakfast at school?
Lucy: No, I don't. I have breakfast at home.
Alex: Do you have lunch at school?
Lucy: Yes, I do. I have lunch at school. But I don't have dinner at school. I have dinner at home.
Auntie Vicky: And it's time for dinner now!
Lucy: Great.
Alex: I'm hungry!

Draw three of your routines in the diagram. Ask and say.

- Children draw three of their own routines in the diagram.
- Children take turns asking and saying the daily routines they do at home and at school.

Activity Book p 39

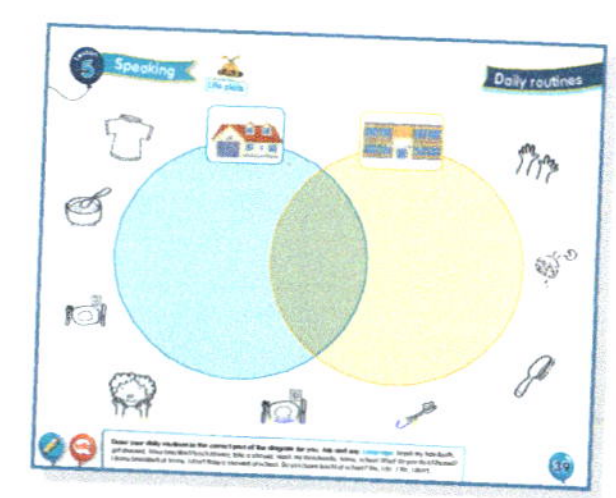

Draw your daily routines in the correct part of the diagram for you.

- Children draw their routines in the correct place on the diagram, depending on whether they do the action at home, school or both.

Ask and say.

- Children ask and answer questions about where they do their daily routines.

Closing time

Learning review (see TB p 18)
Closing routines (see TB p 16)
Goodbye song and puppet (CD1 Track 3; see TB p 17 & 21)

Use the **Navio App** to watch the video, and encourage children to do the same at home.

Lesson 6

Values Having a daily routine

Daily routines

2:26

hello

Listen, point and sing *I sleep, I eat, I learn, I play*. Check (✔) the daily routines you do. Say. Language: brush my teeth, drink water, eat, learn, play, sleep, take a shower, wash my hands; I (drink water) every day.

SOCIAL AND EMOTIONAL LEARNING

40

Daily routines

Learning objectives

- Recognize the value of having a daily routine
- Sing the values song *I sleep, I eat, I learn, I play*
- Identify your own healthy routines

Materials

- Class CDs, flashcards, *Ferris Wheel* mat, Mimi puppet

Main vocabulary

- brush my teeth, drink water, eat, learn, play, sleep, take a shower, wash my hands

Key language

- I (drink water) every day.

Teacher's tip: Understanding healthy routines

Life skills

Instil the importance of a healthy routine by encouraging the class to count how many of the healthy routines they do every day.

Circle time

Hello song and puppet (CD1 Track 2; see TB p 17 & 21)

Opening routines (see TB p 16)

Recycling activity *(Do you (have lunch) at (school)? Yes, I do. / No, I don't.)* (see TB p 19)

Lesson aims (see TB p 18)

Watch the *Giant Joe* story video.

- Play the story video.
- Take the part of the narrator, Grandma and Grandpa yourself. Encourage children to join in acting out the story in two groups (Mimi and Dylan).
- Ask e.g. *Does Giant Joe have a daily routine? Is it important to have a daily routine? Why?* Listen to the children's responses and introduce the idea of a healthy daily routine.

***I sleep, I eat, I learn, I play* song**

CD2 Track 26

- Elicit children's ideas of healthy routines and use this to remind them of vocabulary as necessary.
- Ask *How many healthy daily routines can you hear in the song?* Play the audio once or twice. Children listen.
- Check the answer (eight) and children name the daily routines.
- Play the audio again. Children do actions to show the different daily routines and join in singing the song.
- Ask children if they can tell you other healthy daily routines not in the song and listen to their response e.g. wash my face, brush my hair.

Table time

Student's Book p 40

Listen, point and sing *I sleep, I eat, I learn, I play.*

CD2 Track 26

- Play the song. Children sing and point to the pictures of Harry and Zoe.

Check (✔) the daily routines you do. Say.

- Children choose the daily routines that they do.
- Children take turns showing their pictures and saying e.g. *I wash my face. / I sleep.*

Activity Book p 40

Draw and color pictures of two of your daily routines.

- Children draw two of their own daily routines.

Point and say.

- Children point and say the daily routines.

Closing time

Learning review (see TB p 18)

Closing routines (see TB p 16)

Goodbye song and puppet (CD1 Track 3; see TB p 17 & 21)

Use the **Navio App** to listen to the song, and encourage children to do the same at home.

1 2 3 4

1

Listen and point. Match and number the photos in order. Say. Circle the pictures to show when we need to wash our hands. Language: faucet, soap, towel, water; clean; wash my hands; numbers 1–4; I (wash my hands) with (soap).

41

Learning objectives

- Learn about how and when to wash your hands
- Listen and identify what you need to wash your hands
- Order the stages of washing your hands

Materials

- Class CDs, printable content flashcards, *Ferris Wheel* mat, Mimi puppet

Main vocabulary

- faucet, soap, towel, water; clean; wash my hands; numbers 1 4

Key language

- I (wash my hands) with (soap).

Teacher's tip: Washing your hands

Life skills

Teaching children about washing their hands early on is an important mechanism against the spread of germs. Remind them to wash their hands before snack time and after recess. Encourage them to say the sentences from the video as they wash their hands, e.g. *I turn on the faucet. I wet my hands with water,* etc.

Circle time

Hello song and puppet (CD1 Track 2; see TB p 17 & 21)
Opening routines (see TB p 16)
Recycling activity (see TB p 19)
Lesson aims (see TB p 18)

Introduce content vocabulary.

- Ask *Is it important to wash your hands? What do you need to wash your hands?*
- Use the puppet and the printable flashcards to introduce the new words *(clean, soap, water, towel, faucet).* Children repeat the words.
- Ask e.g. *Why do we need to wash our hands?* Listen to the children's responses and reinforce the idea of washing hands to keep clean and healthy.

Mime washing your hands.

- Put the flashcards face up on the floor or board.
- Say e.g. *Let's wash our hands together!* Point to the flashcards, say sentences (as in the audio on this page) and get children to mime the actions with you.
- Repeat once or twice. Once children are confident, leave out words and children supply them, e.g. *I turn on the … (faucet).*

Think and say.

- Ask children *When do we need to wash our hands?* Listen to their ideas and be ready to recast in English, e.g. *when we go to the bathroom / before lunch / when we touch animals / when our hands are dirty.*

Table time

Student's Book p 41

Listen and point.

- Say *Alex and Lucy are talking to Auntie Vicky about washing their hands.*
- Children look at the photos and identify what's happening at each stage.
- Play the audio. Children listen and point to the photos.

CD2 Track 27

Lucy:	Why do we wash our hands, Auntie Vicky?
Auntie Vicky:	We wash our hands to keep clean and healthy. Come on. Let's wash our hands together! I turn on the faucet. I wet my hands with water. I wash my hands with soap. I rinse my hands with water. I turn off the faucet. I dry my hands with a towel.
Alex:	All done!
Lucy:	My hands are clean. Great!

Match and number the photos in order. Say.

- Play the audio again. Use the pause button. Children number the photos in order. Children repeat the sentences.

Circle the pictures to show when we need to wash our hands.

- Children circle the pictures to show when they need to wash their hands. Point to each picture in turn and say e.g. *We wash our hands before lunch.*

Activity Book p 41

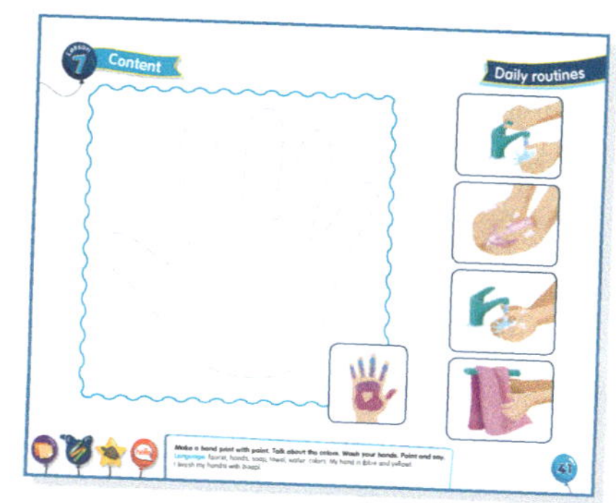

Make a hand print with paint. Talk about the colors.

- Children make a hand print with paint and say the colors.

Wash your hands. Point and say.

- Children then wash their hands. They point and say the stages of washing their hands.

Closing time

Learning review (see TB p 18)
Closing routines (see TB p 16)
Goodbye song and puppet (CD1 Track 3; see TB p 17 & 21)

Use the **Navio App** to play the vocabulary and language games, and encourage children to do the same at home.

Lesson 8 Culture

2:28

Watch. Listen and point to the story *Goldilocks and the three bears*. Draw and color a picture to show what you think happens next. Say. Language: bed, bowl, chair; big, small, tiny; Mommy, Daddy, Baby Bear; This (bowl) is (small).

Learning objectives

- Watch, understand and enjoy the traditional story *Goldilocks and the three bears*
- Mime characters from the story
- Predict how the story ends

Materials

- Class CDs, printable story cards, flashcards, *Ferris Wheel* mat, Mimi puppet

Main vocabulary

- bed, bowl, chair; big, small, tiny; Mommy, Daddy, Baby Bear

Key language

- This (bowl) is (tiny).

Teacher's tip: Listening skills

Sometimes children appear to be listening but are not fully paying attention. Introduce the idea of "whole body listening." Say *Eyes are watching* and demonstrate looking. Say *Ears are listening* and point to your ears. Say *Brain is thinking. Feet and hands are still* and point to your head, place your feet together and fold your arms. Finally say, *Mouth is closed* and mime zipping it closed.

Circle time

Hello song and puppet (CD1 Track 2; see TB p 17 & 21)
Opening routines (see TB p 16)
Recycling activity (see TB p 19)
Lesson aims (see TB p 18)

Introduce the story *Goldilocks and the three bears*.

- Explain that children are going to watch and listen to a traditional story, *Goldilocks and the three bears.*
- Ask if children know the story. Give clues, e.g. *Goldilocks is a little girl. The three bears are Mommy Bear, Daddy Bear and Baby Bear.*
- If children know the story, ask *Do you want to watch and listen to the story in English?*

Watch and listen to the story.

CD2 Track 28

- Ask *What does Goldilocks do in the bears' house? What happens at the end?* Encourage children to guess.
- Play the video. Children watch and listen to the story.
- Ask the pre-questions again and children respond.
- Play the video again. Use the pause button. Ask questions, e.g. *Is the tiny bowl of porridge delicious? Is the big chair perfect?*
- Ask *Who's your favorite character? Can you imagine what happens next? Do the bears see Goldilocks again?*

Mime the bears and say a chant.

- Say *I'm Daddy Bear.* Make yourself big and speak with a deep voice. Say in a rhythmic way *I'm Daddy Bear. My bowl is big. My chair is big. My bed is big.* Make gestures to show a big bowl, big chair and big bed. Repeat and children join in.
- Repeat for Mommy Bear (small) and Baby Bear (tiny). Ask children which is their favorite bear.

Table time

Student's Book p 42

Watch. Listen and point to the story *Goldilocks and the three bears*.

Story questions

Picture 1
What do Daddy Bear, Mommy Bear and Baby Bear eat for breakfast? *(Porridge)*
Is Baby Bear happy to go for a walk? *(Yes)*

Picture 2
Does Goldilocks eat the big bowl of porridge? *(No)*
Does Goldilocks like the tiny chair? *(Yes)*

Picture 3
Is Goldilocks sleepy? *(Yes)*
Does Goldilocks go to sleep in the tiny bed? *(Yes)*

Picture 4
Who comes back to the house? *(The Bears)*
Is Goldilocks in Baby Bear's bed? *(Yes)*

CD2 Track 28

- Play the story. Children listen and point to the pictures.
- Say e.g. *Find the (big bowl)* and children respond.
- Play the audio again. *Ask Who wants Goldilocks to stay and play? Do the bears see Goldilocks again?*

Draw and color a picture to show what you think happens next. Say.

- Children draw and color a picture to show what they imagine happens after the end of the story.
- Children take turns showing each other their pictures and saying what they think happens.

Activity Book p 42

Match the bowls, chairs and beds to the bears. Color Daddy Bear's things red, Mommy Bear's things green, and Baby Bear's things blue.

- Children match the items to the bears and then color.

Point and say.

- They point and name the bears' things.

Closing time

Learning review (see TB p 18)
Closing routines (see TB p 16)
Goodbye song and puppet (CD1 Track 3; see TB p 17 & 21)

Use the **Navio App** to watch the video, and encourage children to do the same at home.

Review

Daily routines

I can …

Vocabulary

Story

Speaking

Content

Circle the routines you know. Listen, point and say. Listen and answer. Ask and say. Complete the faces to show what you can do. **Language:** brush my hair/teeth, get dressed, get up, have breakfast/lunch/dinner, take a shower, wash my face/hands; I (get up). I don't (have dinner). Do you (have lunch) at (home)?

43

Daily routines

Learning objectives

- Review what you have learned in this unit
- Complete a self-evaluation
- Ask and answer questions about daily routines

Materials

- Class CDs, flashcards, *Ferris Wheel* mat, Mimi puppet

Main vocabulary

- brush my hair/teeth, get dressed, get up, breakfast/lunch/dinner, take a shower, wash my face/hands

Key language

- I (get up). I don't (have dinner). Do you (have lunch) at (home)?

Teacher's tip: Reviewing vocabulary cooperatively

COOPERATIVE LEARNING

Encourage the children to complete the review with a partner. Have them compare the faces that they have drawn. Remind them to be positive and help each other with the task.

Circle time

Hello song and puppet (CD1 Track 2; see TB p 17 & 21)
Opening routines (see TB p 16)
Recycling activity (see TB p 19)
Lesson aims (see TB p 18)

Daily routine flashcard games

- Choose one or two flashcard games with the *Ferris Wheel* mat and/or the puppet (see TB p 20 & 21).

Sing *What do you do every day?*

CD2 Track 20

- Put the daily routine flashcards on the board.
- Play the audio. Children sing, point and do the actions.
- Use the puppet to ask *What do you do every day?*

Game: *Say and mime!*

- Organize children into pairs. The first child says a sentence e.g. *I brush my teeth.* The second child does the mime.

Game: *At school or at home?*

- Choose one side of the classroom to be "home" and the opposite side to be "school." Ask e.g. *Do you wash your face at school?* Children answer *No, I don't.* and move to the "home" side of the classroom. Ask *Do you learn at school?* Children answer *Yes, I do.* and move to the "school" side of the classroom.

Watch the story video.

- Children watch the story video. Ask e.g. *Who tells Mimi and Dylan a story? What is the story about?*

Table time

Student's Book p 43

Circle the routines you know.

- Explain and demonstrate the activity.

Listen, point and say.

- Play the audio. Children check the words they know, point to the pictures and repeat the words.

CD2 Track 29

Mimi: I'm the teacher! Can you remember the daily routines, Dylan?
Dylan: Yes, I can. Get up.
Mimi: Get up.
Dylan: Get dressed.
Mimi: Get dressed.
Dylan: Brush my teeth.
Mimi: Brush my teeth.
Dylan: Brush my hair.
Mimi: Brush my hair.
Dylan: Wash my hands.
Mimi: Wash my hands.
Dylan: Wash my face.
Mimi: Wash my face.
Dylan: Take a shower.
Mimi: Take a shower.
Dylan: Have breakfast.
Mimi: Have breakfast.
Dylan: Have lunch.
Mimi: Have lunch.
Dylan: Have dinner.
Mimi: Have dinner. Well done, Dylan!
Both: Fantastic!

Listen and answer. Ask and say.

- Play the audio. Children listen to the questions.

CD2 Track 30

Mimi: What do you do every day?
Do you have lunch at school?
Do you brush your teeth every day?
Do you have breakfast at home?
Do you wash your hands at school?
Do you have dinner at home?

- Play the audio again. Children listen, repeat and answer the questions.
- Children ask and answer about their daily routines.

Complete the faces to show what you can do.

- Explain the four pictures: *I can name daily routines; I can understand the story; I can name daily routines at home and at school; I know how and when to wash my hands.*
- Remind children they should complete each face with a smile or frown depending on how well they think they have done.

Activity Book p 43

Complete the faces to show your daily routines. Ask and say.

- Children complete the faces with a smile if they do the routine.
- Children ask and answer about their daily routines.

Think and circle the number to show your progress.

- Children circle the number.

Closing time

Learning review (see TB p 18)
Closing routines (see TB p 16)
Goodbye song and puppet (CD1 Track 3; see TB p 17 & 21)

Use the **Navio App** to review what children have learned in this unit, and encourage them to do the same at home.

Project

COOPERATIVE LEARNING

Daily routines

hello

Trace and color a picture of one of Giant Joe's daily routines. Put your pictures together to make a book, *Giant Joe's Day*. Ask and say. Language: brush my hair/teeth, get dressed, get up, have breakfast, take a shower, wash my face/hands; What do you do every day? I (get up). I don't (wash my face). Do you (get dressed)? Yes, I do. / No, I don't.

44

Daily routines

Learning objectives

- Work together to do a collaborative project
- Trace and color a picture for the book
- Talk about daily routines
- Make a daily routine wheel

Materials

- Class CDs, Mimi puppet, photocopiable templates, pencils, crayons, glue

Main vocabulary

- brush my hair/teeth, get dressed, get up, have breakfast, take a shower, wash my face/hands

Key language

- What do you do every day? I (get up). I don't (wash my face). Do you (get dressed)? Yes, I do. / No, I don't.

Teacher's tip: Home-school link: Taking a class (or group) book home

COOPERATIVE LEARNING

The class (or group) book that the children make is an ideal way to create a link between the school and home. Allow the children to take turns taking it home to show their parents and telling them about Giant Joe. Encourage them to draw one of their own routines and add it to the book.

Circle time

Hello song and puppet (CD1 Track 2; see TB p 17 & 21)
Opening routines (see TB p 16)
Recycling activity (see TB p 19)
Lesson aims (see TB p 18)

Prepare for your project.

- Say *Let's do a project. Let's make a class (or group) book of Giant Joe's daily routines!*
- Show children the large empty home-made book(s) (or bought scrapbook(s)) that you have prepared for the purpose and the daily routine template.
- Explain that children should trace and color one of Giant Joe's daily routines.
- Explain and demonstrate that children will then glue their pictures in the book to make a class (or group) book of daily routines. Depending on the size of your class, you may like children to make one book per group, or table(s), of e.g. 8–12 children.

Table time

COOPERATIVE LEARNING

Student's Book p 44

Trace and color a picture of one of Giant Joe's daily routines. Put your pictures together to make a book, *Giant Joe's Day*.

- Say e.g. *We're going to make a class (or group) book of daily routines like this. Look at what we need for our project: a template of Giant Joe's daily routines, a pencil, crayons, glue.* Children listen and point to the pictures.
- Use the flashcards to remind children of Giant Joe's daily routines.
- Elicit other daily routines children know as well, e.g. sleep, drink water.
- Children choose a daily routine. Give a copy of this project template to each child. Make sure children have a pencil and crayons available.
- Children trace around and color the picture of Giant Joe's daily routine.
- When they are ready, invite children to come and glue their pictures into the class or group book you have prepared.

Ask and say.

- Talk about the daily routines class or group book(s) using language of the unit and other language children know. Show and "read" the completed book(s) to the class.
- Ask children *Do you like our class (or group) book(s) of daily routines?* Make the point that everyone has helped make the class or group book(s) and that they couldn't have made such a beautiful book on their own.

Activity Book p 44

Make a daily routine wheel. Draw and color pictures to show what you do every day.

- Children draw and color pictures on the wheel to show what routines they do every day.

Ask and say.

- Children ask and answer questions about their daily routines and say what they do and don't do every day.

Closing time

Learning review (see TB p 18)
Closing routines (see TB p 16)
Goodbye song and puppet (CD1 Track 3; see TB p 17 & 21)

Meals

Toast, toast, toast!

Vocabulary and language

- **Main vocabulary:** chicken, fish, pancakes, pizza, rice, salad, soup, spaghetti, toast, yogurt
- **Key language:** What do you have for (dinner)? I have (soup). Do you want (chicken)? Yes, please. / No, thank you. I want/don't want (fish).
- **Content language:** fruit, vegetables; apples, bananas, candy, carrots, chips, cupcakes, ice cream, oranges, peas, plums, tomatoes; (Oranges) are good for you. (Candy) isn't good for you. (Cupcakes) aren't good for you.
- **Other language:** breakfast, lunch, dinner; food; pan; catch, cook, mix; toss; I want (toast), please. I like/don't like (soup). I don't like (orange) food. (Mix) the pancake. (Yogurt) is good for you. Do you like (fish)? Yes, I do. / No, I don't.

Unit objectives

- Identify and name food for meals
- Sing the language song *What do you have for breakfast?*
- Ask and say food you have for different meals
- Understand and act out the story *Toast, toast, toast*
- Sing and act out the story song *The toast song*
- Ask and say what you want for (lunch)
- Understand a story about being willing to try food
- Recognize the value of willingness to try food
- Learn about food that is and isn't good for you
- Sing and act out the traditional song *Mix a pancake*
- Review your learning and progress
- Participate in a collaborative project

Story

CD3 Track 7

Picture 1

Narrator: Mimi and Dylan are at Grandma and Grandpa's house.
Grandma: What do you have for breakfast?
Dylan: I have pancakes and yogurt.
Mimi: I have toast.
Grandpa: What do you have for lunch?
Dylan: Mmm. I have chicken and rice.
Mimi: I have toast.
Grandma: What do you have for dinner?
Dylan: Mmm. I have soup and spaghetti.
Mimi: I have toast.

Picture 2

Narrator: It's time for breakfast.
Grandma: Do you want pancakes and yogurt, Dylan?
Dylan: Oh, yes, please, Grandma. Mmm. Delicious.
Grandma: Do you want pancakes and yogurt, Mimi?
Mimi: No, thank you. I want toast, please.

Picture 3

Narrator: It's time for lunch.
Grandpa: Do you want chicken and rice, Dylan?
Dylan: Oh, yes, please, Grandpa. Mmm. Delicious.
Grandpa: Do you want chicken and rice, Mimi?
Mimi: Err … no, thank you. I want toast, please.

Picture 4

Narrator: It's time for dinner.
Grandma: Do you want soup and spaghetti, Dylan?
Dylan: Oh, yes, please, Grandma. Mmm. Delicious.
Grandma: Do you want soup and spaghetti, Mimi?
Mimi: Err … no, thank you. I want toast, please.
Grandpa: Oh, no, toast again!
Grandma: I have an idea!

Picture 5

Narrator: The next day it's time for lunch …
Grandma: Here's fish and peas for you, Dylan.
Dylan: Mmm, delicious. Thank you!
Grandpa: And here's toast for you, Mimi.
Mimi: Um … thank you.

Picture 6

Narrator: And now it's time for dinner.
Grandma: Here's pizza and salad for you, Dylan.
Dylan: Mmm, delicious. Thank you!
Grandpa: And here's toast for you, Mimi.
Mimi: Umm. Can I have pizza and salad too, please?
Grandpa: Oh yes, of course, you can, Mimi. Here you are.
Mimi: Mmm, delicious. Thank you. Toast is boring all the time!
Grandpa: Ha, ha. Yes, you're right, Mimi. Toast is boring all the time! Well done, Grandma!

Songs and story

Language song

What do you have for breakfast? CD3 Track 5

What do you have for breakfast? (Shrug)
I have toast for breakfast. (Point to flashcard)
I have yogurt and pancakes, too. (Point to flashcards)
Toast, yogurt, pancakes. (Point to flashcards)
Oh, delicious! What about you? (Rub tummy and point to a child)

What do you have for lunch? (Shrug)
I have fish and salad for lunch. (Point to flashcards)
I have chicken and rice too. (Point to flashcards)
Fish and salad, chicken and rice. (Point to flashcards)
Oh, delicious! What about you? (Rub tummy and point to a child)

What do you have for dinner? (Shrug)
I have soup for dinner. (Point to flashcard)
I have pizza and spaghetti too. (Point to flashcards)
Soup, pizza, spaghetti. (Point to flashcards)
Oh, delicious! What about you? (Rub tummy and point to a child)

Story song

The toast song CD3 Track 8

Do you want pancakes? (Point to pancake flashcard)
No, thank you, no! (Waggle your finger and shake your head)
Do you want yogurt? (Point to yogurt flashcard)
No, thank you, no! (Waggle your finger and shake your head)
All I want is toast, toast, toast! (Point to toast flashcard)
I like toast the most, most, most! (Raise arms up in air)

Do you want chicken? No, thank you, no!
Do you want rice? No, thank you, no! (Point to rice flashcard)

(Chorus)

Do you want soup? No, thank you, no!
Do you want spaghetti? No, thank you, no!

(Chorus)

Do you want pizza?
Yes, please, yes! (Thumbs up and nod)
Do you want salad?
Yes, please, yes! (Thumbs up and nod)
I don't want toast, toast, toast (Waggle finger and shake your head)
I like pizza and salad the most, most, most! (Raise arms up in air)

Values story

CD3 Track 11

Picture 1

Narrator: Dad's making lunch.
Zoe: I'm hungry.
Dad: Do you want peas, Zoe?
Zoe: Yes, please.
Dad: Do you want peas, Harry?
Harry: No, thank you. I don't like green food.
Dad: But peas are delicious.

Picture 2

Dad: Do you want carrots, Harry?
Harry: Yes, please.
Dad: Do you want carrots, Zoe?
Zoe: No, thank you. I don't like orange food.
Dad: But carrots are delicious.

Picture 3

Dad: Do you want tomatoes, Zoe?
Zoe: Yes, please.
Dad: Do you want tomatoes, Harry?
Harry: No, thank you. I don't like red food.
Dad: But tomatoes are delicious.

Picture 4

Narrator: Lunch is ready.
Dad: Do you want to try the soup, Zoe?
Zoe: Yes, please.
Dad: Do you want to try the soup, Harry?
Harry: Oh, yes, please. I like soup. Mmm. This soup is delicious.
Zoe: What's in the soup, Dad?
Dad: Peas, carrots and tomatoes!
Zoe: Ha, ha. So you like green food and red food, Harry!
Harry: Ha, ha. And you like orange food, Zoe!
Zoe: Oh, yes! I like carrots!
Harry: And I like peas and tomatoes! They're delicious!

Culture song

Mix a pancake CD3 Track 13

Mix a pancake (Mime holding a bowl and mixing)
Mix a pancake (Mime holding a bowl and mixing)
Pop it in the pan (Mime pouring the mixture out)
Cook the pancake (Mime cooking)
Toss the pancake (Mime tossing the pancake in the air)
Catch it if you can! (Mime trying to catch it)
(Repeat)

Meals
Toast, toast, toast!
Vocabulary
Lesson 1
3:01
hello
3:02
3:03
Listen, point and repeat. Listen and stick the food stickers. Listen and play *Memory*. Circle the food you like. Say. Language: chicken, pancake, rice, salad, toast, yogurt; blue, green, orange, pink, red, yellow
45

Learning objectives

- Identify and name food for meals
- Listen and point to food
- Remember food in a memory game

Materials

- Class CDs, flashcards, *Ferris Wheel* mat, Mimi puppet

Main vocabulary

- chicken, pancake, rice, salad, toast, yogurt; blue, green, orange, pink, red, yellow

Teacher's tip: Pre-reading skills: using an initial sound clue

Once children are familiar with the new vocabulary, place the flashcards around the classroom. Say e.g. *I like y…* using only the initial sound and not the complete word. Children say the complete word and point to the item.

Circle time

Hello song & puppet (CD1 Track 2; see TB p 17 & 21)
Opening routines (see TB p 16)
Lesson aims (see TB p 18)

Introduce the food vocabulary.

- Use the puppet and flashcards to introduce six food words. Children repeat the words.
- Put the *Ferris Wheel* mat on the floor or board with the food flashcards face down (one on each color). Use the puppet to turn them over and name them. The children repeat the words.

Game: *Say the color!*

- Name the food on the Ferris Wheel and children name the color. Then the reverse.

Game: *Repeat if it's true!*

- Use the puppet to point to a flashcard and say e.g. *I like toast!* or *I don't like yogurt!* Children repeat the sentence if it is true for them and fold their arms and stay silent if not.
- Repeat with all the food and different sentences in random order.

Table time

Student's Book p 45

Listen, point and repeat.

- Play the audio. The children listen, point to each food as the hear it, and repeat the words.

CD3 Track 1

Mimi: Look Dylan! Toast … chicken … pancake … yogurt … salad. Repeat, Dylan!
Dylan: Yes, Mimi. Toast … chicken … pancake … yogurt … salad.
Mimi: Very good, Dylan! Let's name the food together!
Both: Toast … chicken … pancake … yogurt … salad. Fantastic!

- Draw children's attention to the question mark in their books. They identify the missing food (rice).

Listen and stick the food stickers.

- Play the audio. The children listen and point to the food in their books.

CD3 Track 2

Where's the toast? It's on … red.
Where's the chicken? It's on … blue.
Where's the yogurt? It's on … pink.
Where's the pancake? It's on … orange.
Where's the salad? It's on … green.
Where's the rice? Can you guess? It's on … yellow.
Yes, yes, yes!
The rice is on yellow. Yes, yes, yes!

- Ask questions about all the food in the same way and children respond.
- Play the audio again. Children listen and stick the food stickers.

Listen and play *Memory*.

- Demonstrate covering your eyes with your hands. Get children to do the same.
- Play the audio. Children listen and try to remember the food on each color on the wheel.

CD3 Track 3

Close your eyes	*Red … toast!*
One, two, three	*Yellow … rice!*
Say the words	*Green … salad!*
Play memory!	*Pink … yogurt!*
Blue … chicken!	*Orange … pancake!*

- Play the game with you and/or individual children naming colors and responding with the food.

Circle the food you like. Say.

- Children circle the food they like. They point and say the words.

Activity Book p 45

Look and match.

- Children look and match the food pictures.

Trace and color the food. Point and say.

- They trace and color the food, then point and say the words.

Closing time

Learning review (see TB p 18)
Closing routines (see TB p 16)
Goodbye song and puppet (CD1 Track 3; see TB p 17 & 21)

Use the **Navio App** to play the vocabulary game, and encourage children to do the same at home.

Listen and find the new food words. Listen, point and sing *What do you have for breakfast?* Match the food to Alex and Lucy. Ask and say. Language: chicken, fish, pancakes, pizza, rice, salad, soup, spaghetti, toast, yogurt; breakfast, lunch, dinner; What do you have for (dinner)? I have (soup).

46

Learning objectives

- Talk about food for meals
- Identify and name four new foods
- Sing the language song *What do you have for breakfast?*
- Ask and say what you have for different meals

Materials

- Class CDs, flashcards, *Ferris Wheel* mat, Mimi puppet

Main vocabulary

- chicken, fish, pancakes, pizza, rice, salad, soup, spaghetti, toast, yogurt; breakfast, lunch, dinner

Key language

- What do you have for (dinner)? I have (soup).

Teacher's tip: Pronunciation: slow drilling

If you find children are having any difficulty with pronunciation of the new words, use the puppet to say them very slowly, exaggerating any tricky parts of the word e.g. "sssssspaaaagheeetiiii." This will help children focus on the position of their mouth and practice the pronunciation.

Circle time

Hello song & puppet (CD1 Track 2; see TB p 17 & 21)
Opening routines (see TB p 16)
Recycling activity (six food words from lesson 1) (see TB p 19)
Lesson aims (see TB p 18)

Introduce the new food words.

- Put all ten flashcards of food on the floor or board. Children identify the four new words. Use the puppet to point to and say the words. Children repeat.
- Turn the four new food flashcards face down. Mix them up. Point to one and ask *Is it soup, fish, pizza, or spaghetti?* Children guess. Repeat several times.
- Children say if they like or don't like the foods.

Introduce *What do you have for (breakfast)? I have (pancakes).*

- Check that children know or remember the three main meals of the day: breakfast, lunch, dinner.
- Children name all the food flashcards.
- Say e.g. *I have pancakes for breakfast.* Ask children *What do you have for breakfast?* Encourage children to point and respond e.g. *I have toast.*
- Be ready for children to say other foods as well e.g. *cereal, cookies, banana, milk* and remind them of the words if necessary. Group the flashcards of food children have for breakfast together.
- Repeat the procedure for lunch and dinner.
- Recap by asking the questions again.

Game: *Breakfast, lunch or dinner?*

- Hold up the food flashcards in turn and say the words. Children respond by naming the meal they personally have the food for e.g. *Toast! / Breakfast!* Be ready for variations in the answers. If they never eat the food, children fold their arms and stay silent.

***What do you have for breakfast?* song**

CD3 Track 5

- Put the flashcards in groups on the board to reflect the three verses of the song.
- Put the Alex flashcard by the food in verse 1 and 3, and the Lucy flashcard by the food in verse 2. Children listen and point to the flashcards.
- Play the audio again. Children point to the flashcards and join in singing the song.
- Ask *What does (Alex) have for (breakfast)?* Hold up the flashcards and prompt children to repeat what Alex and Lucy say about each meal e.g. *I have toast. / I have fish.*
- Remember that you can use the karaoke version of the song when children are confident.

Table time

Student's Book p 46

Listen and find the new food words.

- Children listen and find the four new food words. Repeat and children say the words.

CD3 Track 4

One, two, Which words are new?
Soup! Soup! *Pizza! Pizza!*
Fish! Fish! *Spaghetti! Spaghetti!*

Listen, point and sing
What do you have for breakfast?

- Play the song again. The children listen, point to the photos of food and sing the song.

Match the food to Alex and Lucy.

- Play the audio again with pauses. Demonstrate that children should match the photos of food to Alex and Lucy having breakfast, lunch or dinner.
- Play the audio again with pauses. Check answers.

Ask and say.

- Children pretend to be Alex or Lucy and ask about and say what they have for all three meals.

Activity Book p 46

Draw food you have for breakfast, lunch and dinner.

- Demonstrate that children should draw and color food they have for each meal in the frames. Make sure they realize there are no correct answers.

Ask and say.

- Children ask and say what they eat.

Closing time

Learning review (see TB p 18)
Closing routines (see TB p 16)
Goodbye song and puppet (CD1 Track 3; see TB p 17 & 21)

Use the **Navio App** to listen to the song, and encourage children to do the same at home.

Lesson 3 Story

3:07

Watch. Listen to the story *Toast, toast, toast!* Circle the food Mimi wants for every meal. Stick the story sticker.
Language: chicken, fish, pancakes, peas, pizza, rice, salad, soup, spaghetti, toast, yogurt; breakfast, lunch, dinner; What do you have for (breakfast)? I have (yogurt). Do you want (pancakes)? I want (toast), please.

47

Learning objectives

- Watch, understand and enjoy the story
- Make a prediction about the story *Toast, toast, toast!*
- Identify the food Mimi wants

Materials

- Class CDs, printable story cards, flashcards, *Ferris Wheel* mat, Mimi puppet

Main vocabulary

- chicken, fish, pancakes, peas, pizza, rice, salad, soup, spaghetti, toast, yogurt; breakfast, lunch, dinner

Key language

- What do you have for (breakfast)? I have (yogurt). Do you want (pancakes)? I want (toast), please.

Teacher's tip: Identifying the story frame

After completing the page in the Student's Book, describe things you can see in each frame and encourage the children to say the corresponding frame number.

Circle time

Hello song and puppet (CD1 Track 2; see TB p 17 & 21)
Opening routines (see TB p 16)
Recycling activity (*What do you have for (lunch)?* and food words) (see TB p 19)
Lesson aims (see TB p 18)

Introduce the story *Toast, toast, toast!*

- Say *It's story time!* Play the *Story rhyme* (CD1 Track 4; see TB p 17)
- Say *Alex and Lucy are watching a story about Mimi and Dylan. Mimi and Dylan are at Grandma and Grandpa's house. What do Mimi and Dylan have for (breakfast)?* Listen to children's answers.

Watch and listen to the story *Toast, toast, toast!*.

CD3 Track 7

- Watch the video, play the audio or read the story using the printable story cards. Pause, repeat words, point to the pictures, ask questions.
- Play the audio again. Use the pause button and children name the food Mimi and Dylan have for breakfast, lunch and dinner in the story.
- Repeat the story. Use the pause button. Encourage children to join in with the words and phrases.
- Ask *What does Mimi want for dinner? Do you like the story? Is it important to be willing to try different food?*

Game: *I want toast, please!*

- Hold up the flashcards in turn and ask children e.g. *Do you want yogurt?* Children respond *No, thank you.* As soon as you hold up the flashcard of toast, they open their arms wide and say *I want toast, please!* Repeat several times going faster each time.
- Get children to ask the puppet questions about the flashcards in chorus in the same way.

Table time

Student's Book p 47

Watch. Listen to the story *Toast, toast, toast!*

Story questions

Picture 1
Are Mimi and Dylan with Mommy and Daddy? *(No)*
What does Mimi have for breakfast, lunch and dinner? *(Toast)*

Picture 2
Does Dylan want pancakes and yogurt for breakfast? *(Yes)*
Does Mimi want pancakes and yogurt for breakfast? *(No)*

Picture 3
Does Dylan want chicken and rice for lunch? *(Yes)*
What does Mimi want for lunch? *(Toast)*

Picture 4
Does Dylan want soup and spaghetti for dinner? *(Yes)*
Does Mimi want soup and spaghetti for dinner? *(No)*

Picture 5
Does Dylan have fish and peas for lunch? *(Yes)*
Is Mimi happy to have toast for lunch? *(No)*

Picture 6
Does Mimi want toast for dinner? *(No)*
Is Mimi happy to have pizza and salad for dinner? *(Yes)*

CD3 Track 7

- Read or play the audio again (see TB p 120). Children listen and point to the pictures.

Circle the food Mimi wants for every meal. Stick the story sticker.

- Demonstrate circling the food Mimi wants for every meal (apart from dinner) and sticking the story sticker.
- Ask *What does Mimi have for dinner at the end of the story? Is it important to eat a variety of food?*

Activity Book p 47

Draw pictures to show what Dylan and Mimi want for breakfast, lunch and dinner in the story. Ask and say.

- Children draw the meals Mimi and Dylan want for breakfast, lunch and dinner on the plates.
- Children ask and answer about what they want to eat.

Closing time

Learning review (see TB p 18)
Closing routines (see TB p 16)
Goodbye song and puppet (CD1 Track 3; see TB p 17 & 21)

Use the **Navio App** to watch the video, and encourage children to do the same at home.

Story Song

Watch. Listen, point and sing *The toast song*. Circle 🙂 or ☹ to show the food Mimi wants and doesn't want. Ask and say. **Language:** chicken, pancakes, pizza, rice, salad, soup, spaghetti, toast, yogurt; Do you want (chicken)? Yes, please. / No, thank you. I want (toast). I don't want (chicken).

Learning objectives

- Watch, sing and act out the story song *The toast song*
- Listen to the story again and play a memory game
- Identify and say foods
- Ask and say what you want to eat

Materials

- Class CDs, printable story cards, flashcards, *Ferris Wheel* mat, Mimi puppet

Main vocabulary

- chicken, pancakes, pizza, rice, salad, soup, spaghetti, toast, yogurt

Key language

- Do you want (chicken)? Yes, please. / No, thank you. I want (toast). I don't want (chicken).

Teacher's tip: Personalizing the story

Personalize by asking the children if there's any food that they like to eat most, like Mimi in the story. Compare the children's responses and find out how many foods they choose are the same.

Circle time

Hello song and puppet (CD1 Track 2; see TB p 17 & 21)
Opening routines (see TB p 16)
Recycling activity (food words) (see TB p 19)
Lesson aims (see TB p 18)

Retell the *Toast, toast, toast!* story.

- Play the audio or video, or read the story using the printable story cards.
- Demonstrate that children should wave their arms in the air every time they hear a food word in the story.

Game: *Dylan or Mimi?*

- Ask *What do you have for breakfast?* Pause and then say *Mimi*. Children answer for Mimi e.g. *I have toast.*
- Repeat for the other meals changing between Mimi and Dylan e.g. *What do you have for lunch? … Dylan!* Children answer *I have chicken and rice.*

The toast song

CD3 Track 8

- Put the flashcards of food in each verse of the song in pairs on the board and put the flashcard of toast in the middle. Play the audio. Children listen and point to the flashcards.
- Play the audio again. Children listen, sing and act out the song.

Game: *Do you want pizza?*

- Use the puppet to pass a flashcard around the circle. The puppet asks a child *Do you want pizza?* The child responds *Yes, please* or *No, thank you*, takes the flashcard and asks the same question to the next child in the circle, and so on. Repeat with different flashcards.

Table time

Student's Book p 48

Watch. Listen, point and sing *The toast song*.

CD3 Track 8

- Children identify Mimi eating toast and the other food in the pictures.
- Play the song (see TB p 121). Children listen, sing and point to the food.
- Remember that you can use the karaoke version of the song when children are confident.

Circle or to show the food Mimi wants and doesn't want.

- Children circle the smiley faces to show the food Mimi wants in the song.
- Play the audio again. Children check their answers and join in singing the song.

Ask and say.

- Children ask and answer questions about all the food.

Activity Book p 48

Draw the next food in the sequence. Color the food Mimi wants.

- Children draw the next food in each sequence, then color the food Mimi wants.

Ask and say.

- Children ask and answer questions about what they want to eat.

Closing time

Learning review (see TB p 18)
Closing routines (see TB p 16)
Goodbye song and puppet (CD1 Track 3; see TB p 17 & 21)

Use the **Navio App** to watch the video, and encourage children to do the same at home.

Watch. Listen and point. Match the characters to what they want for lunch. Draw a picture of what you want for lunch. Ask and say. **Language:** chicken, fish, pizza, rice, salad, spaghetti; Do you want (chicken)? Yes, please. / No, thank you. I want (fish). I don't want (pizza).

Learning objectives
- Ask and say what you want for (lunch)
- Watch, understand and enjoy a video
- Identify food in the video

Materials
- Class CDs, flashcards, *Ferris Wheel* mat, Mimi puppet

Main vocabulary
- chicken, fish, pizza, rice, salad, spaghetti

Key language
- Do you want (chicken)? Yes, please. / No, thank you. I want (fish). I don't want (pizza).

Teacher's tip: Setting a time limit Life skills

Encourage children to begin to take responsibility for finishing their work in a reasonable amount of time. Set a time limit as part of the instructions. Telling them how much time is left can help them remain focused on the activity in hand.

Circle time

Hello song and puppet (CD1 Track 2; see TB p 17 & 21)
Opening routines (see TB p 16)
Recycling activity (story song) (CD3 Track 8; see TB p 19)
Lesson aims (see TB p 18)

Game: *Stand up if you want (chicken) for lunch.*
- Put the flashcards on the board.
- Point and say e.g. *Stand up if you want chicken for lunch!* Demonstrate that children who like the idea of chicken for lunch stand up and say *I want chicken, please!*
- Repeat with other food.

Game: *Guess what Mimi wants for lunch!*
- Use the puppet to point to or hold a flashcard so children can't see the food.
- Children ask the puppet in chorus e.g. *Do you want pizza for lunch?* and the puppet responds *Yes, I do. / No, I don't.* depending on the flashcard.
- Repeat with different flashcards. Once children are confident, encourage them to guess and ask questions individually.

Watch the video.
- Explain that Alex, Lucy and Auntie Vicky are having lunch in a restaurant.
- Ask *What does Lucy / Auntie Vicky / Alex want for lunch?* Children guess.
- Play the video of Lucy, Alex and Auntie Vicky once or twice.
- Ask the questions again and children respond. Put the flashcards for each character on the board.
- Watch again. Pause and children repeat what each character says they want for lunch.
- Ask *What do you want for lunch?* and listen to children's responses.

Table time

Student's Book p 49 Life skills

Watch. Listen and point. Match the characters to what they want for lunch.
- Children identify Lucy, Alex, Auntie Vicky and the three dishes in the photos. Demonstrate matching the dishes to the characters.
- Play the audio or video. Use the pause button. Children match what the characters want for lunch.

CD3 Track 10

Lucy:	Mmm. I'm hungry.
Alex:	Me too!
Auntie Vicky:	Let's look at the menu. What do you want for lunch, Alex? Pizza … chicken …?
Alex:	Mmm. I don't know.
Auntie Vicky:	What about you, Lucy? Do you want chicken?
Lucy:	Oh, yes, please. I want chicken and salad. What do you want for lunch, Auntie Vicky?
Auntie Vicky:	I want fish and rice. What do you want, Alex?
Alex:	I don't know.
Waiter:	Can I help you?
Auntie Vicky:	Oh, yes, please. We want one chicken and salad, one fish and rice, and one … Alex, do you want pizza or chicken?
Alex:	Mmm. I don't want pizza and I don't want chicken.
Waiter:	Do you want spaghetti?
Alex:	Oh yes! I want spaghetti please! Yummy!

Draw a picture of what you want for lunch. Ask and say.
- Children draw a picture of what they want for lunch.
- Children take turns showing their pictures and asking and saying what they want for lunch.

Activity Book p 49

Draw food you want and don't want for lunch.
- Children draw food they want in the box with the smile and food they don't want in the box with the frown.

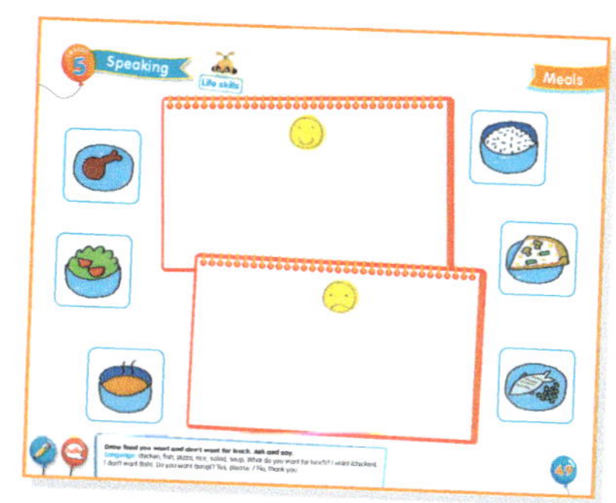

Ask and say.
- Children ask and answer questions about what they want to eat.

Closing time

Learning review (see TB p 18)
Closing routines (see TB p 16)
Goodbye song and puppet (CD1 Track 3; see TB p 17 & 21)

Use the **Navio App** to watch the video, and encourage children to do the same at home.

Lesson 6

Values Willingness to try food

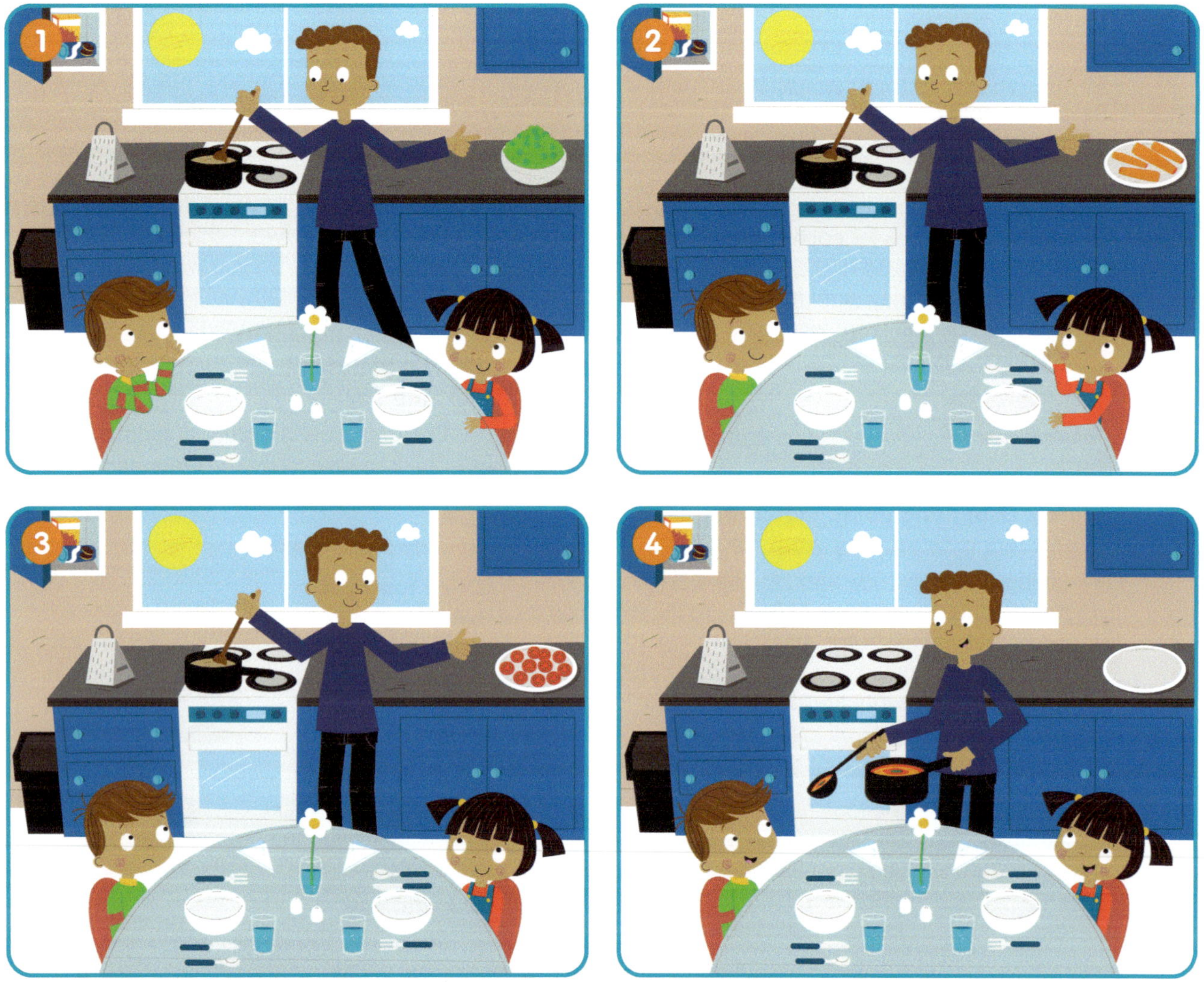

Listen and point to the story. Draw a picture of food you want to try. Ask and say.
Language: carrots, food, peas, soup, tomatoes; green, orange, red; Do you want (peas)? Yes, please. / No, thank you. I like (soup). I don't like (orange) food.

3:11

hello

SOCIAL AND EMOTIONAL LEARNING

50

Learning objectives

- Watch, sing and act out the story song *Dinosaurs in space*
- Listen to the story again and order the story cards
- Identify and say activities in town
- Ask and say what you want to do

Materials

- Class CDs, printable story cards, flashcards, *Ferris Wheel* mat, Mimi puppet

Main vocabulary

- movie theater; books, dinosaurs, space, toys; go, learn, play, read

Key language

- I want to play with (dinosaur) toys. I want to learn about (animals).

Teacher's tip: Being positive about one another's ideas

When the children are showing each other their pictures of what they want to learn about, encourage them to say *Good idea!* or *Great!*, etc. Make sure all the comments are positive and discourage any negativity.

Circle time

Hello song and puppet (CD1 Track 2; see TB p 17 & 21)
Opening routines (see TB p 16)
Recycling activity (places in town) (see TB p 19)
Lesson aims (see TB p 18)

Retell the story *A day out*.

- Play the audio, video or read the story using the printable story cards.
- Demonstrate that children should move their arms as if walking like a dinosaur every time they hear the word "dinosaur" and put the tips of their fingers together and swoosh them up into the air like a rocket every time they hear the word "space."

Order the story cards.

- Put the printable story cards face up in jumbled order on the board. Invite children to take turns putting the cards in the correct order.
- Use the story cards to reconstruct a brief version of the story encouraging children to join in.

***Dinosaurs in space* song**

CD3 Track 23

- Play the video. Children say who sings each verse.
- Play the video again. Children do actions for *dinosaur* and *space* as previously and join in singing the song.
- Ask e.g. *Do you like the song?* and children respond.

Think and say.

- Say e.g. *Mimi wants to learn about dinosaurs. Dylan wants to learn about space. I want to learn about …* and name something the children know e.g. *dogs, cars, soccer, elephants.*
- Ask *What do you want to learn about?* And listen to children's responses. Be ready to recast their answers as necessary. Don't pressure children to respond if they don't want to.

Table time

Student's Book p 58

Watch. Listen, point and sing *Dinosaurs in space.*

CD3 Track 23

- Play the song (see TB p 143). Children listen, sing and point to the pictures.
- Remember that you can use the karaoke version of the song when children are confident.

Match Mimi and Dylan to what they want to do. Point and say.

- Children match Mimi and Dylan to what they want to do. They point to and say what Mimi and Dylan want to do.

Draw a picture of something you want to learn about.

- Children draw a picture to show what they want to learn about.
- Children take turns showing each other their pictures and saying sentences e.g. *I want to learn about flowers.*

Activity Book p 58

Trace and color the movie *Dinosaurs in space.*

- Children trace and color the scene from *Dinosaurs in space.*

Say.

- Children say what they want to do.

Closing time

Learning review (see TB p 18)
Closing routines (see TB p 16)
Goodbye song and puppet (CD1 Track 3; see TB p 17 & 21)

Use the **Navio App** to watch the video, and encourage children to do the same at home.

Lesson 5 **Speaking** Life skills

Watch. Listen and point. Match Alex and Lucy's pictures to the parts of the museum. Color the things you want to see. Ask and say. Language: dinosaur, fish, ocean, planet, space; museum; Do you want to see (the fish)? Yes. / No. Where do you want to go? I want to go to (a museum).

Lesson 5 Speaking

Learning objectives
- Ask and say what you want to do in town
- Watch, understand and enjoy a video
- Identify places in town in the video

Materials
- Class CDs, flashcards, *Ferris Wheel* mat, Mimi puppet

Main vocabulary
- dinosaur, fish, ocean, planet, space; museum

Key language
- Do you want to (see the fish)? Yes. / No. Where do you want to go? I want to go to (a museum).

Teacher's tip: Practicing listening and memory skills Life skills

Place all the flashcards on the floor or board. With the children in pairs, name five places you want to go to, e.g. *I want to go to the museum. I want to go to the swimming pool,* etc. Have the children whisper the places to their partner. When both children have finished, they should raise their hands. One pair takes the named cards and the class checks that they remembered correctly.

Circle time

Hello song and puppet (CD1 Track 2; see TB p 17 & 21)
Opening routines (see TB p 16)
Recycling activity (story song) (CD3 Track 23; see TB p 19)
Lesson aims (see TB p 18)

Game: *Guess where Alex and Lucy go!*
- Put the town flashcards on the board. Explain that Alex and Lucy go on a day out with Auntie Vicky.
- Children take turns guessing where they go.
- Explain that they go to a natural history museum to learn about dinosaurs, space and the ocean.

Watch the video.
- Explain that Auntie Vicky, Alex and Lucy want to visit three parts of the museum.
- Ask *Where do they want to go?* and encourage children to guess.
- Play the video. Ask the question again.
- Watch again. Pause and children say what they see in each part of the museum.
- Ask *Do you want to go to the museum?*

Table time

Student's Book p 59 Life skills

Watch. Listen and point.
- Children identify the parts of the museum in the photos and Alex and Lucy's pictures.
- Play the audio or video. Children listen and point to the photos and pictures when they hear the words.

Match Alex and Lucy's pictures to the parts of the museum.
- Children match Alex and Lucy's pictures to the parts of the museum.
- Play the audio again for children to check.

CD3 Track 25

Auntie Vicky: Let's go out today. Where do you want to go, Alex?
Alex: I want to go to a museum. I want to learn about space.
Auntie Vicky: Where do you want to go, Lucy?
Lucy: I want to go to a museum, too. I want to see the dinosaurs.
Alex: Do you want to see the dinosaurs, Auntie Vicky?
Auntie Vicky: Oh, yes! And I want to learn about life in the ocean.
Lucy: Great!
Auntie Vicky: OK. So let's look for a museum about space, dinosaurs and life in the ocean. Here we go! Look at this!
Lucy and Alex: Awesome!
Alex: Oh, wow! Look at this dinosaur. I want to see the dinosaurs.
Lucy: Oh, wow! Look at this fish. I want to see the fish.
Lucy: Oh, wow! Look at this planet. I want to see the planets.
Alex: This museum is amazing, Auntie Vicky.
Auntie Vicky: Yes, it's perfect! Come on. Put on your coats. Let's go!

Color the things you want to see. Ask and say.
- Children color one or more pictures to show where they want to go in the museum.
- Children take turns showing each other their pictures and asking and saying where they want to go.

Activity Book p 59

Plan your visit to the museum. Draw a line to show your route.
- Children draw a path on the museum map to show what they want to see first, second and third.

Write numbers to show the order.
- They write the numbers on the map to show the order.

Ask and say.
- They ask and answer questions about where they want to go in the museum.

Closing time

Learning review (see TB p 18)
Closing routines (see TB p 16)
Goodbye song and puppet (CD1 Track 3; see TB p 17 & 21)

Use the **Navio App** to watch the video, and encourage children to do the same at home.

Lesson 6

Values Interest in learning

Listen, point and sing *I find out about my world*. Check (✓) the ways you learn. Draw a picture to show a way you like to learn. Say. Language: ask questions, find out about my world, go to school, look at books, play games, talk to friends, watch movies/TV; I want to learn. Do you?

SOCIAL AND EMOTIONAL LEARNING

60

Learning objectives

- Recognize the value of being interested in learning
- Sing the values song *I find out about my world*
- Talk about your favorite way of learning

Materials

- Class CDs, flashcards, *Ferris Wheel* mat, Mimi puppet

Main vocabulary

- ask questions, find out about my world, go to school, look at books, play games, talk to friends, watch movies/TV

Key language

- I want to learn. Do you?

Teacher's tip: Using non-fiction books to encourage learning

If you have any simple, non-fiction picture books about space or dinosaurs or other topics in units covered so far, bring them in and allow the children to look at them and identify the topics. Ask them if they enjoy learning things from books and which ones they think look most interesting.

Circle time

Hello song and puppet (CD1 Track 2; see TB p 17 & 21)

Opening routines (see TB p 16)

Recycling activity (*Do you want to...? Yes, I do. / No, I don't.*) (see TB p 19)

Lesson aims (see TB p 18)

Watch the *A day out* story video.

- Play the story video.
- Take the part of the narrator and Daddy yourself. Encourage children to join in acting out the story in two groups (Mimi, Dylan).
- Ask *Is Mimi interested in learning about dinosaurs? Is Dylan interested in learning about space? Are Mimi and Dylan curious about the world?* Explain what you mean by "curious" (they want to learn). (Yes).
- Ask *Is it important to be curious and interested in learning about the world? Why?* and listen to the children's responses.

***I find out about my world* song**

CD3 Track 26

- Say the title of the song. Ask *How can we learn about the world?* Listen to children's ideas and use these to pre-teach or remind children of words and phrases in the song, e.g. ask questions, *play games*, watch films, look at books, etc.
- Ask *How do the singers in the song say they learn?* Give an example to clarify what you mean.
- Play the audio. Children listen.
- Repeat the question and children respond with some of the ways.
- Play the audio again. Use the pause button and children identify all the ways of learning.
- Play the audio a third time. Children join in singing the song.
- Make the point that it is important to be curious about the world and that there are many ways of learning.
- Ask *How do you learn?* and children respond with ideas from the song.

Table time

Student's Book p 60

Listen, point and sing *I find out about my world.*

CD3 Track 26

- Play the song. Children sing and point to the pictures of Harry and Zoe in their books.

Check (✔) the ways you learn.

- Children choose the pictures to show the ways they learn.

Draw a picture to show a way you like to learn. Say.

- Children draw a picture to show their favorite way of learning. Children take turns showing their pictures and saying sentences e.g. *I talk to my big brother.*

Activity Book p 60

Trace the pictures of children learning.

- Children trace the children who are learning.

Choose and color a picture that shows how you like to learn. Say.

- They color the picture of how they like to learn and say.

Closing time

Learning review (see TB p 18)

Closing routines (see TB p 16)

Goodbye song and puppet (CD1 Track 3; see TB p 17 & 21)

Use the **Navio App** to listen to the song, and encourage children to do the same at home.

1 2 3 4

Listen and point. Match and number the photos to show how to cross the street safely. Say. **Language:** cars, crosswalk, sidewalk, stoplights, street; stop, look, listen; black, green, orange, red, white; numbers 1–4; The (stoplights) are (red).

Learning objectives

- Learn about how to cross the street safely
- Listen and order the stages of crossing a street
- Talk about crossing the street safely

Materials

- Class CDs, printable content flashcards, *Ferris Wheel* mat, Mimi puppet

Main vocabulary

- cars, crosswalk, sidewalk, stoplights, street; stop, look, listen; black, green, orange, red, white; numbers 1–4

Key language

- The (stoplights) are (red).

Teacher's tip: Crossing the street safely

Crossing the street safely is an important life skill. If toy cars and dolls are available in the children's classroom, set up an area in the classroom where they can role-play crossing the road safely.

Circle time

Hello song and puppet (CD1 Track 2; see TB p 17 & 21)
Opening routines (see TB p 16)
Recycling activity (see TB p 19)
Lesson aims (see TB p 18)

Introduce content vocabulary.

- Ask children what transportation you see when you go into town e.g. cars, bike, motorcycles. Say *It's important to cross streets safely.*
- Show the printable flashcards in turn and say the words *(cars, sidewalk, street, stoplights, crosswalk).* Children repeat the words.
- Ask questions e.g. *Where do we walk in town? (sidewalk) Where do cars and motorcycles go? (street) Where do we cross the street? (crosswalk) How do we know when we can cross the street? (stoplights) What colors are stoplights? (red, orange and green)*

Make a 'crocodile' and act out crossing the road.

- Children stand up and make a "crocodile," i.e. they line up holding hands in pairs.
- Stand at the front of the "crocodile." Use the flashcards to explain where things are. Say *We're in town. We're on the sidewalk. This is the street. There is the crosswalk and the stoplights.*
- Use language as in the audio and act out crossing the street safely with the children.
- Repeat once or twice. Ask questions as you do this e.g. *What do we do at the crosswalk? (wait on the sidewalk, look at the stoplights) What color are the stoplights when it's safe to cross? (The stoplights for the cars are red but the light for us is green).*

Table time

Student's Book p 61

Listen and point.

- Say *Look at the photos of Auntie Vicky, Lucy and Alex. Find the sidewalk / street / crosswalk / stoplights* and children respond.
- Play the audio. Children listen and point to the photos in order.

CD3 Track 27

Auntie Vicky:	Come on, Lucy and Alex. Hold my hand. Stay on the sidewalk. Let's walk to the crosswalk. It's black and white. It has stoplights.
Alex:	Look, there it is!
Auntie Vicky:	Yes! Wait on the sidewalk. Look at the stoplights – green, orange … Now the stoplights are red! The man is green. Wait for the cars to stop. Look and listen. Is it safe now?
Lucy:	Yes, Auntie Vicky.
Auntie Vicky:	OK. Great. Let's cross the street.
Lucy and Alex:	Hurray.

Match and number the photos to show how to cross the street safely.

- Play the audio again. Use the pause button.
- Children match the numbers and photos.
- Children number the photos in order.

Say.

- Children say sentences about the photos and stages, e.g. *The crosswalk is black and white.*

Activity Book p 61

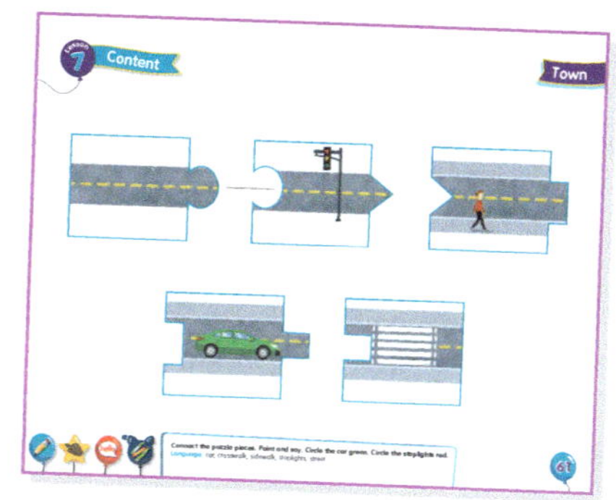

Connect the puzzle pieces. Point and say.

- Children connect the pieces of the puzzle. Then they point and say the words.

Circle the car green. Circle the stoplights red.

- They circle the car in green and the stoplights in red.

Closing time

Learning review (see TB p 18)
Closing routines (see TB p 16)
Goodbye song and puppet (CD1 Track 3; see TB p 17 & 21)

Use the **Navio App** to play the vocabulary and language games, and encourage children to do the same at home.

Lesson 8 Culture

Watch. Listen and point to the story *The enormous carrot.* Color the things in the story. Say. **Language:** carrot; boy, girl, man, woman; pull; Do you want to help? Yes, of course. The (man) pulls the (woman).

62

Learning objectives

- Watch, understand and enjoy the traditional story *The enormous carrot*
- Act out the story
- Identify the characters in the story

Materials

- Class CDs, printable story cards, flashcards, *Ferris Wheel* mat, Mimi puppet

Main vocabulary

- carrot; boy, girl, man, woman; pull

Key language

- Do you want to help? Yes, of course. The (man) pulls the (woman).

Teacher's tip: Acting out the story and choosing roles

Divide the class into groups of five. Have the groups decide their roles: the man, woman, girl, boy and carrot. Tell the story again and have the children join in when it's their turn.

Circle time

Hello song and puppet (CD1 Track 2; see TB p 17 & 21)
Opening routines (see TB p 16)
Recycling activity (see TB p 19)
Lesson aims (see TB p 18)

Introduce the story *The enormous carrot*.

- Explain that children are going to watch and listen to a traditional story, "The enormous carrot."
- Ask if children if they know the story. Give clues, e.g. *The enormous carrot is a very big vegetable. The woman who grows the carrot can't pull it out of the ground* (demonstrate what you mean) *and asks other people to help.*
- If children know the story, ask *Do you want to watch and listen to the story in English?*

Watch and listen to the story.

CD3 Track 28

- Ask *Who helps the woman pull the carrot out of the ground? What happens at the end?* Encourage children to guess and listen to their ideas.
- Play the video. Children watch and listen to the story.
- Ask the pre-questions again and children respond.
- Play the video again. Pause and ask questions, e.g. *Who pulls the carrot? Does the carrot move?*
- Ask *Do you like the story? Do you think they have a delicious dinner? Do you like carrots?*

Act out the story *The enormous carrot*.

- Take the part of the woman. Say *I'm hungry. I want to cook the carrot.* Mime pulling the carrot and indicate that it doesn't move. Ask *Do you want to help … ?* and name a child to stand behind you and hold your waist. Say *Pull, pull, pull.* Again, the carrot doesn't move.
- Repeat with other children.
- At the end, the carrot comes out. Say *We have the carrot. Let's have dinner together.*

Table time

Student's Book p 62

Watch. Listen and point to the story *The enormous carrot*.

Story questions

Picture 1
What vegetable grows in the garden? *(A carrot)*
Is the woman hungry? *(Yes)*

Picture 2
Who wants to help pull the carrot? *(A man)*
Does the carrot move? *(No)*

Picture 3
Who wants to help to pull the carrot? *(A girl)*
Does the carrot move? *(No)*

Picture 4
Who wants to help to pull the carrot now? *(A boy)*
Does the carrot come out? *(Yes)*

CD3 Track 28

- Play the audio. Children listen and point to the pictures.
- Say *Find the woman, man, girl, boy, carrot* and children respond.
- Play the audio again. Ask *Who wants to help? Who has dinner together at the end of the story?*

Color the things in the story. Say.

- Children color the things in the story. They point and say the words.

Activity Book p 62

Connect the dots to complete the picture. Color the enormous carrot.

- Children connect the dots to complete the enormous carrot and color it.

Point and say.

- They point and say the story events.

Closing time

Learning review (see TB p 18)
Closing routines (see TB p 16)
Goodbye song and puppet (CD1 Track 3; see TB p 17 & 21)

Use the **Navio App** to watch the video, and encourage children to do the same at home.

Review

I can …

Vocabulary

Story

Speaking

Content

3:29 hello 3:30

Circle the town words you know. Listen, point and say. Listen and answer. Ask and say. Complete the faces to show what you can do. Language: bookstore, mall, movie theater, museum, park, restaurant, supermarket, swimming pool, toy store, zoo; Do you want to go to (the zoo)? Yes, I do. / No, I don't. I want to go to (the park).

63

Learning objectives

- Review what you have learned in this unit
- Complete a self-evaluation
- Ask and answer questions about where you want to go in town

Materials

- Class CDs, flashcards, *Ferris Wheel* mat, Mimi puppet

Main vocabulary

- bookstore, mall, movie theater, museum, park, restaurant, supermarket, swimming pool, toy store, zoo

Key language

- Do you want to go to the (zoo)? Yes, I do. / No, I don't. I want to go to the (park).

Teacher's tip: Working with different partners

Working with a partner helps children learn to cooperate. Encourage them to complete the first part of the review with their neighbor, checking that they know the vocabulary before circling the pictures. Once they have completed the review, they change partners and compare their results.

Circle time

Hello song and puppet (CD1 Track 2; see TB p 17 & 21)
Opening routines (see TB p 16)
Recycling activity (see TB p 19)
Lesson aims (see TB p 18)

Town flashcard games

- Play one or two flashcard games (see TB p 20 & 21).

Sing *Do you want to go to the zoo?*

CD3 Track 20

- Put the flashcards in the song in pairs on the board.
- Play the audio. Children sing, point to the flashcards and shake their index finger for "no" and nod their head for "yes" in each verse.

Game: *Where do you want to go?*

- Give a child a flashcard to hold facing them.
- Encourage children to ask questions, e.g. *Do you want to go to the (mall)?* The child answers, *No, I don't* until the class guesses.

Watch the story video.

- Children watch the story video. Ask e.g. *What does Mimi / Dylan want to learn about?*

Table time

Student's Book p 63

Circle the town words you know.

- Explain and demonstrate the activity.

Listen, point and say.

- Play the audio. Children check the words they know, point to the pictures and repeat the words.

CD3 Track 29

Mimi: I'm the teacher! Can you remember the places in town, Dylan?
Dylan: Yes, I can. Supermarket.
Mimi: Supermarket.
Dylan: Mall.
Mimi: Mall.
Dylan: Museum.
Mimi: Museum.
Dylan: Zoo.
Mimi: Zoo.
Dylan: Swimming pool.
Mimi: Swimming pool.
Dylan: Movie theater.
Mimi: Movie theater.
Dylan: Restaurant.
Mimi: Restaurant.
Dylan: Toy store.
Mimi: Toy store.
Dylan: Bookstore.
Mimi: Bookstore.
Dylan: Park.
Mimi: Park. Well done, Dylan.
Both: Fantastic!

Listen and answer. Ask and say.

- Play the audio. Children listen to the questions.

CD3 Track 30

Mimi: Where do you want to go?
Do you want to go to the zoo?
Do you want to go to a museum?
Do you want to go to the park?
Do you want to go to the swimming pool?
Do you want to go to the movie theater?
Do you want to go to the supermarket?

- Play the audio again. Children listen, repeat and answer the questions.

Complete the faces to show what you can do.

- Explain the four pictures: *I can name places in town; I can understand the story; I can ask and say where I want to go; I understand how to cross the street safely.*
- Remind children they should complete each face with a smile or frown depending on how well they think they have done.

Activity Book p 63

Complete the faces to show places you want to go to in your town. Ask and say.

- Children complete the faces with a smile if they want to go to that place in their town.
- Children ask and answer questions about places they want to go.

Think and circle the number to show your progress.

- Children circle the number.

Closing time

Learning review (see TB p 18)
Closing routines (see TB p 16)
Goodbye song and puppet (CD1 Track 3; see TB p 17 & 21)

Use the **Navio App** to review what children have learned in this unit, and encourage them to do the same at home.

Project

COOPERATIVE LEARNING

1

2

3

Choose and color a place. Put the places together to make a map of Mimi's town. Ask and say. Language: bookstore, movie theater, park, restaurant, supermarket, swimming pool, toy store, zoo; Where do you want to go? I want to go to (the supermarket). I don't want to go to (the restaurant). Do you want to go to (the zoo)? Do you like (the toy store)? Yes, I do. / No, I don't. I like (the park).

64

Town

Learning objectives

- Work together to do a collaborative project
- Make a place for the town project
- Talk about the places in the town
- Design a town

Materials

- Class CDs, Mimi puppet, photocopiable templates, crayons or paints, glue, colored card

Main vocabulary

- bookstore, movie theater, park, restaurant, supermarket, swimming pool, toy store, zoo

Key language

- Where do you want to go? I want to go to (the supermarket). I don't want to go to (the restaurant). Do you want to go to (the zoo)? Do you like (the toy store)? Yes, I do. / No, I don't. I like (the park).

Teacher's tip: Giving positive feedback about one another's work

COOPERATIVE LEARNING

Once the children have finished their drawings, encourage them to look at each other's work in the imaginary town display. Encourage them to comment and give each other positive feedback e.g. I like the park. *It's lovely / I want to go to the swimming pool. It's fantastic etc.* Make sure all the comments are positive and discourage any negativity.

Circle time

Hello song and puppet (CD1 Track 2; see TB p 17 & 21)
Opening routines (see TB p 16)
Recycling activity (see TB p 19)
Lesson aims (see TB p 18)

Prepare for your project.

- Say *Let's do a project. Let's make a map of an imaginary town!*
- Show children the template of places in town. Explain that children should choose a place and color it.
- Explain and demonstrate that children will then use their pictures to make a street map of their imaginary town.

Table time

COOPERATIVE LEARNING

Student's Book p 64

Choose and color a place.

- Say e.g. *We're going to make a map of an imaginary town like this. Look at what we need for our project: a picture of a place in town, crayons* (or paints), *glue and colored card.* Children listen and point to the pictures.
- Children choose a place in town. Give a copy of this project template to each child. Make sure children have crayons (or paints) available.
- Children color or paint the picture of the place they have chosen.

Put the places together to make a map of Mimi's town. Ask and say.

- When they are ready, invite children to come and glue their pictures onto the map, with a simple pattern of streets, a crosswalk and stoplights, that you have prepared. If appropriate, you can have more than one map, e.g. one per group of 8–12 children.
- Talk about the imaginary towns using language of the unit and other language children know.
- Ask children *Do you like our imaginary town? Make the point that everyone has helped make the map and that they couldn't have made such a beautiful map on their own.*

Activity Book p 64

Design a town. Choose and draw four places in your town.

- Children design a town. They choose and draw four places on the map of a town.

Ask and say.

- They ask and answer questions about where they want to go.

Closing time

Learning review (see TB p 18)
Closing routines (see TB p 16)
Goodbye song and puppet (CD1 Track 3; see TB p 17 & 21)

Music
Mimi's band

Unit objectives

- Identify and name musical instruments and activities
- Sing the language song *Listen, clap, dance!*
- Ask and say what you're doing
- Understand and act out the story *Mimi's band*
- Sing and act out the story song *Welcome to our show*
- Ask and say what you like doing
- Understand a story about willingness to practice
- Recognize the value of being willing to practice
- Recognize and reproduce a musical rhythm
- Sing and act out the traditional song *I am the music man*
- Review your learning and progress
- Participate in a collaborative project

Vocabulary and language

- **Main vocabulary:** drum, guitar, maracas, piano, recorder, tambourine; clap, dance, listen, sing
- **Key language:** What are you doing? I'm (playing the piano). I'm (singing). Do you like playing the (guitar)? Yes, I do. / No, I don't. I like (playing the drum).
- **Content language:** fast, slow, loud, quiet; It's (loud). Clap the rhythm.
- **Other language:** trombone, violin; I'm practicing. What can you play? I play the (violin). My maracas are (red and blue). I like the (green) maracas.

Story CD4 Track 7

Picture 1

Narr: Mrs. Cat's class is preparing a show. The children are excited.
Mrs. C: I have a drum, a recorder, a tambourine and maracas. Do you like playing the drum, Dylan?
Dylan: Oh, yes, I do.
Mrs. C: Here you go. A drum for Dylan.
Dylan: Oh, thank you, Mrs. Cat.
Mrs. C: Do you like playing the recorder, Katy?
Katy: Oh, yes, I do.
Mrs. C: Here you go. A recorder for Katy.
Katy: Oh, thank you, Mrs. Cat.

Picture 2

Mrs. C: Do you like playing the tambourine, Leo?
Leo: Oh, yes, I do.
Mrs. C: Here you go. A tambourine for Leo.
Leo: Oh thank you, Mrs. Cat.
Mrs. C: Do you like playing the maracas, Zara?
Zara: Oh, yes, I do.
Mrs. C: Here you go. Maracas for Zara.
Zara: Oh, thank you, Mrs. Cat.
Mrs. C: Do you like playing the maracas, Mimi?
Mimi: Oh, yes, I do. Thank you, Mrs. Cat.

Picture 3

Mrs. C: Great! So now we're ready. Let's practice! I'm playing the piano.
Dylan: I'm playing the drum. This is great!
Katy: I'm playing the recorder. Brilliant!
Leo: I'm playing the tambourine. What fun!
Zara: I'm playing the maracas. Fantastic!
Mimi: I'm playing the maracas, too! This is great!
Mrs. C: Uh-hmm. Oh … I have an idea. Let's change instruments.

Picture 4

Mrs. C: OK everyone. Let's try again. What are you doing, Dylan?
Dylan: I'm playing the maracas.
Mrs. C: What are you doing, Katy?
Katy: I'm playing the maracas, too.
Mrs. C: What are you doing, Leo?
Leo: I'm playing the recorder.
Mrs. C: What are you doing, Zara?
Zara: I'm playing the drum
Mrs. C: And what are you doing, Mimi?
Mimi: I'm playing the tambourine.
Mrs. C: Very good! Here we go! One, two, three.
Mrs. C: Umm. That's a little better, but …

Picture 5

Mimi: I know! Let's write a song for our show, Mrs. Cat.
Mrs. C: Oh, that's a great idea, Mimi!
All: Oh yes! Great! Fantastic!
Mrs. C: Come on. Let's begin …
Leo: Hello, hello …
Zara: Welcome to our show!
Katy: We want you to know …
Mimi: We love you so!
Mrs. C: Oh, yes! Well done, children! Do you like singing, Mimi?
Mimi: Yes, I do.
Mrs. C: Great! You can be the singer in the band!
Mimi: Oh, thank you, Mrs. Cat.
Mrs. C: Come on now. Let's practice!

Picture 6

Narr: It's the day of the show. All the mommies and daddies come to watch. The children are excited.
Katy: Mrs. Cat's class is happy to present …
Leo: Mimi's band!
Mommy: Bravo!
Daddy: Fantastic!
Parents: Good job, Mrs. Cat's class! And good job, Mimi!

Songs and story

Language song

Listen, clap, dance! CD4 Track 5

Listen, clap, dance! (Cup your ear, clap once, move your arms)
What are you doing? (Open arms questioningly)
Can you guess? (Point to head with index finger)
I'm playing the … Guitar! (Mime strumming a guitar)
I'm playing the guitar! (Mime strumming a guitar)
Yes, yes, yes! (Punch arms in the air three times)

(Chorus)

I'm playing the … Piano! (Mime playing a piano)
I'm playing the piano! (Mime playing a piano)
Yes, yes, yes! (Punch arms in the air three times)

(Chorus)

I'm playing the … Tambourine! (Shake your fist back and forth)
I'm playing the tambourine! (Shake your fist back and forth)
Yes, yes, yes! (Punch arms in the air three times)

(Chorus)

I'm lalalala … (Mime holding a microphone)
I'm singing! (Mime holding a microphone)
Yes, yes, yes! (Punch arms in the air three times)

Values story

CD4 Track 11

Picture 1

Narrator: Harry's practicing the recorder for the class show.
Mom: What are you doing, Harry?
Harry: I'm playing the recorder. I'm practicing for the show.
Mom: Good boy!
Harry: I'm not very good.
Mom: Keep practicing! You can do it!

Picture 2

Narrator: Zoe's practicing the piano for the school show.
Dad: What are you doing, Zoe?
Zoe: I'm playing the piano. I'm practicing for the show.
Dad: Good girl!
Zoe: I'm not very good.
Dad: Keep practicing! You can do it!

Picture 3

Narrator: Harry and Zoe practice every day.
Mom: That's good.
Zoe: Thank you, Mom!
Dad: You're better every day!
Harry: Oh, great! Thanks, Dad!

Picture 4

Narrator: And now it's time for the class show. Harry and Zoe are nervous and excited.
Zoe: Good luck, Harry.
Harry: Good luck, Zoe.
Voice: Welcome to our class show!
Mom: Hurray!
Dad: Bravo!
Mom: Well done, Harry!
Dad: Well done, Zoe!
Mom: You see! Keep practicing and you can do it!

Story song

Welcome to our show CD4 Track 8

Hello, hello (Wave)
Welcome to our show (Make a beckoning gesture)
We want you to know (Point outward with both hands)
We love you so! (Hug yourself)

I'm playing the drum. One, two, three. (Mime playing a drum)
I'm playing the recorder. Listen to me! (Mime playing a recorder, then open arms wide)
I'm playing the tambourine. One, two, three. (Mime playing a tambourine)
I'm playing the maracas. Listen to me! (Mime playing maracas)

I'm singing, I'm dancing. One, two, three. (Mime singing and dancing)
I'm singing, I'm clapping. Listen to me! (Mime singing and clapping)

(Chorus)

Culture song

I am the music man CD4 Track 13

I am the music man. (Gesture to self with both thumbs)
I come from far away and I can play. (Gesture far away with one hand)
What can you play? (Open arms questioningly)
I play the piano. (Mime playing the piano)
Pia pia piano, piano piano. Pia pia piano, pia piano

(Chorus)

I play the violin. (Mime playing the violin)
Vio vio violin, violin violin. Vio vio violin, vio violin (etc)
(Chorus)

I play the trombone. (Mime playing the trombone)
Trom trom trom trom trom trombone, trom trombone, trom trombone (etc)

(Chorus)

I play the big bass drum. (Mime banging on a big drum)
Big bass big bass big bass drum, big bass drum, big bass drum (etc)

Music
Mimi's band

Vocabulary Lesson 1

Listen, point and repeat. Listen and stick the music stickers. Listen and play *Memory*. Circle the musical instruments you like. Say. Language: drum, guitar, maracas, piano, recorder, tambourine; blue, green, orange, pink, red, yellow

65

Learning objectives

- Identify and name musical instruments
- Listen and point to musical instruments
- Remember musical instruments in a memory game

Materials

- Class CDs, flashcards, *Ferris Wheel* mat, Mimi puppet

Main vocabulary

- drum, guitar, maracas, piano, recorder, tambourine; blue, green, orange, pink, red, yellow

Teacher's tip: Predicting vocabulary

As an alternative to using the flashcards to introduce the musical instruments, use mime and make the sound each instrument makes, bringing in an element of prediction. As children respond in their shared language, name the instrument in English and show the flashcard.

Circle time

Hello song and puppet (CD1 Track 2; see TB p 17 & 21)
Opening routines (see TB p 16)
Lesson aims (see TB p 18)

Introduce the musical instruments.

- Use the puppet and flashcards to introduce the musical instruments. Ask children what instruments they know. As they respond in their shared language, introduce the words in English. Children repeat the words.
- Put the *Ferris Wheel* mat on the floor or board with the musical instrument flashcards face down (one on each color). Use the puppet to turn them over and name them. The children repeat the words.

Game: *Say the color!*

- Name the musical instruments on the Ferris Wheel and children name the color. Then the reverse.

Game: *Take a photo!*

- Stick the flashcards at the children's height on different walls around the classroom.
- Ask a few children to stand up. Say e.g. *Take a photo of the … (guitar)!* Children walk to the flashcard, pretend to take a photo and say the word.

Table time

Student's Book p 65

Listen, point and repeat.

- Play the audio. The children listen, point to and repeat each musical instrument.

CD4 Track 1

Mimi: Look Dylan! Guitar … recorder … tambourine … piano … maracas. Repeat, Dylan.
Dylan: Yes, Mimi. Guitar … recorder … tambourine … piano … maracas.
Mimi: Very good, Dylan! Let's name the musical instruments together!
Both: Guitar … recorder … tambourine … piano … maracas. Fantastic!

- Draw attention to the question mark in their books. They identify the missing instrument (drum).

Listen and stick the music stickers.

- Play the audio. The children listen and point to the musical instruments in their books.

CD4 Track 2

Where's the tambourine? It's on … orange.
Where are the maracas? They're on … green.
Where's the guitar? It's on … red.
Where's the recorder? It's on … blue.
Where's the piano? It's on … yellow.
Where's the drum? Can you guess? It's on … pink.
Yes, yes, yes!
The drum is on pink. Yes, yes, yes!

- Ask questions about all the musical instruments in the same way and children respond.
- Play the audio again. Children listen and stick the music stickers.

Listen and play *Memory*.

- Children copy you covering your eyes with your hands. Play the audio. Children listen and remember the musical instrument on each color on the wheel.

CD4 Track 3

Close your eyes
One, two, three
Say the words
Play memory!
Blue … recorder!
Red … guitar!
Yellow … piano!
Green … maracas!
Pink … drum!
Orange … tambourine!

- Play the game.

Circle the musical instruments you like. Say.

- Children circle the musical instrument they like. They point and say the words.

Activity Book p 65

Draw the next musical instrument in the sequence.

- Children draw the next instrument in each sequence.

Point and say.

- Children point and name the musical instruments.

Closing time

Learning review (see TB p 18)
Closing routines (see TB p 16)
Goodbye song and puppet (CD1 Track 3; see TB p 17 & 21)

Use the **Navio App** to play the vocabulary game, and encourage children to do the same at home.

4:04 4:05 hello

Listen and find the new music words. Listen, point and sing *Listen, clap, dance!* Check (✓) the things Alex and Lucy are doing in the song. Ask and say. Language: drum, guitar, piano, recorder, tambourine; clap, dance, listen, sing; What are you doing? I'm (playing the piano). I'm (singing).

Learning objectives

- Talk about music
- Identify and name four new musical activities
- Sing the language song *Listen, clap, dance!*
- Ask and say what you're doing

Materials

- Class CDs, flashcards, *Ferris Wheel* mat, Mimi puppet

Main vocabulary

- drum, guitar, piano, recorder, tambourine; clap, dance, listen, sing

Key language

- What are you doing? I'm (playing the piano). I'm (singing).

Teacher's tip: Singing the song with different partners

COOPERATIVE LEARNING

Have the children interact with different partners when they sing the song. Get them to stand in two lines facing each other. They should sing the chorus and first verse of the song to the child standing opposite them. When the first verse finishes, one line stays still and the other line moves along one. The last child comes around to the front. They then sing the chorus and next verse to their new partner.

Circle time

Hello song and puppet (CD1 Track 2; see TB p 17 & 21)
Opening routines (see TB p 16)
Recycling activity (six musical instruments from lesson 1) (see TB p 19)
Lesson aims (see TB p 18)

Introduce the musical activities.

- Put all ten music flashcards on the floor or board. Ask the children to identify the four new words.
- Uses the puppet to point to and say the words in turn. Children repeat in chorus.
- Turn the four new food flashcards face down. Mix them up. Point to one and ask *Listen, clap, sing or dance?* Children guess. Repeat several times.
- Mime or do each activity and children say the words.

Introduce *What are you doing? I'm … ing.*

- Put the flashcards face up on the floor or board. Mime playing the guitar. Children mime with you. Say *I'm playing the guitar.* Children repeat the sentence.
- Repeat with different flashcards and mimes.
- Ask a confident child or pair to choose one of the flashcards and mime in the same way. The class ask *What are you doing?* and the child or children respond e.g. *I'm playing the drum.*
- Repeat several times with different children.

Game: *Guess what I'm doing!*

- Show a flashcard secretly to a pair or group of children. Children mime the activity. The rest of the class take turns guessing e.g. *Playing the piano?* If the guess is correct, the children say *Yes! I'm playing the piano!* The child who guesses correctly is included in the next turn to mime an activity.
- Repeat several times using different flashcards.

***Listen, clap, dance!* song**

CD4 Track 5

- Put the music flashcards face up on the floor or board.
- Children listen and point to the flashcards with you as they hear them in the song. Check the words and instruments in the song.
- Play the audio again. Children do actions and join in singing the song.
- Remember that you can use the karaoke version of the song when children are confident.

Table time

Student's Book p 66

Listen and find the new music words.

- The children listen and find the four new words. Repeat and children say the words.

CD4 Track 4

One … two … Which words are new?
Listen! Listen! *Sing! Sing!*
Clap! Clap! *Dance! Dance!*

Listen, point and sing *Listen, clap, dance!*

- Play the song. Children listen and point to the pictures, and join in singing the song.

Check (✓) the things Alex and Lucy are doing in the song.

- Play the audio again. Use the pause button. Demonstrate that children should choose the pictures that show what the characters are doing in the song.
- Play the audio. Children check answers and sing.

Ask and say.

- Children ask and answer about all the pictures.

Activity Book p 66

Circle your favorite music activity. Draw a picture of you doing it.

- Children circle their favorite music activity. Then they draw a picture of themselves doing it.

Ask and say.

- Children take turns showing each other their pictures and asking and saying what they're doing.

Closing time

Learning review (see TB p 18)
Closing routines (see TB p 16)
Goodbye song and puppet (CD1 Track 3; see TB p 17 & 21)

Use the **Navio App** to listen to the song, and encourage children to do the same at home.

Lesson 3 Story

4:07

Watch. Listen to the story *Mimi's band*. Circle the musical instruments in the class show. Stick the story sticker. **Language:** drum, maracas, piano, recorder, tambourine; sing; What are you doing? I'm (playing the recorder). Do you like (playing the maracas)? Yes, I do. / No, I don't.

Learning objectives

- Watch, understand and enjoy the story *Mimi's band*
- Make a prediction about the story
- Identify musical instruments in the story

Materials

- Class CDs, printable story cards, flashcards, *Ferris Wheel* mat, Mimi puppet

Main vocabulary

- drum, maracas, piano, recorder, tambourine; sing

Key language

- What are you doing? I'm (playing the recorder). Do you like (playing the maracas)? Yes, I do. / No, I don't.

Teacher's tip: Asking questions to maintain focus

Asking comprehension questions helps maintain the children's focus on the story. If children are distracted, pause the audio or video or your telling of the story to ask specific questions or elicit a personal response.

Circle time

Hello song and puppet (CD1 Track 2; see TB p 17 & 21)

Opening routines (see TB p 16)

Recycling activity (*What are you doing? I'm …* and music words) (see TB p 19)

Lesson aims (see TB p 18)

Introduce the story *Mimi's band*.

- Say *It's story time!* Play the *Story rhyme* (CD1 Track 4; see TB p 17)
- Say *Alex and Lucy are watching a story about Mimi and Dylan. Mrs. Cat's class is preparing a show.* (Explain meaning) *Who's in the show?* Listen to children's answers.

Watch and listen to the story *Mimi's band*.

CD4 Track 7

- Watch the video, play the audio or read the story using the printable story cards. Pause, repeat words, point to the pictures, ask questions.
- Ask *Who's in the show?* again and check the answer (Dylan, Katy, Zara, Leo, Mimi). Ask e.g. *Who's playing the drum?* and children respond.
- Play the story again. Pause and ask e.g. *What idea does Mimi have? (to write a song for the show) Does Mrs. Cat think it's a good idea? (Yes)*
- Repeat the story. Encourage children to join in with the words and phrases.
- Ask *Do the mommies and daddies like the show? (Yes) What do they say about the show? (Bravo! Fantastic! Good job!)*

Game: *Mime the music!*

- Ask e.g. *Dylan! What are you doing?* Children respond by pretending to play the drum and say *I'm playing the drum.*
- Repeat with the other characters (Katy, Leo, Zara, Mimi).

Table time

Student's Book p 67

Story questions

Picture 1
What does Dylan like playing? *(The drum)*
What does Katy like playing? *(The recorder)*

Picture 2
What does Leo like playing? *(The tambourine)*
What does Zara like playing? *(The maracas)*

Picture 3
What is Mrs. Cat playing? *(The piano)*
What is Mimi playing? *(The maracas)*

Picture 4
Is Dylan playing the drum now? *(No)*
Who is playing the maracas now? *(Katy)*

Picture 5
What do the children write for the show? *(A song)*
Does Mimi like singing? *(Yes)*

Picture 6
Are the children excited for the show? *(Yes)*
Who is singing in the band? *(Mimi)*

Watch. Listen to the story *Mimi's band*.

CD4 Track 7

- Read or play the audio of the story again. Children listen and point to the pictures in their books.

Circle the musical instruments in the class show. Stick the story sticker.

- Demonstrate circling the musical instruments in the class show and sticking the story sticker.
- Ask *Are Mommy, Daddy, Mimi and Dylan happy at the end of the story? Is Mrs. Cat happy?*

Activity Book p 67

Trace the musical instruments. Match them to the characters who play them in the class show in the story.

- Children trace the instruments, then match them to the characters who play them in the class show.

Point and say.

- Children pretend to be the character, point and say what they are doing.

Closing time

Learning review (see TB p 18)

Closing routines (see TB p 16)

Goodbye song and puppet (CD1 Track 3; see TB p 17 & 21)

Use the **Navio App** to watch the video, and encourage children to do the same at home.

Lesson 4 Story Song

Music

Watch. Listen, point and sing *Welcome to our show*. Follow and draw the paths through the maze to show what the characters are doing in the show. Ask and say. **Language:** drum, maracas, recorder, tambourine; clap, dance, listen, sing; What are you doing? I'm (playing the recorder). I'm (singing).

68

Learning objectives

- Watch, sing and act out the story song *Welcome to our show*
- Listen to the story again
- Identify and say musical instruments and activities
- Ask and say what you're doing

Materials

- Class CDs, printable story cards, flashcards, *Ferris Wheel* mat, Mimi puppet

Main vocabulary

- drum, maracas, recorder, tambourine; clap, dance, listen, sing

Key language

- What are you doing? I'm (playing the recorder). I'm (singing).

Teacher's tip: Tuning into sounds

Making different vocal sounds can help children with articulation. Encourage them to make the sounds of each instrument as well as doing the mime. In addition, once they finish the page in their Student's Book, they can make the noise and guess the instrument in pairs. Be ready with your quiet signal if noise levels get too high!

Circle time

Hello song and puppet (CD1 Track 2; see TB p 17 & 21)
Opening routines (see TB p 16)
Recycling activity (music words) (see TB p 19)
Lesson aims (see TB p 18)

Retell the story *Mimi's band*.

- Play the audio, video or read the story using the printable story cards. Demonstrate that children should wave their arms in the air every time they hear the name of a musical instrument or a musical activity (sing, dance, listen, clap).

Game: *Spot the deliberate mistake!*

- Mime and say *I'm playing the drum*. Children wave their arms in the air and say *Yes! (You're) playing the drum!* Repeat with different instruments.
- Once you're confident children recognize the names of the instruments and actions, mime playing the piano but say *I'm playing the guitar*. Children say *No! (You're) playing the piano!* Repeat with different instruments, sometimes saying the correct sentence and sometimes making deliberate mistakes.

***Welcome to our show* song**

CD4 Track 8

- Say *We're going to learn the song children sing in Mrs. Cat's class show.* Ask *What are the children doing in the song?*
- Play the video. Ask the question again and check the answer.
- Play the video again. Children mime and join in singing the song.
- Ask e.g. *Do you like the song?* and children respond.

Act out the song.

- Divide the class into groups of five children and assign roles to each child: Mimi (sing, dance, clap), Dylan (drum), Zara (maracas), Leo (tambourine), Katy (recorder).
- Check children know what their character does in the show.
- Play the song. Children act out and sing the song with their groups.
- Repeat once or twice, getting children to change roles within their group each time.

Table time

Student's Book p 68

Watch. Listen, point and sing *Welcome to our show*.

CD4 Track 8

- Play the song (see TB p 165). Children listen, sing and point to the pictures.
- Remember that you can use the karaoke version of the song when children are confident.

Follow and draw the paths through the maze to show what the characters are doing in the show.

- Children draw lines to follow the maze and show what each character does in the show.

Ask and say.

- Children take turns pretending to be the characters and asking and saying e.g. *What are you doing? I'm playing the drum.*

Activity Book p 68

Choose and circle an instrument. Draw a picture of you playing the instrument in the class show.

- Children choose and circle one of the instruments. Then they draw themselves playing the instrument in Mimi's band.

Point and say.

- Children point and say what they are doing.

Closing time

Learning review (see TB p 18)
Closing routines (see TB p 16)
Goodbye song and puppet (CD1 Track 3; see TB p 17 & 21)

Use the **Navio App** to watch the video, and encourage children to do the same at home.

Lesson 5 **Speaking** Life skills

Watch. Listen and point. Match Auntie Vicky, Alex and Lucy to the instrument they like playing. Circle the instrument(s) you like playing. Ask and say. **Language:** drum, guitar, maracas, piano, recorder, tambourine; Do you like (playing the guitar)? Yes, I do. / No, I don't. I like (playing the drum).

Learning objectives

- Ask and say what you like doing
- Watch, understand and enjoy a video
- Identify musical instruments in the video

Materials

- Class CDs, flashcards, *Ferris Wheel* mat, Mimi puppet

Main vocabulary

- drum, guitar, maracas, piano, recorder, tambourine

Key language

- Do you like playing the (guitar)? Yes, I do. / No, I don't. I like (playing the drum).

Teacher's tip: Encouraging communication

Life skills

Have children ask and answer the question *Do you like playing (the drum)?* as a mingling activity. Have the children stand up and find a partner. Children greet each other and ask and answer the question. On finishing, they should raise their hand. They repeat with a new partner.

Circle time

Hello song and puppet (CD1 Track 2; see TB p 17 & 21)
Opening routines (see TB p 16)
Recycling activity (story song) (CD4 Track 8; see TB p 19)
Lesson aims (see TB p 18)

Game: *Guess the flashcard*

- Give out the music flashcards to individual children without others seeing.
- Children take turns miming their flashcard. Other children guess the flashcard.
- Ask children if they have music lessons or play musical instruments. If they answer yes, ask *Do you like playing the (drum)?*

Watch the video.

- Explain that Auntie Vicky, Alex and Lucy are talking about musical instruments they like playing.
- Ask *What instruments do Auntie Vicky, Alex and Lucy like playing?* and encourage children to guess.
- Play the video. Ask the questions again.
- Watch again. Pause and children repeat the questions and answers about each instrument.
- Ask *Do you like listening to the music Auntie Vicky, Alex and Lucy play?*

Table time

Student's Book p 69 Life skills

Watch. Listen and point.

- Children identify the musical instruments in the photos.
- Play the audio or video. Children listen and point to the instruments when they hear the words.

Match Auntie Vicky, Alex and Lucy to the instrument they like playing.

- Play the audio again. Use the pause button and children match the characters to the instruments they like playing.
- Check children have matched the instruments and characters correctly.

CD4 Track 10

Auntie Vicky: I have a guitar lesson today.
Alex: Do you like playing the guitar, Auntie Vicky?
Auntie Vicky: Yes, I do. Do you like playing the recorder, Lucy?
Lucy: No, I don't.
Auntie Vicky: Do you like playing the tambourine?
Lucy: Yes, I do.
Auntie Vicky: Do you like playing the tambourine, Alex?
Alex: No, I don't.
Auntie Vicky: Do you like playing the drum?
Alex: Yes, I do.
Auntie Vicky: I have an idea! Let's play together!
Lucy: Oh, yes!
Alex: Great idea!
Lucy: Oh brilliant! I like playing the tambourine!
Alex: And I like playing the drum!
Auntie Vicky: And I like playing the guitar. Let's play again!

Circle the instrument(s) you like playing.

- Children circle the instrument(s) they like playing.

Ask and say.

- Children ask and answer questions about all the instruments e.g. *Do you like playing the maracas? Yes, I do. / No, I don't.*

Activity Book p 69

Color the musical instruments you like playing.

- Children choose and color the musical instruments they like playing.

Ask and say.

- Children ask and answer questions about the instruments they like playing.

Closing time

Learning review (see TB p 18)
Closing routines (see TB p 16)
Goodbye song and puppet (CD1 Track 3; see TB p 17 & 21)

Use the **Navio App** to watch the video, and encourage children to do the same at home.

Lesson 6 Values Willingness to practice

Music

Listen and point to the story. Color the pictures of things you practice. Ask and say.
Language: piano, recorder; practice; What are you doing? I'm (playing the recorder). I'm (practicing).

4:11

SOCIAL AND EMOTIONAL LEARNING

70

Learning objectives

- Recognize the value of being willing to practice
- Understand and enjoy a story about willingness to practice
- Say what you practice

Materials

- Class CDs, flashcards, *Ferris Wheel* mat, Mimi puppet

Main vocabulary

- piano, recorder; practice

Key language

- What are you doing? I'm (playing the recorder). I'm practicing.

Teacher's tip: Encouraging practice

Life skills

Point out to the children that everything improves with practice, not only music. Use the language from the story to encourage them with their drawing, coloring or pencil skills. Say *Keep practicing! You can do it!* if they are finding something difficult.

Circle time

Hello song and puppet (CD1 Track 2; see TB p 17 & 21)

Opening routines (see TB p 16)

Recycling activity (*Do you like (playing the guitar)? Yes, I do. / No, I don't.*) (see TB p 19)

Lesson aims (see TB p 18)

Watch the *Mimi's band* story video.

- Play the story video.
- Take the part of the narrator and Mrs. Cat yourself. Encourage children to join in acting out the story in five groups (Mimi, Dylan, Katy, Zara and Leo).
- Ask *Do the children practice for the show in the story? Is it important to practice?* and listen to the children's responses.

Story about willingness to practice from *Little Book of Values*

CD4 Track 11

- Use the Mimi puppet to remind children of the *Little Book of Values* with stories about a brother and sister called Harry and Zoe. In this story, Harry and Zoe are practicing for a school show.
- Say *Listen and find out. What is Harry doing? (Practicing the recorder) What is Zoe doing? (Practicing the piano).*
- Play the audio. Ask the questions again. Check the answers.
- Play the audio again. Ask e.g. *What does Dad say to Zoe? What does Mom say to Harry? (Keep practicing) What do Zoe and Harry do? Are they better every day? Is the class show good? Why?*

Table time

Student's Book p 70

Listen and point to the story.

CD4 Track 11

- Play the audio of the story. Children listen and point to the pictures.
- Ask questions e.g. *What is Harry doing? What is Zoe doing? What does Dad say to Zoe? What does Mom say to Harry? What do Zoe and Harry do? Are they better every day? Is the class show good? Why?*
- Make the point that if you want to do something well, you need to practice like Harry and Zoe in the story.

Color the pictures of things you practice.

- Ask children *What do you practice?* and listen to their responses e.g. *playing the recorder, drawing, coloring, writing, reading, swimming,* etc.
- Look at the pictures and say the activities (riding my bike, writing, playing the recorder, playing soccer). Children color the activities they practice.

Ask and say.

- Children take turns showing the pictures they colored and saying e.g. *I'm practicing playing the recorder.*

Activity Book p 70

Draw a picture of you practicing something.

- Children draw a picture of themselves practicing something.

Ask and say.

- Children ask and answer questions about what they are doing.

Closing time

Learning review (see TB p 18)

Closing routines (see TB p 16)

Goodbye song and puppet (CD1 Track 3; see TB p 17 & 21)

Use the **Navio App** to listen to the story, and encourage children to do the same at home.

Content

Music

1 2 3 4

1

Listen and point. Clap the rhythm. Number the pictures in order. Color the circle of your favorite rhythm. Say. Language: fast, slow, loud, quiet; numbers 1–4; It's (loud). Clap the rhythm.

Lesson 7 Content

Learning objectives

- Recognize and reproduce a musical rhythm
- Listen and identify different rhythms
- Talk about your favorite rhythm
- Invent and draw a new rhythm

Materials

- Class CDs, printable content flashcards, *Ferris Wheel* mat, Mimi puppet

Main vocabulary

- fast, slow, loud, quiet; numbers 1–4

Key language

- It's (loud). Clap the rhythm.

Teacher's tip: Using rhythm

Bring rhythm into other areas of your lesson. Once children are familiar with the new vocabulary (*loud, quiet, fast, slow*) have them practice e.g. counting, saying the days of the week or singing a familiar song using a loud or quiet voice or with fast or slow rhythm.

Circle time

Hello song and puppet (CD1 Track 2; see TB p 17 & 21)
Opening routines (see TB p 16)
Recycling activity (see TB p 19)
Lesson aims (see TB p 18)

Introduce content vocabulary.

- Say *We're going to learn about rhythm!* Explain that rhythm is the pattern of sounds in music. Demonstrate this by clapping a simple rhythm, e.g. two slow claps, followed by three quick ones, and get the children to repeat this.
- Show the printable flashcards of quiet, loud, fast, slow in turn and introduce the words. Demonstrate what each one means by repeating the rhythm you clapped previously in a quiet, loud, fast or slow way. Say the words and children repeat the rhythm.

Clap the rhythm!

- Give an instruction, e.g. *Loud!* Children repeat the rhythm you have taught them in a loud way. Repeat with different instructions.
- Clap the rhythm yourself in different ways and children say e.g. *Fast!* Repeat several times.
- Ask e.g. *Do you like the fast rhythm?*

Table time

Student's Book p 71

Listen and point. Clap the rhythm.

- Say *Look at the photos of Lucy, Alex and Auntie Vicky. What are Lucy and Alex doing? (clapping the rhythm) What is Auntie Vicky doing? (singing)*
- Have children identify the pictures representing: *fast, slow, loud, quiet.* Point and say e.g. *It's slow.*
- Play the audio. Children listen and point.

CD4 Track 12

Auntie Vicky: Rhythm is the pattern of sounds in music. I sing: "Listen to the tambourine." Can you clap the rhythm? Very good. "Listen to the tambourine." Great. Now can you make the rhythm loud? Good. Now can you make the rhythm quiet? Great. Now can you make the rhythm fast? Great. Now can you make the rhythm slow?
Lucy: This is fun, Auntie Vicky!
Alex: It's great! I like rhythm!

- Play the audio again. Use the pause button. Children point to the pictures and join in clapping the rhythm with the characters.

Number the pictures in order.

- Play the audio again. Use the pause button and children match the numbers and pictures.
- Check the answers by asking *What's number one? (It's loud.)*

Color the circle of your favorite rhythm.

- Children choose and color the circle to show their favorite rhythm.

Say.

- Ask e.g. *What's your favorite rhythm? (It's fast!)*

Activity Book p 71

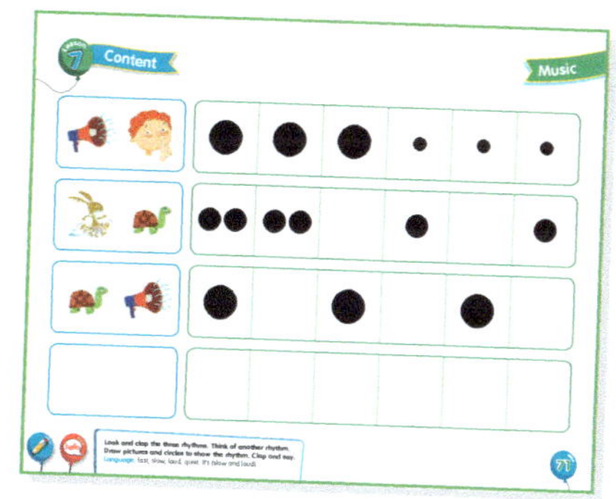

Look and clap the three rhythms.

- Children look and clap the three rhythms.

Think of another rhythm. Draw pictures and circles to show the rhythm. Clap and say.

- They draw pictures and circles to show a new rhythm. They clap the rhythm and describe it.

Closing time

Learning review (see TB p 18)
Closing routines (see TB p 16)
Goodbye song and puppet (CD1 Track 3; see TB p 17 & 21)

Use the **Navio App** to play the vocabulary and language games, and encourage children to do the same at home.

Lesson 8 Culture

Watch. Listen, point and sing *I am the music man*. Trace the instruments. Color your favorite instrument. Ask and say. **Language:** drum, piano, trombone, violin; What can you play? I play the (violin).

Learning objectives

- Watch, sing and act out the traditional song *I am the music man*
- Talk about your favorite musical instrument

Materials

- Class CDs, flashcards, *Ferris Wheel* mat, Mimi puppet

Main vocabulary

- drum, piano, trombone, violin

Key language

- What can you play? I play the (violin).

Teacher's tip: Singing the song in groups

Once the children are familiar with the song, divide them into four groups. Each group represents one of the instruments and sings and acts out their verse. Make sure that the groups who are not singing are listening, watching and paying attention in order to begin singing their verse when it's their turn. Encourage the groups to prompt each other to join in. At the end, encourage the children to give each group positive feedback on their "performance," e.g. *I like the piano. It's fantastic!*

Circle time

Hello song and puppet (CD1 Track 2; see TB p 17 & 21)
Opening routines (see TB p 16)
Recycling activity (see TB p 19)
Lesson aims (see TB p 18)

Game: *Freeze!*

- Say e.g. *I am the music man!* march around swinging your arms and get children to join in. Say e.g. *Very good! I come from far away.* Gesture far away with your hand. Say, *I play the piano.* Get the children to join in miming playing a piano.
- Say *Stop!* and demonstrate that children should freeze in position to show the musical instrument they are playing.
- Repeat with the instruments from the song, making sure children know what these are. You may also like to include other instruments children know. When children freeze, comment e.g. *Very good. You can play the trombone well!* and ask questions e.g. *Do you like playing the trombone?* and children respond.

***I am the music man* song**

CD4 Track 13

- Say *Let's learn the song "I am the music man."*
- Play the audio. Children listen and do the actions with you (as in the previous activity).
- Play the audio again. Children do the actions and join in singing the song.

Watch the *I am the music man* song video.

- Children watch the video and join in singing the song and doing the actions with Alex and Lucy.
- Ask e.g. *Do you like playing the violin?* and children respond.

Table time

Student's Book p 72

Watch. Listen, point and sing *I am the music man.*

CD4 Track 13

- Play the audio (see TB p 165). Children listen, point to the pictures and join in singing the song.

Trace the instruments. Color your favorite instrument.

- Children trace the instruments in the song and color their favorite instrument.
- Play the audio again. Children sing and pretend to play the instruments like Alex and Lucy.

Ask and say.

- At the end ask e.g. *Do you like the song? Which instrument is your favorite?* and children respond.

Activity Book p 72

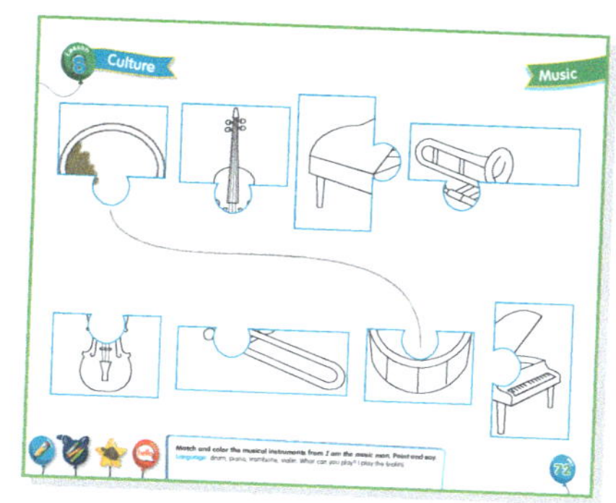

Match and color the musical instruments from *I am the music man.*

- Children match the instrument halves, then color them.

Point and say.

- They point and say what they can play.

Closing time

Learning review (see TB p 18)
Closing routines (see TB p 16)
Goodbye song and puppet (CD1 Track 3; see TB p 17 & 21)

Use the **Navio App** to watch the video, and encourage children to do the same at home.

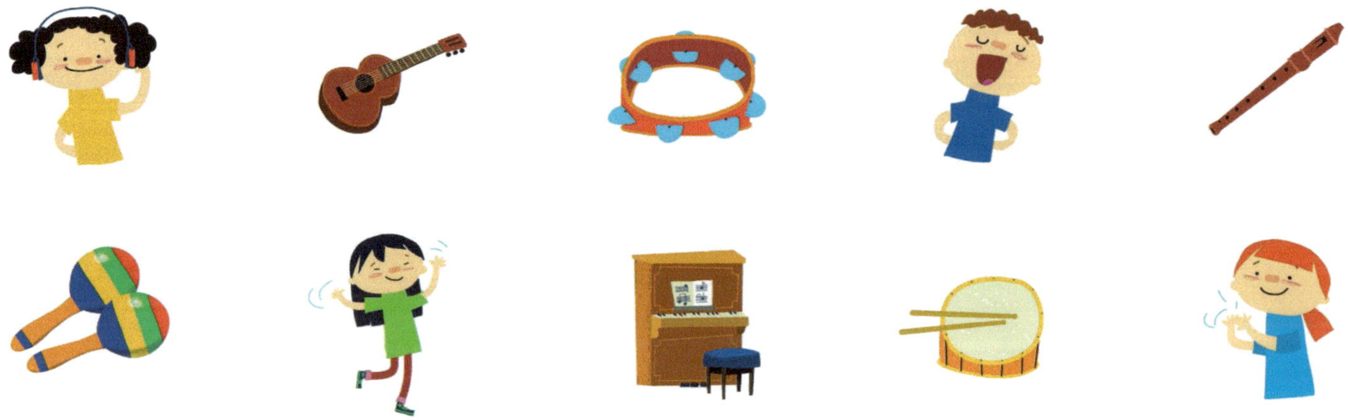

I can ...

Vocabulary

Story

Speaking

Content

Circle the music words you know. Listen, point and say. Listen and answer. Ask and say. Complete the faces to show what you can do. Language: drum, guitar, maracas, piano, recorder, tambourine; clap, dance, listen, sing; What are you doing? I'm (playing the piano). Do you like (playing the drum)? I like (playing the guitar).

Learning objectives

- Review what you have learned in this unit
- Complete a self-evaluation
- Ask and answer questions about musical instruments and activities

Materials

- Class CDs, flashcards, *Ferris Wheel* mat, Mimi puppet

Main vocabulary

- drum, guitar, maracas, piano, recorder, tambourine; clap, dance, listen, sing

Key language

- What are you doing? I'm (playing the piano). Do you like (playing the drum)? I like (playing the guitar).

Teacher's tip: Lively games

If children are sleepy and need livening up, play the flashcard games with the children standing on one leg. The last child to put their leg down is the winner.

Circle time

Hello song and puppet (CD1 Track 2; see TB p 17 & 21)
Opening routines (see TB p 16)
Recycling activity (see TB p 19)
Lesson aims (see TB p 18)

Music flashcard games

- Choose one or two flashcard games with the *Ferris Wheel* mat and/or the puppet (see TB p 20 & 21).

Sing *Listen, clap, dance!*

CD4 Track 5

- Put the music flashcards on the board.
- Play the audio. Children point to the flashcards as they hear the words and sing the song.

Game: *What am I doing?*

- Choose a volunteer and place a flashcard on his / her head so that everybody except the volunteer can see it. The class does the corresponding mime and the child guesses by saying e.g. *I'm playing the drums!*

Play a guessing game.

- Hide a flashcard behind your back. Children ask e.g. *Do you like playing the (recorder)?* Answer, *No, I don't* until the children guess correctly.

Watch the story video.

- Children watch the story video. Children say what each character does in the show e.g. *Dylan – I'm playing the drum.*

Table time

Student's Book p 73

Circle the music words you know.

- Explain and demonstrate the activity.

Listen, point and say.

- Play the audio. Children check the words they know, point to the pictures and repeat the words.

CD4 Track 14

Mimi: I'm the teacher! Can you remember the music words, Dylan?
Dylan: Yes, I can. Guitar.
Mimi: Guitar.
Dylan: Piano.
Mimi: Piano.
Dylan: Drum.
Mimi: Drum.
Dylan: Recorder.
Mimi: Recorder.
Dylan: Maracas.
Mimi: Maracas.
Dylan: Tambourine.
Mimi: Tambourine.
Dylan: Listen.
Mimi: Listen.
Dylan: Sing.
Mimi: Sing.
Dylan: Dance.
Mimi: Dance.
Dylan: Clap.
Mimi: Clap. Well done, Dylan!
Both: Fantastic!

Listen and answer. Ask and say.

- Play the audio. Children listen to the questions.

CD4 Track 15

Mimi: What are you doing?
What are you doing?
What are you doing?
Do you like playing the maracas?
Do you like playing the tambourine?
Do you like singing?

- Play the audio again. Children listen, repeat and answer the questions.

Complete the faces to show what you can do.

- Explain the four pictures: *I can name musical instruments and activities; I can understand the story; I can ask and say what I like doing; I understand rhythm in music.*
- Remind children they should complete each face with a smile or frown depending on how well they think they have done.

Activity Book p 73

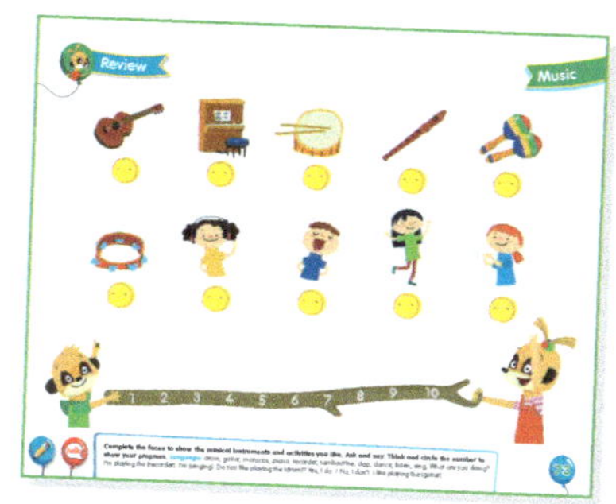

Complete the faces to show the musical instruments and activities you like. Ask and say.

- Children complete the faces with a smile if they like the instrument or activity.
- Children ask and answer about what they like to do.

Think and circle the number to show your progress.

- Children circle the number.

Closing time

Learning review (see TB p 18)
Closing routines (see TB p 16)
Goodbye song and puppet (CD1 Track 3; see TB p 17 & 21)

Use the **Navio App** to review what children have learned in this unit, and encourage them to do the same at home.

Project

COOPERATIVE LEARNING

Music

1

2

3

Make and decorate maracas. Play your maracas together and invent a rhythm. Ask and say. **Language:** maracas; loud, quiet, fast, slow; colors; What are you doing? I'm playing my (maracas). Do you like playing your (maracas)? Yes, I do. / No, I don't. My maracas are (red and blue). I like the (green) maracas. I like playing my (maracas).

Learning objectives

- Work together to do a collaborative project
- Make maracas and invent a rhythm
- Talk about your maracas
- Make a collage of musical instruments

Materials

- Class CDs, Mimi puppet, plastic pots or cardboard tubes, rice, beans or pasta, paints, colored paper and tissue paper, tape, glue, stickers
- optional: photocopiable templates, crayons

Main vocabulary

- maracas; loud, quiet, fast, slow; colors

Key language

- What are you doing? I'm (playing my maracas). Do you like (playing your maracas)? Yes, I do. / No, I don't. My maracas are (red and blue). I like the (green) maracas. I like playing my (maracas).

Teacher's tip: Pre-reading skills: becoming aware of differences in sounds

COOPERATIVE LEARNING

Use the maracas to raise children's awareness of sounds around them and to develop their listening skills. In groups, have them move the finished maracas and use their shared language to compare the sounds they make. The maracas will contain varying amounts of rice, so the pitch of the sounds produced will be different. Children can also take turns moving their maracas in different ways (loud, quiet, fast, slow) and identifying the rhythms.

Circle time

Hello song and puppet (CD1 Track 2; see TB p 17 & 21)

Opening routines (see TB p 16)

Recycling activity (see TB p 19)

Lesson aims (see TB p 18)

Prepare for your project.

- Say *Let's do a project. Let's make musical maracas!* Show children the musical maracas you have prepared.
- Explain and demonstrate that when children have made their maracas, they will play them together and invent a rhythm.

Table time

Student's Book p 74

COOPERATIVE LEARNING

Make and decorate maracas. Play your maracas together and invent a rhythm.

- Say e.g. *We're going to make maracas like this. Look at what we need for our project: a pot for our maracas, rice, beans or pasta, paints, colored paper and tissue paper, tape, glue and stickers.* Children listen and point to the pictures.
- Give out a clean, empty yogurt pot or similar to each child. Make sure children have paints, colored paper and tissue paper, stickers and glue available.
- Children put some dry rice, beans or small pasta shapes in their pot and use tape to stick paper over the top of the pot and seal it. Be ready to help with this.
- Children decorate their maracas either by painting them or by sticking colored paper and tissue paper and stickers, such as stars, on them.
- When they are ready, children practice playing their maracas and inventing a rhythm. If you like, play the karaoke version of a song children know and encourage children to play their maracas rhythmically to the music. If possible, take a photo of the children playing their maracas to use as a class display.

Ask and say.

- Ask children *Do you like playing your maracas?* Make the point that when the class play their maracas, everyone works together to keep the rhythm and make a great sound.

Alternative version of project

- Children could color or paint the photocopiable templates and use these to decorate their maracas.

Activity Book p 74

Find photos and make a collage of musical instruments.

- Children find and glue photos of musical instruments to make a collage.

Circle and color the instruments in your collage. Point and say.

- Children circle and color the instruments that are in their collage. Then they point and describe their instruments.

Closing time

Learning review (see TB p 18)

Closing routines (see TB p 16)

Goodbye song and puppet (CD1 Track 3; see TB p 17 & 21)

Bugs

Honey for dinner

Vocabulary and language

- **Main vocabulary:** ant, bee, butterfly, ladybug, snail, worm; legs, spots, stripes, wings
- **Key language:** Does (a snail) have (spots)? Yes, it does. / No, it doesn't. Does it have (legs)? It has (wings). It doesn't have (stripes). A (ladybug)'s (red and black). It's (black and yellow).
- **Content language:** butterfly, caterpillar, chrysalis, egg, leaf; They're eggs on a leaf.
- **Other language:** animals, bugs, family, flowers, friends, nature, trees; grasshopper; summer, winter; happy, hungry, sad; play, work; food; Where are the (bees)? I don't know. Ask the (ladybug), please. I care for (nature). I want to (play). I'm (hungry). I have (food). I don't have (food). I like the (butterfly). Do you like the (snail)? Yes, I do. / No, I don't.

Unit objectives

- Identify and name bugs
- Sing the language song *Does a butterfly have wings?*
- Ask about and describe bugs
- Understand and act out the story *Honey for dinner*
- Sing and act out the story song *We want to get some honey*
- Sing the values song *I care for our world*
- Recognize the value of caring for our world
- Learn about the life cycle of a butterfly
- Understand the traditional story *The ant and the grasshopper*
- Review your learning and progress
- Participate in a collaborative project

Story

CD4 Track 22

Picture 1

Narrator: Mimi and Dylan's friend, Bruno, is coming for dinner. Bruno loves honey.
Mimi: I have an idea. Bees make honey. Let's find the bees and get some honey for dinner!
Dylan: Great idea! But where are the bees?
Mimi: I don't know. Let's find out.

Picture 2

Narrator: Along comes a wiggly worm.
Mimi: Hello, Worm. We want to get some honey. Where are the bees?
Worm: I don't know. Ask the ladybug.
Dylan: But what's a ladybug?
Mimi: A ladybug? Oh, Dylan! A ladybug's red and black. It has spots.
Dylan: Oh wow! Does it have wings?
Mimi: Yes, it does.
Dylan: Does it have legs?
Mimi: Yes, it does. It has six legs.
Dylan: Amazing!

Picture 3

Dylan: Oh, look, Mimi. Here comes the ladybug.
Mimi: Hello, Ladybug. We want to get some honey. Where are the bees?
Ladybug: I don't know. Ask the snail.
Dylan: But what's a snail?
Mimi: A snail? Oh, Dylan! A snail's brown and white. It has stripes.
Dylan: Oh wow! Does it have wings?
Mimi: No, it doesn't.
Dylan: Does it have legs?
Mimi: No, it doesn't.
Dylan: Amazing!

Picture 4

Dylan: Oh, look, Mimi. Here comes the snail.
Mimi: Hello, Snail. We want to get some honey. Where are the bees?
Snail: I don't know. Ask the butterfly.
Dylan: But what's a butterfly?
Mimi: A butterfly? Oh, Dylan! A butterfly has a lot of different colors. It sometimes has spots and stripes, too.
Dylan: Oh wow! Does it have wings?
Mimi: Yes, it does.
Dylan: Does it have legs?
Mimi: Yes, it does. It has six legs.
Dylan: Amazing!

Picture 5

Dylan: Oh, look, Mimi. Here comes the butterfly.
Mimi: Hello, Butterfly. We want to get some honey. Where are the bees?
Butterfly: Follow me! Come and see!
Mimi: Thank you, Butterfly.

Picture 6

Dylan: Oh wow! It's Bruno!
Mimi: Hello, Bruno!
Bruno: Hello, Mimi. Hello, Dylan. Here are the bees. And here's the honey! It's for you. It's yummy!
Mimi: Oh, wow! Thank you, Bruno.
Dylan: And thank you, bees!
Mimi & Dylan: Let's go home and have dinner!

Songs and story

Language song

Does a butterfly have wings? CD4 Track 20

Does a butterfly have wings? (Flutter both hands in the air)
Let's look and see. (Point to your eyes)
Does a butterfly have legs like you and me? (Point to your legs, a child, then yourself)

Does a ladybug have spots? (Pinch thumb and fingers together)
Let's look and see.
Does a ladybug have legs like you and me?

Does a bee have stripes? (Zoom pinched fingers around quickly)
Let's look and see.
Does a bee have legs like you and me?

Does a snail have wings? (Move about slowly like a snail)
Let's look and see.
Does a snail have legs like you and me?

Does an ant have spots? (Walk two fingers across your other palm)
Let's look and see.
Does an ant have legs like you and me?

Does a worm have stripes? (Wiggle your finger like a worm)
Let's look and see.
Does a worm have legs like you and me?

Story song

We want to get some honey CD4 Track 23

Hello, Worm. We want to get some honey. *(Wave and rub tummy)*
Where are the bees? *(Hold up arms and look around)*
I don't know. Ask the ladybug, please. *(Shrug shoulders, then point to the ladybug)*
Hello, Ladybug. We want to get some honey. Where are the bees?
I don't know. Ask the snail, please.
Hello, Snail. We want to get some honey. Where are the bees?
I don't know. Ask the butterfly, please.
Hello, Butterfly. We want to get some honey. Where are the bees?
Oh, I know. Follow me, please.
Hello, Bruno. We want to get some honey. Here are the bees
And here is the honey
Yummy, yummy, yummy!

Values song

I care for our world CD4 Track 26

I care for our world. I care for nature, too. (Gesture all around you, then mime a tree)
I care for animals. I care for you. (Mime stroking a dog, then point to a child)
Please care for our world today. (Gesture all around you)
It's so special in every way. (Make a heart with your hands)

I care for my family. I care for friends, too. (Hug yourself, then point to the children)
I care for other children. I care for you. (Gesture to all the children)
(Chorus)

I care for trees. I care for flowers, too. (Mime a tree, then mime smelling a flower)
I care for little bugs. I care for you. (Flutter your hands like a butterfly, then point to a child)
(Chorus)

Culture story

The ant and the grasshopper CD4 Track 28

Picture 1

Narrator: It's summer. Ant and Grasshopper are friends. Grasshopper plays in the sun.
Grasshopper: Hee, hee, hee! This is fun.
Narrator: Ant collects food for winter.
Ant: Phew! I'm busy!

Picture 2

Grasshopper: Come and play, Ant!
Ant: No, I want to collect food for winter.
Grasshopper: Don't worry, Ant. We have a lot of food!
Ant: We have food now, Grasshopper. But in winter …
Grasshopper: Never mind. I want to play.

Picture 3

Narrator: Ant works and collects food for the winter.
Ant: Oh, good. I'm ready for winter. I have a lot of food.
Narrator: Grasshopper plays all day.
Grasshopper: Hee, hee, hee! This is fun.

Picture 4

Narrator: And now it's winter. It's very cold and there's no food.
Ant: I'm happy. I have food for the winter.
Grasshopper: I'm sad. I'm hungry. I don't have food for the winter. Ant is right!
Ant: Oh, dear …

Vocabulary Lesson 1

Bugs

Honey for dinner

Listen, point and repeat. Listen and stick the bug stickers. Listen and play *Memory*. Circle the bugs you sometimes see. Say. Language: ant, bee, butterfly, ladybug, snail, worm; blue, green, orange, pink, red, yellow

75

Learning objectives

- Identify and name bugs
- Listen and point to bugs
- Remember bugs in a memory game

Materials

- Class CDs, flashcards, *Ferris Wheel* mat, Mimi puppet

Main vocabulary

- ant, bee, butterfly, ladybug, snail, worm; blue, green, orange, pink, red, yellow

Teacher's tip: Reviewing vocabulary with a partner

Once the children have finished the activity in their Student's Book, have them take turns finding and pointing to the bugs with a partner. One child names a bug and the other points to it in their book.

Circle time

Hello song and puppet (CD1 Track 2; see TB p 17 & 21)
Opening routines (see TB p 16)
Lesson aims (see TB p 18)

Introduce bug vocabulary.

- Use the puppet and flashcards to introduce the bugs. Say the words and children repeat them.
- Put the *Ferris Wheel* mat on the floor or board with the bug flashcards face down (one on each color). Use the puppet to turn them over and name them. The children repeat the words.

Game: *Say the color!*

- Name the bugs on the Ferris Wheel and children name the color. Then the reverse.

Game: *Binoculars!*

- Stick the flashcards on different walls around the room.
- Use your hands to mime looking through binoculars.
- Say the words and children turn to the flashcard you name and mime looking at it through their "binoculars."
- Invite individual children to take turns giving instructions and others turning toward the flashcards and miming in the same way.

Table time

Student's Book p 75

Listen, point and repeat.

- Play the audio. The children listen, point to each bug as they hear it, and repeat the words.

CD4 Track 16

Mimi: Look, Dylan! Ladybug … butterfly … snail … bee … worm. Repeat, Dylan!
Dylan: Yes, Mimi. Ladybug … butterfly … snail … bee … worm.
Mimi: Very good, Dylan! Let's name the bugs together!
Both: Ladybug … butterfly … snail … bee … worm … Fantastic!

- Draw children's attention to the question mark in their books. They identify the missing bug (ant).

Listen and stick the bug stickers.

- Play the audio. The children listen and point to the bugs in their books.

CD4 Track 17

Where's the ladybug? It's on … red. Where's the butterfly? It's on … blue. Where's the bee? It's on … yellow. Where's the worm? It's on … pink.
Where's the snail? It's on … orange. Where's the ant? Can you guess? It's on … green. Yes, yes, yes! The ant is on green. Yes, yes, yes!

- Ask questions about all the bugs in the same way and children respond. Play the audio again. Children listen and stick the bug stickers.

Listen and play *Memory*.

- Children copy you covering your eyes with your hands. Play the audio. Children listen and remember the bug on each color on the wheel.

CD4 Track 18

Close your eyes	*Red … ladybug!*
One, two, three	*Yellow … bee!*
Say the words	*Green … ant!*
Play memory!	*Pink … worm!*
Blue … butterfly!	*Orange … snail!*

- Play the game.

Circle the bugs you sometimes see. Say.

- Children circle the bugs they sometimes see. They point and say the words.

Activity Book p 75

Find and circle the bugs.

- Children find and circle the bugs.

Point and say. Color.

- Children point to the pictures and say the words. They color the bugs.

Closing time

Learning review (see TB p 18)
Closing routines (see TB p 16)
Goodbye song and puppet (CD1 Track 3; see TB p 17 & 21)

Use the **Navio App** to play the vocabulary game, and encourage children to do the same at home.

Language

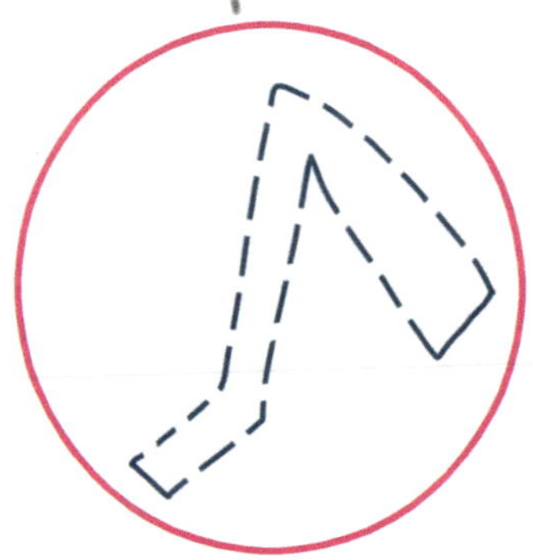

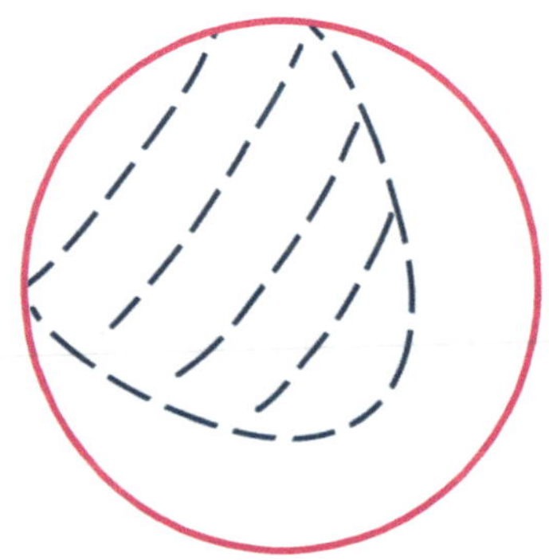

Listen and find the new bug words. Listen, point and sing *Does a butterfly have wings?* Match the bugs to the pictures. Trace and color. Ask and say. Language: ant, bee, butterfly, ladybug; legs, spots, stripes, wings; Does a (snail) have (spots)? Yes, it does. / No, it doesn't.

76

Learning objectives

- Talk about bugs
- Identify and name four new parts of bugs
- Sing the language song *Does a butterfly have wings?*
- Ask about and describe bugs

Materials

- Class CDs, flashcards, *Ferris Wheel* mat, Mimi puppet

Main vocabulary

- ant, bee, butterfly, ladybug, snail, worm; legs, spots, stripes, wings

Key language

- Does a (snail) have (spots)? Yes, it does. / No, it doesn't.

Teacher's tip: Pronunciation: loud and quiet drilling

When practicing the pronunciation of the new words add variety by asking the children to say the words in quiet and then loud voices. Alternate between quiet and loud, using quiet to decrease volume at the end.

Circle time

Hello song and puppet (CD1 Track 2; see TB p 17 & 21)
Opening routines (see TB p 16)
Recycling activity (six bugs from lesson 1) (see TB p 19)
Lesson aims (see TB p 18)

Introduce the new bug vocabulary.

- Use the puppet to put the four new bug flashcards on the floor or board. As you do this, say *Some bugs have legs / wings / spots / stripes.*
- Use the puppet to point to and say the words in turn. Children repeat in chorus.
- Turn the four new flashcards face down. Mix them up. Point to one and ask *Wings, legs, spots or stripes?* Children guess. Repeat several times.
- Make a gesture to indicate each one and children say the words.

Introduce *Does a butterfly have ...? Yes, it does. / No, it doesn't.*

- Put the flashcards of bugs and features of bugs separately on the board. Point to one of the features e.g. wings. Children say the word. Then point to the bugs in turn and ask *Does a butterfly have wings?* Encourage children to respond e.g. *Yes, it does. / No, it doesn't.*
- Repeat for all the different features and bugs.

Game: *Guess the bug!*

- Leave the flashcards of bug features face up on the floor or board. Collect the other flashcards.
- Use the puppet to hold one flashcard without children seeing what it is. Point to the features in turn and get the children to ask with you in chorus e.g. *Does it have wings?* Get the puppet to respond *Yes, it does. / No, it doesn't.* and children guess the bug.
- Once children are confident, play the game with pairs of children secretly choosing a bug and the rest of the class asking questions and guessing.

***Does a butterfly have wings?* song**

CD4 Track 20

- Put the flashcards face up on the floor or board.
- Explain that Alex and Lucy are looking at a book about bugs.
- Play the audio. Children listen and point to the flashcards with you as they hear them in the song.
- Play the audio again. Children make gestures for each feature, point to a friend and themselves for the words *like you and me*, and join in singing the song.
- Remember that you can use the karaoke version of the song when children are confident.

Table time

Student's Book p 76

Listen and find the new bug words.

- Play the audio. Children listen and find the four new words. Repeat and children say the words.

CD4 Track 19

One … two … Which words are new?
Wings! Wings! *Spots! Spots!*
Legs! Legs! *Stripes! Stripes!*

Listen, point and sing *Does a butterfly have wings?*

- Play the song. Children listen and point to the pictures, and join in singing the song.

Match the bugs to the pictures. Trace and color.

- Children match the bugs to their body parts and trace and color them.

Ask and say.

- Children ask and answer about all the bugs.

Activity Book p 76

Look and match.

- Children look and match what's missing from each bug.

Draw and color what's missing from each bug.

- Children draw and color to complete the pictures.

Ask and say.

- Children ask and answer questions about all the bugs e.g. *Does a worm have legs? No, it doesn't.*

Closing time

Learning review (see TB p 18)
Closing routines (see TB p 16)
Goodbye song and puppet (CD1 Track 3; see TB p 17 & 21)

Use the **Navio App** to listen to the song, and encourage children to do the same at home.

Story

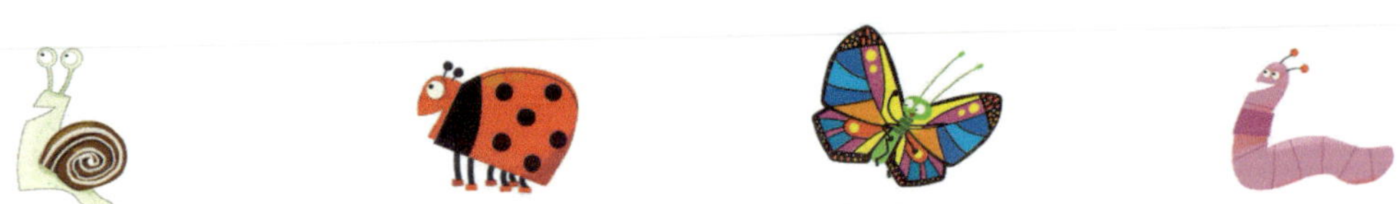

Watch. Listen to the story *Honey for dinner.* Circle the bug who knows where the bees are. Stick the story sticker. **Language:** bee, butterfly, ladybug, snail, worm; legs, spots, stripes, wings; colors; A (ladybug)'s (red and black). It has (spots). Does it have (legs)? Yes, it does. / No, it doesn't.

Learning objectives

- Watch, understand and enjoy the story *Honey for dinner*
- Make a prediction about the story
- Identify the bug who helps them in the story

Materials

- Class CDs, printable story cards, flashcards, *Ferris Wheel* mat, Mimi puppet

Main vocabulary

- bee, butterfly, ladybug, snail, worm; legs, spots, stripes, wings; colors

Key language

- A (ladybug)'s (red and black). It has (spots). Does it have (legs)? Yes, it does. / No, it doesn't.

Teacher's tip: Checking comprehension in pairs

Have children work with a partner to randomly name the different bugs in each story frame. Their partner should point and say the frame number.

Circle time

Hello song and puppet (CD1 Track 2; see TB p 17 & 21)

Opening routines (see TB p 16)

Recycling activity (*Does it have ... ?* and bugs words) (see TB p 19)

Lesson aims (see TB p 18)

Introduce the story *Honey for dinner*.

- Say *It's story time!* Play the *Story rhyme* (CD1 Track 4; see TB p 17)
- Say *Alex and Lucy are watching a story about Mimi and Dylan. Mimi and Dylan are hungry. They want honey for dinner. Who makes honey? Who can help them find honey for dinner?* Listen to children's answers.

Watch and listen to the story *Honey for dinner*.

CD4 Track 22

- Watch the video, play the audio or read the story using the printable story cards. Pause, repeat words, point to the pictures, ask questions.
- Ask the questions again and check answers *Who makes honey? (bees) Who can help them find honey for dinner? (butterfly).* Ask e.g. *Who else likes honey for dinner?*
- Play the video again. Pause and ask e.g. *Who does Mimi ask? What does the ladybug say? Does a snail have spots?*
- Repeat the story. Use the pause button. Encourage children to join in asking and answering questions about the bugs in the story.
- Ask *Who is having dinner with the bees? Do Mimi and Dylan like honey? Does Bruno like honey? What do Mimi and Dylan say to Bruno and the bees? Do Mimi and Dylan respect (care for) the bugs?*

Order the bugs in the story.

- Put the bug flashcards on the board. Ask and children point to the flashcards e.g. *Who do Mimi and Dylan ask first? (worm). And then? (ladybug, snail, butterfly).*
- Ask *Who is the bees' friend? (Bruno) Which bug isn't in the story? (ant).*

Story questions

Picture 1
What does Bruno love? *(Honey)*
Who do Mimi and Dylan want to find? *(Bees)*

Picture 2
Who do Mimi and Dylan ask first? *(Worm)*
Does a ladybug have spots? *(Yes)*

Picture 3
Who do Mimi and Dylan ask now? *(Ladybug)*
Does a snail have legs? *(No)*

Picture 4
Who do Mimi and Dylan ask now? *(Snail)*
Does a butterfly have wings? *(Yes)*

Picture 5
Who do Mimi and Dylan ask now? *(Butterfly)*
Does Butterfly know where the bees are? *(Yes)*

Picture 6
Is Bruno with the bees? *(Yes)*
Do the bees have honey? *(Yes)*

Table time

Student's Book p 77

Watch. Listen to the story *Honey for dinner*.

CD4 Track 22

- Read or play the story again (see TB p 186). Children listen and point to the pictures in their books.

Circle the bug who knows where the bees are. Stick the story sticker.

- Demonstrate circling the bug who knows where the bees are in the story and sticking the story sticker.
- Ask *Do you like the story? Do you like honey too?* and children respond.

Activity Book p 77

Number the pictures in order.

- Children number the pictures in order.

Color your favorite bug from the story. Ask and say.

- They color their favorite bug, then ask and answer questions about what it has.

Closing time

Learning review (see TB p 18)

Closing routines (see TB p 16)

Goodbye song and puppet (CD1 Track 3; see TB p 17 & 21)

Use the **Navio App** to watch the video, and encourage children to do the same at home.

Lesson 4 Story Song

Watch. Listen, point and sing *We want to get some honey*. Follow and draw a path through the maze. Color the bugs. Ask and say. **Language:** bee, butterfly, ladybug, snail, worm; Where are (the bees)? I don't know. Ask (the ladybug), please.

Learning objectives

- Watch, sing and act out the story song *We want to get some honey*
- Listen to the story again and order the story cards
- Identify and say bugs
- Ask and answer questions about where things are

Materials

- Class CDs, printable story cards, flashcards, *Ferris Wheel* mat, Mimi puppet

Main vocabulary

- bee, butterfly, ladybug, snail, worm

Key language

- Where are the (bees)? I don't know. Ask the (ladybug), please.

Teacher's tip: Thinking skills: predicting

COOPERATIVE LEARNING

Before you put out the flashcards for the story song, ask children to predict which bugs are in the song. Have children work cooperatively with a partner by sharing their ideas first. Once they have made their decision, they raise their hands to tell the class their guesses. Play the song to check their predictions.

Circle time

Hello song and puppet (CD1 Track 2; see TB p 17 & 21)
Opening routines (see TB p 16)
Recycling activity (bugs words) (see TB p 19)
Lesson aims (see TB p 18)

Retell the story *Honey for dinner*.

- Play the audio, video or read the story using the printable story cards.
- Demonstrate that children should wave their arms every time they hear the name of a bug in the story.

Order the story.

- Put the printable story cards in jumbled order on the board. Hold up the first story card. Say *Mimi and Dylan are hungry. They want to find the bees. Who do they ask?*
- Use the puppet to say *Hello … Where are the bees?* and children name the bug Mimi asks first: worm.
- Repeat and children name the bugs in the order of the story.
- For the last story card, say *Here's … (Bruno) and the … (bees)* and children supply the words.

***We want to get some honey* song**

CD4 Track 23

- Put the bug flashcards in the order of the song on the board.
- Play the audio. Children listen and point to the flashcards.
- Play the audio again. Children stand up, do actions and join in singing the song.
- Ask e.g. *Do you like the song?* and the children respond.

Act out the story song.

- Assign roles to children as follows: Mimi and Dylan, worm, ladybug, snail, butterfly, Bruno. Give out the puppet and flashcards.
- Children with the puppet and flashcards act out the story song at the front of the class. Everyone joins in saying with you and the children in role in chorus e.g. *Hello, Ladybug. We want to get some honey. Where are the bees? / I don't know. Ask the snail, please.* and for the last verse: *Hello Bruno. We want to get some honey. / Here are the bees. And here is the honey. Yummy! Yummy! Yummy!*
- Repeat once or twice with different children taking the roles with the puppet and flashcards at the front of the class each time.

Table time

Student's Book p 78

Watch. Listen, point and sing *We want to get some honey*.

CD4 Track 23

- Play the song (see TB p 187). Children listen, sing and point to the pictures.
- Remember that you can use the karaoke version of the song when children are confident.

Follow and draw a path through the maze. Color the bugs.

- Children draw a line through the maze and color the bugs.

Ask and say.

- Children ask and say e.g. *Hello, Worm. Where are the bees? I don't know. Ask the (ladybug) please.*

Activity Book p 78

Circle the character who is with the bees in *We want to get some honey*. Point, ask and say.

- Children circle the character who is with the bees at the end of the song. Then they point, ask and answer questions about where the characters are.

Draw and color more bees.

- They draw and color more bees.

Closing time

Learning review (see TB p 18)
Closing routines (see TB p 16)
Goodbye song and puppet (CD1 Track 3; see TB p 17 & 21)

Use the **Navio App** to watch the video, and encourage children to do the same at home.

Lesson 5 Speaking

Life skills

Bugs

1 2 3 4

4:25

hello

Watch. Listen and point. Name the bugs. Number the photos in order. Invent and draw a bug. Ask and say. Language: bee, ladybug, snail, worm; legs, spots, stripes, wings; colors; numbers 1–4; Does it have (legs)? Yes, it does. / No, it doesn't. It has (wings). It doesn't have (stripes). It's (black and yellow).

Learning objectives

- Ask and answer questions about bugs
- Watch, understand and enjoy a video
- Identify bugs in the video

Materials

- Class CDs, flashcards, *Ferris Wheel* mat, Mimi puppet

Main vocabulary

- bee, ladybug, snail, worm; legs, spots, stripes, wings; colors; numbers 1–4

Key language

- Does it have (legs)? Yes, it does. / No, it doesn't. It has (wings). It doesn't have (stripes). It's (black and yellow).

Teacher's tip: Communicating with different partners

COOPERATIVE LEARNING

Once the children have drawn their bug, have them pick up their book and stand up in two lines facing each other. They should ask and answer a question about their bug with the child opposite them e.g. *Does it have legs? Yes, it does.* Next, one line stays put while the other line moves along and children ask and answer with a new partner.

Circle time

Hello song and puppet (CD1 Track 2; see TB p 17 & 21)
Opening routines (see TB p 16)
Recycling activity (story song) (CD4 Track 23; see TB p 19)
Lesson aims (see TB p 18)

Game: *Guess the bug!*

- Put the flashcards of bug features face up on the board and children say the words.
- Give the children a bug flashcard without you or the puppet seeing what it is.
- Use the puppet to ask questions e.g. *Does it have wings?* and encourage children to respond *Yes, it does. / No, it doesn't* in chorus. After two or three questions, guess the bug.
- Reverse roles. You and the puppet hold a flashcard the class can't see and children ask you questions.

Watch the video.

- Explain that Alex, Lucy and Auntie Vicky are doing a quiz on bugs on Auntie Vicky's tablet.
- Ask *Which bugs are in the quiz? Can Alex and Lucy answer the questions?* and encourage guesses.
- Play the video. Ask the questions again and children respond. Watch again. Pause and children repeat the questions and answers.
- Ask *Do you like the quiz?* and elicit responses.

Table time

Student's Book p 79 Life skills

Watch. Listen and point. Name the bugs.

- Children identify the bugs in the photos. Play the audio or video. Children listen and point.

Number the photos in order.

- Children number the photos in order. Play the audio again with pauses and children check their answers.

CD4 Track 25

Auntie Vicky: Let's do the bug quiz. Are you ready?
Alex: Number 1.
Lucy: Does it have wings?
Alex: Yes, it does.
Lucy: Does it have stripes?
Alex: Yes, it does. It's black and yellow. It's a …
Lucy: Bee!
Alex: Bee is the correct answer!
Lucy: Great!
Auntie Vicky: Well done, Lucy.
Lucy: OK, my turn. Number 2.
Alex: Does it have legs?
Lucy: No, it doesn't.
Alex: Does it have stripes?
Lucy: No, it doesn't. It's pink. It's a …
Alex: Worm!
Lucy: Worm is the correct answer!
Alex: Great!
Auntie Vicky: Well done, Alex.
Alex: Here's number 3. It has legs. It has wings. It has spots. It's red and black. It's a …
Lucy: Ladybug!
Alex: Ladybug is the correct answer!
Lucy: Great!
Auntie Vicky: Well done, Lucy.
Lucy: And here's number 4. It doesn't have legs. It doesn't have wings. It doesn't have spots. It's brown and white. It's a …
Alex: Snail!
Lucy: Snail is the correct answer!
Alex: Great!
Auntie Vicky: Well done, Alex.

- Invent and draw a bug on the board. When you've finished, point and say, e.g. *Look at my bug! It has four … (legs)* and children supply the words.

Invent and draw a bug. Ask and say.

- Children invent and draw a bug. Then they ask and answer questions about their bugs e.g. *Does it have legs?*

Activity Book p 79

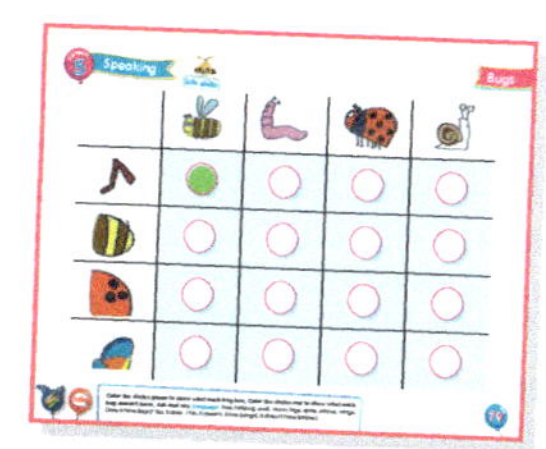

Color the circles green to show what each bug has. Color the circles red to show what each bug doesn't have.

- Children color the circles in the chart green if the bug has the part and red if it doesn't.

Ask and say.

- They ask and answer about the bugs.

Closing time

Learning review (see TB p 18)
Closing routines (see TB p 16)
Goodbye song and puppet (CD1 Track 3; see TB p 17 & 21)

Use the **Navio App** to watch the video, and encourage children to do the same at home.

Values Caring for our world

4:26

hello

Listen, point and sing *I care for our world*. Color the frames of the pictures that show things you care for. Draw a picture of you caring for something. Say.

Language: animals, bugs, family, flowers, friends, nature, trees; I care for (nature).

SOCIAL AND EMOTIONAL LEARNING

80

Learning objectives

- Recognize the value of caring for our world
- Sing the values song *I care for our world*
- Say how you care for our world

Materials

- Class CDs, flashcards, *Ferris Wheel* mat, Mimi puppet

Main vocabulary

- animals, bugs, family, flowers, friends, nature, trees

Key language

- I care for (nature).

Teacher's tip: Caring for our world

Remind the children that Mimi and Dylan are kind to the bugs in the story. Explain that bugs are living things. If any bugs come into the classroom, set a good example by showing them how to help them get outside again by using a plastic container and a piece of card.

Circle time

Hello song and puppet (CD1 Track 2; see TB p 17 & 21)
Opening routines (see TB p 16)
Recycling activity (*Does it have …? Yes, it does. / No, it doesn't.*) (see TB p 19)
Lesson aims (see TB p 18)

Watch the *Honey for dinner* story video.

- Play the story video.
- Take the part of the narrator yourself. Encourage children to join in acting out the story in three groups (Mimi; Dylan; the bugs and Bruno).
- Ask *Are Mimi and Dylan polite and friendly to the bugs? (Yes).* Explain that Mimi and Dylan respect and care for the bugs. They also respect nature and thank the bees for their honey.
- Ask *Is it important to show respect? Who/What do you respect?* and listen to the children's responses. Use this to introduce or remind children of vocabulary in the song.

***I care for our world* song**

CD4 Track 26

- Say *Do you care for your world? What do you care for? …* Children predict the song.
- Play the audio. Children compare their predictions with the song.
- Play the audio again. Children join in doing actions and singing the song.
- Make the point that it's important to care for people, animals and things.

Table time

Student's Book p 80

Listen, point and sing *I care for our world.*

CD4 Track 26

- Children identify Harry and Zoe from the *Little Book of Values.*
- Say e.g. *I care for my family* and children point to the correct picture. Repeat with other sentences and pictures (I care for other children, animals, trees, flowers, little bugs).
- Play the song. Children sing and point to the pictures.

Color the frames of the pictures that show things you care for.

- Children color the frames of the pictures to show what they care for.

Draw a picture of you caring for something.

- Children draw a picture to show what they care for. Monitor and make sure children know the word for what they have drawn.

Say.

- Children take turns showing each other their pictures and saying e.g. *I care for my grandma.*

Activity Book p 80

Color the pictures to show what you care for.

- Children color the pictures to show what they care for.

Point and say.

- Children point and say what they care for.

Closing time

Learning review (see TB p 18)
Closing routines (see TB p 16)
Goodbye song and puppet (CD1 Track 3; see TB p 17 & 21)

Use the **Navio App** to listen to the song, and encourage children to do the same at home.

Lesson 7 Content

Bugs

1 2 3 4

1

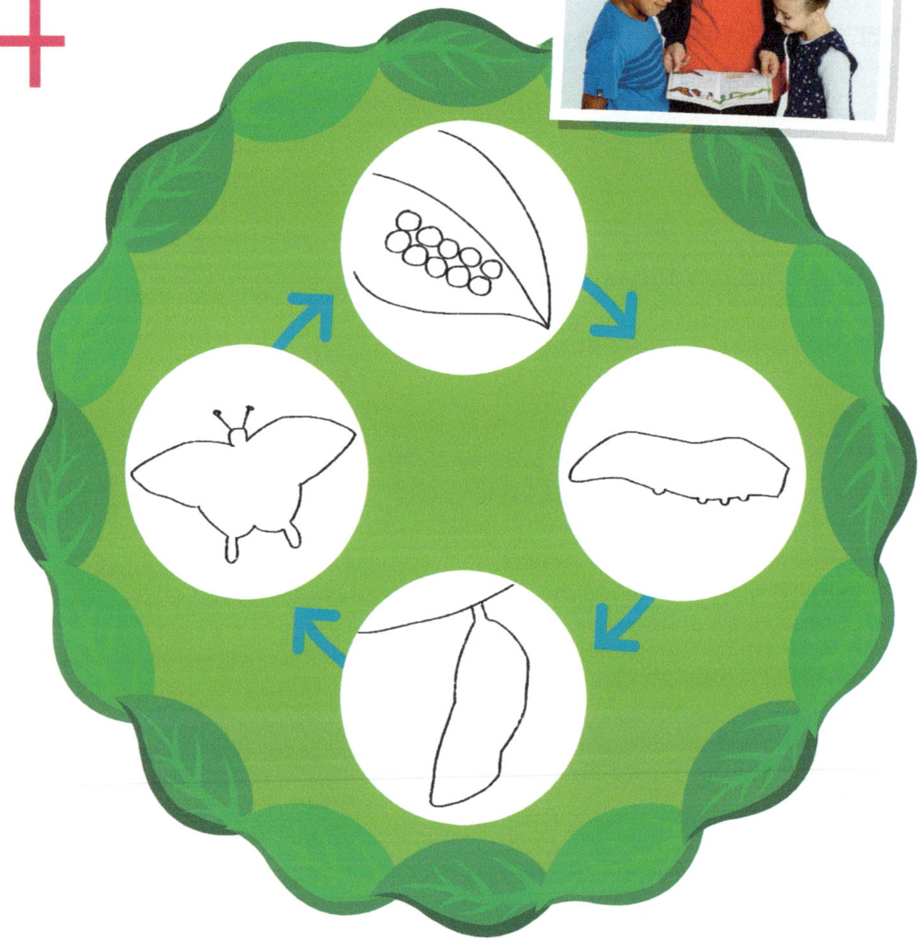

Listen and point. Number the stages in the life cycle of a butterfly. Draw and color the pictures of the life cycle. Say. Language: butterfly, caterpillar, chrysalis, egg, leaf; numbers 1–4; They're eggs on a leaf.

Learning objectives

- Learn about the life cycle of a butterfly
- Listen and order the stages of the life cycle of a butterfly
- Talk about the life cycle of a butterfly

Materials

- Class CDs, printable content flashcards, *Ferris Wheel* mat, Mimi puppet

Main vocabulary

- butterfly, caterpillar, chrysalis, egg, leaf; numbers 1–4

Key language

- They're eggs on a leaf.

Teacher's tip: Cross-curricular link: Art and craft

If there is modeling clay available in the children's classroom, have them make a 3D butterfly life cycle in groups. Roll small balls of modeling clay for eggs. Cut out leaves from green paper to place the eggs on. Roll a sausage shape for the caterpillar and a larger oval shape for the chrysalis. The butterfly is made of a sausage shape, plus the wings. Place all the stages on a paper plate.

Circle time

Hello song and puppet (CD1 Track 2; see TB p 17 & 21)
Opening routines (see TB p 16)
Recycling activity (see TB p 19)
Lesson aims (see TB p 18)

Introduce content vocabulary.

- Hold up the printable flashcard of the butterfly. Say *Let's learn about the life cycle of the butterfly!*
- Show children the printable flashcards in order of the life cycle (*egg, leaf, caterpillar, chrysalis*) and say the words. Children repeat the words.

Mime the life cycle of a butterfly.

- Children stand up. Say *Let's mime the life cycle of a butterfly!*
- Say *You're an egg on a leaf. You're tiny!* Mime curling up in a ball and children do the same.
- Continue e.g. *Now you're a caterpillar* (and mime wriggling around). *You grow and grow* (make yourself bigger). *Now you're in a chrysalis. You stay very still* (freeze in position). *And now …* (mime pushing your way out of the chrysalis) *you're a beautiful butterfly!* (and mime flying).
- Repeat once or twice. Say e.g. *What a tiny egg! What a lovely caterpillar!* as children do their mimes.

Table time

Student's Book p 81

Listen and point. Number the stages in the life cycle of a butterfly.

- Say *Alex, Lucy and Auntie Vicky are looking at the life cycle of the butterfly.*
- Children identify the stages of the life cycle in the photos.
- Play the audio. Children listen and point to the photos.

CD4 Track 27

Auntie Vicky: Let's look at the life cycle of a butterfly. Number 1. They're eggs on a leaf.
Lucy: Oh. Wow. They're tiny.
Auntie Vicky: Yes! Number 2. it's a caterpillar. The caterpillar eats a lot. It grows and grows.
Number 3. The caterpillar makes a chrysalis. The caterpillar's in the chrysalis. It's sleeping.
Number 4. The chrysalis opens and … look! It's a beautiful butterfly.
Alex: Oh, it's amazing! I love butterflies!
Lucy: Me, too!

- Play the audio again. Use the pause button. Children number the stages of the life cycle.

Draw and color the pictures of the life cycle.

- Children draw and color pictures to show the life cycle.

Say.

- Children point to their pictures and say e.g. *It's an egg on a leaf. It's a caterpillar.*

Activity Book p 81

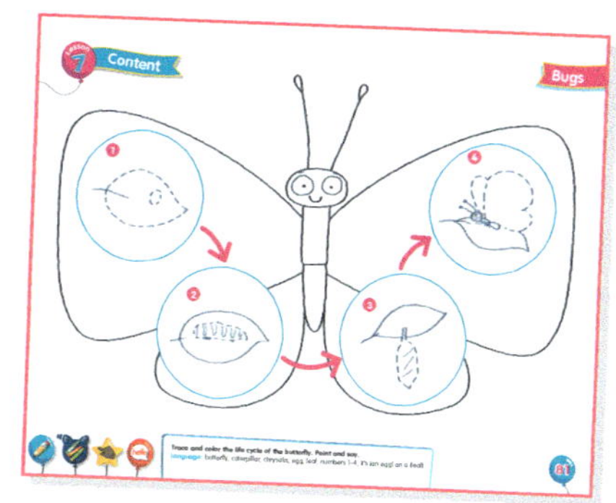

Trace and color the life cycle of the butterfly.

- Children trace and color the stages of the life cycle of the butterfly.

Point and say.

- They point and say the stages.

Closing time

Learning review (see TB p 18)
Closing routines (see TB p 16)
Goodbye song and puppet (CD1 Track 3; see TB p 17 & 21)

Use the **Navio App** to play the vocabulary and language games, and encourage children to do the same at home.

Lesson 8

Culture

Watch. Listen and point to the story *The ant and the grasshopper*. Draw a picture to show what you think happens next. Say. **Language:** ant, grasshopper; summer, winter; happy, hungry, sad; play, work; food; I want to (play). I'm (hungry). I have (food). I don't have (food).

Learning objectives

- Watch, understand and enjoy the traditional story *The ant and the grasshopper*
- Act out the story
- Predict what happens after the story

Materials

- Class CDs, printable story cards, flashcards, *Ferris Wheel* mat, Mimi puppet

Main vocabulary

- ant, grasshopper; summer, winter; happy, hungry, sad; play, work, food

Key language

- I want to (play). I'm (hungry). I have (food). I don't have (food).

Teacher's tip: Making good decisions

Ask the children if the grasshopper makes a good decision in the story. What about the ant? Discuss good decisions that the children can make in the classroom, e.g. cleaning up pencils and crayons after using them, putting paper in the recycling bin, etc.

Circle time

Hello song and puppet (CD1 Track 2; see TB p 17 & 21)
Opening routines (see TB p 16)
Recycling activity (see TB p 19)
Lesson aims (see TB p 18)

Introduce the story *The ant and the grasshopper*.

- Explain that children are going to watch and listen to a traditional story, *The ant and the grasshopper*.
- Ask children if they know the story. Give clues, e.g. *The ant and the grasshopper are friends. In summer, one of them works and collects food for winter. The other one plays.* If children know the story, ask *Do you want to watch and listen to the story in English?*

Watch and listen to the story.

CD4 Track 28

- Ask *Who works hard? Who plays?* Encourage children to guess and listen to their ideas.
- Play the video. Children watch and listen to the story.
- Ask the pre-questions again and children respond.
- Play the video again. Pause and ask questions, e.g. *Who collects food for winter? Who wants to play? What's the weather like in winter? Who has food? Who has no food? Who's happy? Who's sad? Do you think Ant is right? Do you like the story?*

Act out the story *The ant and the grasshopper*.

- Divide the children into two groups: Ant and Grasshopper.
- Retell the story. Children act out either Grasshopper playing or Ant collecting food and repeat words and phrases from the story with you. Then they reverse roles.

Table time

Student's Book p 82

Watch. Listen and point to the story *The ant and the grasshopper*.

CD4 Track 28

- Play the audio of the story. Children listen and point to the pictures.
- Play the audio again. Ask *Who has food at the end of the story? Who has no food at the end of the story?*

Story questions

Picture 1
Is it winter? *(No)*
Does Ant play with Grasshopper? *(No)*

Picture 2
Does Ant want to collect food for summer? *(No)*
What does Grasshopper want to do? *(Play)*

Picture 3
Does Ant have a lot of food for the winter? *(Yes)*
Does Grasshopper collect food for the winter? *(No)*

Picture 4
Is it winter? *(Yes)*
Is Grasshopper happy now? *(No)*

- Ask children to imagine what happens after the end of the story e.g. *Does Ant share his food with Grasshopper? Does Grasshopper find someone else to help him?* and listen to children's ideas.

Draw a picture to show what you think happens next.

- Children draw and color a picture to show what they imagine happens after the end of the story.

Say.

- Children take turns showing each other their pictures and saying their ideas.

Activity Book p 82

Color the circle on the picture of summer green. Color the circle on the picture of winter blue. Color the character who collects food.

- Children color the circle green on the picture of summer and blue on the picture of winter. They then color the character who collects food.

Point and say.

- Children point and say the seasons and what the characters feel.

Closing time

Learning review (see TB p 18)
Closing routines (see TB p 16)
Goodbye song and puppet (CD1 Track 3; see TB p 17 & 21)

Use the **Navio App** to watch the video, and encourage children to do the same at home.

Review

I can ...

Vocabulary

Story

Speaking

Content

4:29 hello 4:30

Color the circles of the bug words you know. Listen, point and say. Listen and answer. Ask and say. Complete the faces to show what you can do. **Language:** ant, bee, butterfly, ladybug, snail, worm; legs, spots, stripes, wings; Does it have (spots)? Yes, it does. / No, it doesn't. It has (stripes). It doesn't have (legs).

Learning objectives

- Review what you have learned in this unit
- Complete a self-evaluation
- Answer questions about bugs

Materials

- Class CDs, flashcards, *Ferris Wheel* mat, Mimi puppet

Main vocabulary

- ant, bee, butterfly, ladybug, snail, worm; legs, spots, stripes, wings

Key language

- Does it have (spots)? Yes, it does. / No, it doesn't. It has (stripes). It doesn't have (legs).

Teacher's tip: Putting things into sets

Putting things into sets is a useful thinking skill. After completing the review activities, encourage children to group the bugs in different ways: those with spots, stripes, those with legs, those that can fly, etc.

Circle time

Hello song and puppet (CD1 Track 2; see TB p 17 & 21)
Opening routines (see TB p 16)
Recycling activity (see TB p 19)
Lesson aims (see TB p 18)

Bug flashcard games

- Choose one or two flashcard games with the *Ferris Wheel* mat and/or the puppet (see TB p 20 & 21).

Sing *Does a butterfly have wings?*

CD4 Track 20

- Put the bug flashcards face up on the floor or board.
- Play the audio. The children listen and point to the flashcards.

Game: *Guess the bug!*

- Put all the bug flashcards on the floor or board. Put the children into pairs. One child secretly chooses a bug. The other asks questions to guess which bug it is, e.g. *Does it have wings? Does it have stripes?*, etc.
- Children change roles and play again.

Watch the story video.

- Children watch the story video.
- Children ask and answer questions about the story e.g. *Does a ladybug have spots? Yes, it does. / No, it doesn't.*

Table time

Student's Book p 83

Color the circles of the bug words you know.

- Explain and demonstrate the activity.

Listen, point and say.

- Play the audio. Children check the words they know, point to the pictures and repeat the words.

CD4 Track 29

Mimi: I'm the teacher! Can you remember the bugs, Dylan?
Dylan: Yes, I can. Worm.
Mimi: Worm.
Dylan: Bee.
Mimi: Bee.
Dylan: Snail.
Mimi: Snail
Dylan: Ant.
Mimi: Ant.
Dylan: Butterfly.
Mimi: Butterfly.
Dylan: Ladybug.
Mimi: Ladybug.
Dylan: Wings.
Mimi: Wings.
Dylan: Legs.
Mimi: Legs.
Dylan: Spots.
Mimi: Spots.
Dylan: Stripes.
Mimi: Stripes. Well done, Dylan!
Both: Fantastic!

Listen and answer. Ask and say.

- Play the audio. Children listen to the questions.

CD4 Track 30

Mimi: Does a butterfly have wings?
Does a worm have legs?
Does a ladybug have spots?
Does a bee have stripes?
Does an ant have legs?
Does a snail have wings?

- Play the audio again. Children listen, repeat and answer the questions.
- Children ask and answer questions about bugs.

Complete the faces to show what you can do.

- Explain the four pictures: *I can name bugs and words to describe bugs; I can understand the story; I can ask about and describe bugs; I understand the life cycle of a butterfly.*
- Remind children they should complete each face with a smile or frown depending on how well they think they have done.

Activity Book p 83

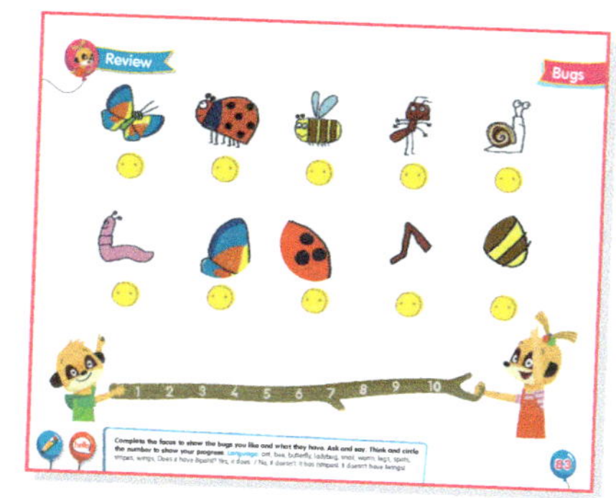

Complete the faces to show the bugs you like and what they have. Ask and say.

- Children complete the faces with a smile to show which bugs they like and what those bugs have.
- Children ask and answer about bugs.

Think and circle the number to show your progress.

- Children circle the number.

Closing time

Learning review (see TB p 18)
Closing routines (see TB p 16)
Goodbye song and puppet (CD1 Track 3; see TB p 17 & 21)

Use the **Navio App** to review what children have learned in this unit, and encourage them to do the same at home.

Project

COOPERATIVE LEARNING

Bugs

1

2

3

Make a bug. Put your bugs together to make a diorama. Ask and say. **Language:** ant, bee, butterfly, ladybug, snail, worm; legs, spots, stripes, wings; colors; Does it have (legs)? Yes, it does. / No, it doesn't. It has (wings). It doesn't have (legs). It's (red and black). I like (the butterfly). Do you like (the snail)? Yes, I do. / No, I don't.

84

Learning objectives

- Work together to do a collaborative project
- Make a bug for the diorama
- Ask and answer questions about the bugs in the diorama
- Draw and color a symmetrical butterfly

Materials

- Class CDs, Mimi puppet, photocopiable templates, paints, colored tissue paper, glue, modeling clay
- optional: crayons

Main vocabulary

- ant, butterfly, snail, worm; legs, wings; colors

Key language

- Does it have (legs)? Yes, it does. / No, it doesn't. It has (wings). It doesn't have (legs). It's (red and black). I like the (butterfly). Do you like the (snail)? Yes, I do. / No, I don't.

Teacher's tip: Sharing responsibility for cleaning up

COOPERATIVE LEARNING

Once the children have finished making their bug, point out the importance of keeping the classroom neat. Remind children that everyone has a responsibility to help and that cleaning up is quicker and easier when everyone works together as a team. Provide a box for any left over tissue paper or spare rolled up balls. Encourage children to make sure there are no bits of paper on the floor or tables at the end of the session.

Circle time

Hello song and puppet (CD1 Track 2; see TB p 17 & 21)
Opening routines (see TB p 16)
Recycling activity (see TB p 19)
Lesson aims (see TB p 18)

Prepare for your project.

- Say *Let's do a project. Let's make a diorama of bugs!*
- Show children the project templates. Explain that children should choose a bug and either stick on balls of tissue paper, paint it or use modeling clay.
- Explain and demonstrate that children will then use their bugs to make a diorama.

Table time

Student's Book p 84

COOPERATIVE LEARNING

Make a bug. Put your bugs together to make a diorama.

- Say e.g. *We're going to make a diorama of bugs. Look at what we need for our project: a picture of a bug, paints, colored tissue paper, glue, modeling clay.* Children listen and point to the pictures.
- Children choose a bug. Give a copy of this project template to each child. Make sure children have paints or colored tissue paper and glue or modeling clay available.
- Children either stick on balls of tissue paper, paint the picture of a bug or make it with modeling clay.
- When they are ready, invite children to come and put their bug in the diorama you have prepared.
- Talk about the bugs in the diorama using language of the unit and other language children know. Count how many of each bug there are in the diorama.

Ask and say.

- Ask children *Do you like our bug diorama?* Make the point that everyone has helped make the diorama and that they couldn't have made such a beautiful diorama on their own.

Alternative version of project

- Children could use crayons instead of finger paints to color their bugs.

Activity Book p 84

Draw the other half of the butterfly. Color your butterfly so both sides are the same.

- Children draw the other side of the butterfly, then color it so both sides are the same.

Ask and say.

- They ask and answer questions about their butterfly and what it has.

Closing time

Learning review (see TB p 18)
Closing routines (see TB p 16)
Goodbye song and puppet (CD1 Track 3; see TB p 17 & 21)

Colors

Listen, point and say. Color the animals the same as in the pictures. Color the circle of your favorite animal. Say. **Language:** black, blue, gray, red, white, yellow; It's (red).

Colors

Black, blue, gray, red, white, yellow

Learning objectives
- Identify and name colors
- Associate colors with animals

Materials
- Class CDs, flashcards, *Ferris Wheel* mat, Mimi puppet

Main vocabulary
- black, blue, gray, red, white, yellow

Key language
- It's (red).

Teacher's tip: Reinforcing colors

In addition to the flashcards, use familiar items of different colors to reinforce the concept e.g. a lemon and a banana for yellow; a tomato and an apple for red etc. Pass the items around and encourage the children to name the color each time.

Circle time

Hello song and puppet (CD1 Track 2; see TB p 17 & 21)
Opening routines (see TB p 16)
Lesson aims (see TB p 18)

Introduce the colors.
- Use the flashcards, puppet and feely bag to introduce or remind children of the colors you are planning to focus on.

Play flashcard games.
- Choose one or two flashcard games with the *Ferris Wheel* mat and/or the puppet (see TB p 20 & 21).
- Ask children to point to, touch or bring you items of different colors in the classroom. Highlight any colors that are new.

Table time

Student's Book p 85

Listen, point and say.
- Hold up your book. Point to the colors in turn.
- Play the audio. Children join in pointing to the animals in their books and naming the colors.

CD4 Track 31

It's red … it's yellow … it's blue … it's black … it's white … it's gray
It's red … it's yellow … it's blue … it's black … it's white … it's gray
It's red … it's yellow … it's blue … it's black … it's white … it's gray

Color the animals the same as in the pictures.
- Children color the animals the same as in the pictures.

Color the circle of your favorite animal.
- Children color the circle to show their favorite animal (of the ones on the page).

Say.
- Children say their favorite color (of the ones on the page).

Activity Book p 85

Match the animals. Use the key to color the animals in the picture.
- Children draw lines to match the animals. Then they color the animals so they are the same as the ones in the key.

Point and say.
- They point and say the animals' colors.

Closing time

Learning review (see TB p 18)
Closing routines (see TB p 16)
Goodbye song and puppet (CD1 Track 3; see TB p 17 & 21)

Cross-curricular activities

- See also the activities in the other Colors lesson (see TB p 211).

Music

Play a track of lively instrumental music. Children pass around the blue flashcard. When you pause the CD, whoever is holding it has to touch a blue object. Say *Touch something blue!*

Math

Give tables or groups of children objects e.g. crayons, blocks, pieces of card in several different colors.

Children sort the objects into sets of different colors and name the colors.

If you wish to focus on numbers as well, children count the number of objects in each color set.

Colors

Listen, point and say. Complete the pattern. Create your own color pattern. Say.
Language: brown, gray, green, orange, pink, purple; It's (orange).

Colors

Learning objectives
- Identify and name colors
- Create a color pattern

Materials
- Class CDs, flashcards, *Ferris Wheel* mat, Mimi puppet

Main vocabulary
- brown, gray, green, orange, pink, purple

Key language
- It's (orange)

Circle time

Hello song and puppet (CD1 Track 2; see TB p 17 & 21)
Opening routines (see TB p 16)
Lesson aims (see TB p 18)

Introduce the colors.
- Use the flashcards, puppet and feely bag to introduce or remind children of the colors you are planning to focus on.

Play flashcard games.
- Choose one or two flashcard games with the *Ferris Wheel* mat and/or the puppet (see TB p 20 & 21).
- Ask children to point to, touch or bring you items of different colors in the classroom. Highlight any colors that are new.

Table time

Student's Book p 86

Listen, point and say.
- Hold up your book. Point to the colors in turn.
- Play the audio. Children join in pointing to the picture in their books and naming the colors.

CD4 Track 32

It's orange … it's purple … it's pink … it's green … it's brown … it's gray
It's orange … it's purple … it's pink … it's green … it's brown … it's gray
It's orange … it's purple … it's pink … it's green … it's brown … it's gray

Complete the pattern.
- Children color the picture following the pattern.

Create your own color pattern.
- Children create their own color pattern.

Say.
- Use the completed picture to review colors. Say e.g. *Point to pink!* and children respond.

Activity Book p 86

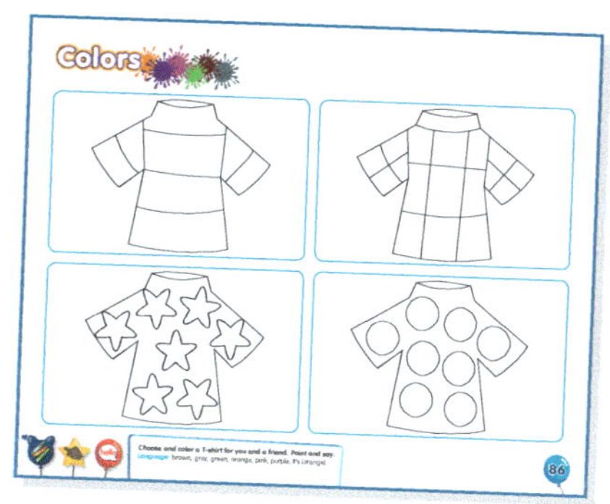

Choose and color a T-shirt for you and a friend.
- Children choose two T-shirts and color their patterns.

Point and say.
- They point and say the T-shirts' colors.

Closing time

Learning review (see TB p 18)
Closing routines (see TB p 16)
Goodbye song and puppet (CD1 Track 3; see TB p 17 & 21)

Cross-curricular activities

- See also the activities in the other Colors lesson (see TB p 209).

Art and craft

Cut out six large balloon shapes (one for each group or table of children). Allow them to choose from the colors introduced.

Children work at their tables or in groups and either color, paint or stick colored tissue paper on each balloon. Alternatively, have them cut out pictures from magazines and stick those of the same color on the balloons.

Display the balloons. Children name the colors.

Science

Use food coloring to make ice cubes in different colors e.g. blue, red, yellow. Place them into glasses of warm water and watch the water take the color. Then add two different colors, e.g. red and blue to make purple etc.

Numbers 10 20 30 40 50 60 70 80 90 100

4:33

Listen, point and say. Draw lines to connect the numbers in order. Circle your favorite number. Say.

Language: numbers 10–100; It's (forty).

Numbers

10–100

Learning objectives
- Learn, reinforce, consolidate or review numbers

Materials
- Class CDs, flashcards, *Ferris Wheel* mat, Mimi puppet

Main vocabulary
- numbers 10–100

Key language
- It's (forty).

Teacher's tip: Identifying numbers

Use wooden or foam numbers from the children's classroom to accustom them to the correct number formation. Place the numbers in a feely bag and encourage the children to guess which number they are touching before they remove it from the bag.

Circle time

Hello song and puppet (CD1 Track 2; see TB p 17 & 21)
Opening routines (see TB p 16)
Lesson aims (see TB p 18)

Introduce the numbers.
- Use the flashcards, puppet and feely bag to introduce or remind children of numbers.

Play flashcard games.
- Choose one or two flashcard games with the *Ferris Wheel* mat and/or the puppet (see TB p 20 & 21).
- Get children to count different classroom objects with you. Highlight any numbers that are new.

Table time

Student's Book p 87

Listen, point and say.
- Hold up your book. Point to the numbers in turn.
- Play the audio. Children join in pointing to the numbers in their books and saying the words.

CD4 Track 33

Ten … twenty … thirty … forty … fifty … sixty … seventy … eighty … ninety … one hundred
Ten … twenty … thirty … forty … fifty … sixty … seventy … eighty … ninety … one hundred
Ten … twenty … thirty … forty … fifty … sixty … seventy … eighty … ninety … one hundred

Draw lines to connect the numbers in order.
- Children draw a line to place the numbers in sequence.

Circle your favorite number. Say.
- Children circle and say their favorite number between 10 and 100 from the ones on the page.

Activity Book p 87

Count and circle groups of ten stars. Count the groups of stars.
- Children circle groups of ten stars and count the groups.

Circle the total number of stars. Point and say.
- Then they circle the total number of stars (50). They point and say the number of stars.

Closing time

Learning review (see TB p 18)
Closing routines (see TB p 16)
Goodbye song and puppet (CD1 Track 3; see TB p 17 & 21)

Cross-curricular activities

- See also the activities in the other Numbers lesson (see TB p 215).

Physical movement

Place the number flashcards (*10, 20, 30,* etc.) around the room. Call out an action and a number e.g. *Hop to eighty!* Children hop to the correct flashcard. When they get there, have them count in tens to the number on the flashcard. Repeat with other numbers and actions, e.g. jump, run, etc.

Math

Give each table or group of children ten small plastic cups with ten small objects e.g. dried chick peas, buttons or bottle tops in each one.

Call out a number between 10 and 100. Children work together and count out the correct number of cups.

Children check they have put the correct number of cups by taking the objects out and counting the ten objects in each one out loud.

Listen, point and say. Match the missing numbers. Say.
Language: numbers 1–50; It's (fifteen).

Numbers

1–50

Learning objectives
- Learn, reinforce, consolidate or review numbers

Materials
- Class CDs, flashcards, *Ferris Wheel* mat, Mimi puppet

Main vocabulary
- numbers 1–50

Key language
- It's (fifteen).

Teacher's tip: Identifying numbers

Use wooden or foam numbers from the children's classroom to accustom them to the correct number formation. Place the numbers in a feely bag and encourage the children to guess which number they are touching before they remove it from the bag.

Circle time

Hello song and puppet (CD1 Track 2; see TB p 17 & 21)
Opening routines (see TB p 16)
Lesson aims (see TB p 18)

Introduce the numbers.

- Use the flashcards, puppet and feely bag to introduce or remind children of numbers.

Play flashcard games.

- Choose one or two flashcard games with the *Ferris Wheel* mat and/or the puppet (see TB p 20 & 21).
- Get children to count different classroom objects with you. Again, highlight any numbers that are new.

Table time

Student's Book p 88

Listen, point and say.

- Hold up your book. Point to the numbers in turn.
- Play the audio. Children join in pointing to the numbers and saying the words.

CD4 Track 34

One … two … three … four … five … six … seven … eight … nine … ten

Eleven … twelve … thirteen … fourteen … fifteen … sixteen … seventeen … eighteen … nineteen … twenty

Twenty-one … twenty-two … twenty-three … twenty-four … twenty-five … twenty-six … twenty-seven … twenty-eight … twenty-nine … thirty

Thirty-one … thirty-two … thirty-three … thirty-four … thirty-five … thirty-six … thirty-seven … thirty-eight … thirty-nine … forty

Forty-one … forty-two … forty-three … forty-four … forty-five … forty-six … forty-seven … forty-eight … forty-nine … Fifty

Match the missing numbers.

- Children match the stones on the left with the empty stones on the path.
- Check the answers. Hold up your book, point and ask e.g. *Where is fifteen?*

Say.

- Children point to the stones in turn and count them.

Activity Book p 88

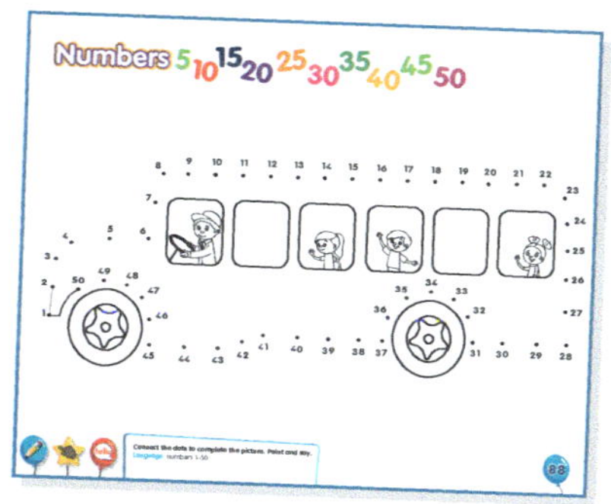

Connect the dots to complete the picture.

- Children connect the dots to complete the picture.

Point and say.

- They point and say the numbers.

Closing time

Learning review (see TB p 18)
Closing routines (see TB p 16)
Goodbye song and puppet (CD1 Track 3; see TB p 17 & 21)

Cross-curricular activities

- See also the activities in the other Numbers lesson (see TB p 213).

Art and craft

Give out plastic bowls, one per pair of children, and write different numbers (1–50) on them. Give out modeling clay.

Check children know the number on their bowl.

Children use the modeling clay to make small balls and put the corresponding number of balls in their bowl.

Children say the numbers and count the balls.

Display the bowls in sequence.

Social science

Write random numbers from 1–50 on different colored card and place each inside a box.

Allocate different boxes to groups of children.

Have the children put the right number of different small classroom items or counters into each box, e.g. 24 pencils, 10 erasers, 38 crayons, 17 books, etc.

Shapes

Listen, point and say. Draw and color the next shape in the sequence. Say.
Language: circle, diamond, oval, rectangle, square, star, triangle; It's a (star).

Shapes

Circle, diamond, oval, rectangle, square, star, triangle

Learning objectives
- Learn, reinforce, consolidate or review shapes

Materials
- Class CDs, flashcards, *Ferris Wheel* mat, Mimi puppet

Main vocabulary
- circle, diamond, oval, rectangle, square, star, triangle

Key language
- It's a (star).

Teacher's tip: Recognizing shapes

Cut shapes out of different materials: sandpaper, card, fabric, etc. Have children touch them, following the shapes with their fingers while they say the name. Ask individual children to take turns closing their eyes. Give them one of the shapes to identify from the shape and the texture of the material used. The rest of the class says if this is correct.

Circle time

Hello song and puppet (CD1 Track 2; see TB p 17 & 21)
Opening routines (see TB p 16)
Lesson aims (see TB p 18)

Introduce the shapes.

- Use the flashcards, puppet and feely bag to introduce or remind children of shapes you are planning to focus on.
- Highlight the new shapes.

Play flashcard games.

- Choose one or two flashcard games with the *Ferris Wheel* mat and/or the puppet (see TB p 20 & 21).
- Get children to identify shapes in any of the classroom posters with you. Again, highlight the shapes that are new.

Table time

Student's Book p 89

Listen, point and say.

- Hold up your book. Point to the shapes in the picture in turn.
- Play the audio. Children join in pointing to the shapes in their books and saying the words.
- Point to the series of shapes and ask what comes next.

CD4 Track 35

It's a star … it's a diamond … it's a circle …
it's a triangle … it's an oval … it's a rectangle …
it's a square
It's a star … it's a diamond … it's a circle …
it's a triangle … it's an oval … it's a rectangle …
it's a square
It's a star … it's a diamond … it's a circle …
it's a triangle … it's an oval … it's a rectangle …
it's a square

Draw and color the next shape in the sequence.

- Children draw and color the next shape in each row.
- Check the answers.

Say.

- Children point to each row in turn and name the shapes in the series.

Activity Book p 89

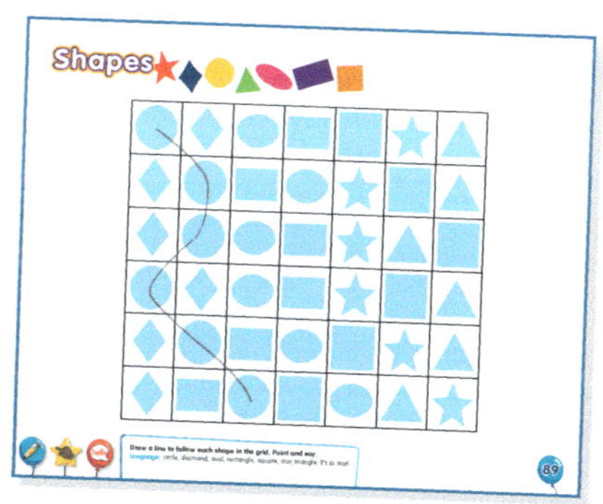

Draw a line to follow each shape in the grid.

- Children draw a line to connect the series of each shape.

Point and say.

- They point and say the shapes.

Closing time

Learning review (see TB p 18)
Closing routines (see TB p 16)
Goodbye song and puppet (CD1 Track 3; see TB p 17 & 21)

Cross-curricular activities

- See also the activities in the other Shapes lesson (see TB p 219).

Physical movement

Put the children into small groups.

Show a shape flashcard and ask children to name it.

Ask them to make the shape together using their bodies.

Alternatively, have the whole group make the shapes.

ICT

Take photos of the whole class shapes with a digital camera.

Shapes

1 2 3 4 5 6 7 8 9 10

Listen, point and say. Count the shapes in the picture. Circle the number and match it to the correct shape. Say. **Language:** circle, diamond, oval, rectangle, square, star, triangle; numbers 1–10; I can see (three) (diamonds).

Shapes

Circle, diamond, oval, rectangle, square, star, triangle

Learning objectives
- Learn, reinforce, consolidate or review shapes

Materials
- Class CDs, flashcards, *Ferris Wheel* mat, Mimi puppet

Main vocabulary
- circle, diamond, oval, rectangle, square, star, triangle; numbers 1–10

Key language
- I can see (three) (diamonds).

Teacher's tip: Recognizing shapes

Draw a selection of shapes on the board and elicit how you say them. Invite a child to the front of the class. Trace a shape with your finger on their back. The child tells you which shape it is. Children play the game with their partner taking turns drawing and guessing the shape.

Circle time

Hello song and puppet (CD1 Track 2; see TB p 17 & 21)
Opening routines (see TB p 16)
Lesson aims (see TB p 18)

Introduce the shapes.

- Use the flashcards, puppet and feely bag to introduce or remind children of shapes you are planning to focus on.
- Highlight the new shapes.

Play flashcard games.

- Choose one or two flashcard games with the *Ferris Wheel* mat and/or the puppet (see TB p 20 & 21).
- Get children to identify shapes in any of the classroom posters with you. Again, highlight the shapes that are new.

Table time

Student's Book p 90

Listen, point and say.

- Hold up your book. Point to the shapes in turn.
- Play the audio. Children join in pointing to the shapes and saying the words.

CD4 Track 35

It's a star … it's a diamond … it's a circle … it's a triangle … it's an oval … it's a rectangle … it's a square
It's a star … it's a diamond … it's a circle … it's a triangle … it's an oval … it's a rectangle … it's a square
It's a star … it's a diamond … it's a circle … it's a triangle … it's an oval … it's a rectangle … it's a square

Count the shapes in the picture. Circle the number and match it to the correct shape.

- Point out that there is more than one of each shape in the picture. Children count each type of shape, circle the number and match it to the shape.

Say.

- Children say how many of each shape there are.

Activity Book p 90

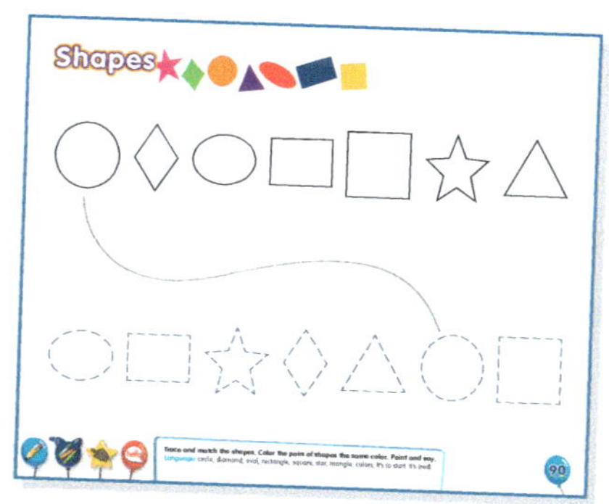

Trace and match the shapes. Color the pairs of shapes the same color.

- Children trace the shapes, match the pairs of shapes, then color the pairs the same color.

Point and say.

- They point and say the shapes and their colors.

Closing time

Learning review (see TB p 18)
Closing routines (see TB p 16)
Goodbye song and puppet (CD1 Track 3; see TB p 17 & 21)

Cross-curricular activities

- See also the activities in the other Shapes lesson (see TB p 217).

Math

Give each table or group of children a set of colored pipe cleaners, straws, toothpicks or wool.

Children use the materials to make different shapes.

Children look at and name the shapes that they and other children have made. If you like, children can then stick their shapes onto colored card and these can be displayed.

Alternatively, have them make the shapes with modeling clay.

Social science

Place some different shaped everyday objects from around the house into a feely bag.

Cut out some large shapes from card and stick them on boxes.

Children identify the shapes by touch, take out the item and place it in the corresponding box.

Concepts

4:36 hello

Listen, point and say. Circle the pictures of hungry children red. Circle the pictures of thirsty children blue. Say.
Language: hungry, thirsty; I'm (hungry).

91

Learning objectives
- Learn, reinforce, consolidate or review concepts

Materials
- Class CDs, flashcards, *Ferris Wheel* mat, Mimi puppet

Main vocabulary
- hungry, thirsty

Key language
- I'm (hungry).

Teacher's tip: Creating a concepts corner

If you have a vocabulary corner in the classroom, you could add a concepts corner. Use contrasting colored card for each pair of concepts and add pictures to illustrate each one.

Circle time

Hello song and puppet (CD1 Track 2; see TB p 17 & 21)
Opening routines (see TB p 16)
Lesson aims (see TB p 18)

Introduce the concepts.

- Use the flashcards, puppet and feely bag to introduce or remind children of the pair of concepts you are planning to focus on.

Play flashcard games.

- Choose one or two flashcard games with the *Ferris Wheel* mat and/or the puppet (see TB p 20 & 21).
- Check that children clearly recognize and understand each concept.

Table time

Student's Book p 91

Listen, point and say.

- Hold up your book. Point to the pictures that show hungry and thirsty in turn.
- Play the audio. Children join in pointing to the pictures in their books and saying the words.

CD4 Track 36

I'm hungry … I'm thirsty … I'm hungry … I'm thirsty
I'm hungry … I'm thirsty … I'm hungry … I'm thirsty
I'm hungry … I'm thirsty … I'm hungry … I'm thirsty

Circle the pictures of hungry children red. Circle the pictures of thirsty children blue.

- Children circle the hungry children red and the thirsty children blue.

Say.

- Check the answers. Children point to the children in the pictures and say if they are hungry or thirsty.

Activity Book p 91

Draw pictures to show food and drink for when you're hungry and thirsty.

- Children draw food and drink in the frames to show what they like when they are hungry and thirsty.

Point and say.

- They point and say how they feel and what they eat and drink.

Closing time

Learning review (see TB p 18)
Closing routines (see TB p 16)
Goodbye song and puppet (CD1 Track 3; see TB p 17 & 21)

Cross-curricular activities

- See also the activities in the other Concepts lessons (see TB p 223 & 225).

Drama

Children stand up. Explain and demonstrate that you're going to say one or other of the concepts you're working on e.g. *Thirsty!* or *Hungry!* and children respond by doing a mime to show they understand e.g. rubbing their tummy to show they're hungry or miming drinking to show they're thirsty.

Alternate giving instructions for the two concepts you're working on and children respond.

Concepts

Listen, point and say. Find and circle six differences in the pictures that show clean and dirty. Say.
Language: clean, dirty; It's (clean).

92

Concepts

Clean, dirty

Learning objectives

- Learn, reinforce, consolidate or review concepts

Materials

- Class CDs, flashcards, *Ferris Wheel* mat, Mimi puppet

Main vocabulary

- clean, dirty

Key language

- It's (clean).

Circle time

Hello song and puppet (CD1 Track 2; see TB p 17 & 21)
Opening routines (see TB p 16)
Lesson aims (see TB p 18)

Introduce the concepts.

- Use the flashcards, puppet and feely bag to introduce or remind children of the pair of concepts you are planning to focus on.

Play flashcard games.

- Choose one or two flashcard games with the *Ferris Wheel* mat and/or the puppet (see TB p 20 & 21).
- Check that children clearly recognize and understand each concept.

Table time

Student's Book p 92

Listen, point and say.

- Hold up your book. Point to the pictures of clean and dirty in turn.
- Play the audio. Children join in pointing to the picture and saying the words.

CD4 Track 37

It's clean … It's dirty … It's clean … It's dirty
It's clean … It's dirty … It's clean … It's dirty
It's clean … It's dirty … It's clean … It's dirty

Find and circle six differences in the pictures that show clean and dirty.

- Children find and circle six differences in the pictures to show clean and dirty. Check the answers.

Say.

- Children point to the pictures they have circled that show clean and dirty and say the words.

Activity Book p 92

Color the frames of the pictures that show clean green. Color the frames of the pictures that show dirty red.

- Children color the frames around the pictures that show clean green and the frames around the pictures that show dirty red.

Point and say.

- They point and say whether the picture shows dirty or clean.

Closing time

Learning review (see TB p 18)
Closing routines (see TB p 16)
Goodbye song and puppet (CD1 Track 3; see TB p 17 & 21)

Cross-curricular activities

- See also the activities in the other Concepts lessons (see TB p 221 & 225).

Art and craft

Take two pieces of card in contrasting colors – one for each of the concepts (hungry/thirsty, old/young, or clean/dirty).

Children cut out pictures from magazines or draw to illustrate the concepts. They classify them by sticking them in the right place.

Concepts

Listen, point and say. Match the old people and animals to the young ones.
Draw a picture of someone old or young in your family. Say.
Language: old, young; He's/She's/It's (old).

Concepts

Learning objectives
- Learn, reinforce, consolidate or review concepts

Materials
- Class CDs, flashcards, *Ferris Wheel* mat, Mimi puppet

Main vocabulary
- old, young

Key language
- He's/She's/It's (old).

Circle time

Hello song and puppet (CD1 Track 2; see TB p 17 & 21)
Opening routines (see TB p 16)
Lesson aims (see TB p 18)

Introduce the concepts.

- Use the flashcards, puppet and feely bag to introduce or remind children of the pair of concepts you are planning to focus on.

Play flashcard games.

- Choose one or two flashcard games with the *Ferris Wheel* mat and/or the puppet (see TB p 20 & 21).
- Check that children clearly recognize and understand each concept.

Table time

Student's Book p 93

Listen, point and say.

- Hold up your book. Point to the pictures of the old and young people in turn.
- Play the audio. Children join in pointing to old and young and saying the words.

CD4 Track 38

She's old … She's young … He's old … He's young … It's old … It's young
She's old … She's young … He's old … He's young … It's old … It's young
She's old … She's young … He's old … He's young … It's old … It's young

Match the old people and animals to the young ones.

- Children draw lines to match the old people and animals to the young ones.

Draw a picture of someone old or young in your family.

- Children draw a picture of an old or young person from their own family.

Say.

- Children point to the pictures of the old and young people and say the words.

Activity Book p 93

Find and circle the old people and animals green. Find and circle the young people and animals red.

- Children circle the old people and animals in green and the young people and animals in red.

Point and say.

- They point and say the words.

Closing time

Learning review (see TB p 18)
Closing routines (see TB p 16)
Goodbye song and puppet (CD1 Track 3; see TB p 17 & 21)

Cross-curricular activities

- See also the activities in the other Concepts lessons (see TB p 221 & 223).

Social science

Ask questions and give prompts to encourage children to think about and say how the concept applies to them e.g. *Name someone old / young in your family. Are you hungry / thirsty? What do you want to eat / drink? Are your hands clean / dirty?* etc.

Festivals

World Book Day

Listen, point and say. Listen and sing *We love books.* Match the books. Choose and color the cover of the book you like best. Say. **Language:** animals, people, pictures, stories, words, world; I like books about (people). I like books with (pictures).

World Book Day

Learning objectives
- Name World Book Day vocabulary
- Sing and act out the song *We love books*
- Participate in celebrating a special day

Materials
- Class CDs, flashcards, *Ferris Wheel* mat, Mimi puppet

Main vocabulary
- animals, people, pictures, stories, words, world

Key language
- I like books about (people). I like books with (pictures).

Teacher's tip: Browsing books
If you have access to suitable books in English with illustrations, bring them in and set up a book corner in the classroom. Allow the children to look at them with a partner and decide which are about people, animals, the world etc. and which ones they like.

Circle time

Hello song and puppet (CD1 Track 2; see TB p 17 & 21)
Opening routines (see TB p 16)
Lesson aims (see TB p 18)

Introduce World Book Day.
- Introduce the idea of World Book Day by showing them some books suitable for their age group. Ask the children if they want to celebrate World Book Day in English.
- Use the puppet to introduce the new words (people, animals, the world). Say each word and children repeat it.
- Put the *Ferris Wheel* mat on the floor or board with the flashcards face down (on different colored pods). Use the puppet to turn them over and name them. The children repeat the words.

Game: *Say the color!*
- Name the words and children say the color of the wheel. Then the reverse.

Game: *Guess and say!*
- Turn the flashcards face down and mix them up.
- Use the puppet to point to one of the flashcards and children guess what it is. Turn the flashcard over and see if they're correct. Repeat several times.

***We love books* song**
- Say *Let's listen to the song "We love books".*
- Ask *What books do you think are in the song?* Children guess.
- Children listen and say the books. Check the answer (pictures, words, animals, people, stories, the world).
- Play the audio again. Children listen and join in singing the song.
- The children stand up. Play the audio again. The children join in with the actions.

CD4 Track 40

We love books with pictures. (Mime reading)
We love books with words, too. (Raise both arms in the air)
We love books with animals. (Mime an elephant)
Do you? Do you? Do you? (Point to different children)
Yes, Yes, yes, we do!

We love books with people.
We love books with stories, too.
We love books about the world. (Make a ball with your hands)
Do you? Do you? Do you?
Yes, Yes, yes, we do!

We love to read books at school.
We love to read books at home, too.
We love to read books together. (Gesture to the whole class)
Do you? Do you? Do you?
Yes, Yes, yes, we do!

Table time

Student's Book p 94

Listen, point and say.
- Hold up your book. Point to the pictures in turn.
- Play the audio. Children join in pointing to the pictures in their books and saying the words.

CD4 Track 39

It's World Book Day.
Look! Stories and books about people… animals … the world.
I like books with pictures and words.

Listen and sing *We love books*.

CD4 Track 40
- Play the song. Children point to the pictures and join in singing the song.

Match the books. Choose and color the cover of the book you like best. Say.
- Children match the books and then color the cover of the book they like best.
- Children say the book they like best e.g. *I love books with pictures.*
- Say *Happy World Book Day!* and encourage children to say this to each other and to you.

Activity Book p 94

Draw and color your favorite book.
- Children draw and color their favorite book.

Point and say.
- They point and say the words.

Closing time

Learning review (see TB p 18)
Closing routines (see TB p 16)
Goodbye song and puppet (CD1 Track 3; see TB p 17 & 21)

Festivals

World Animal Day

Listen, point and say. Listen and sing *Save the rhino*. Find and circle the animals in the song. Draw and color an animal you want to save. Say.
Language: elephant, gorilla, panda, polar bear, rhino, tiger; Save the (panda).

World Animal Day

Learning objectives
- Name World Animal Day vocabulary
- Sing and act out the song *Save the rhino*
- Participate in celebrating a special day

Materials
- Class CDs, flashcards, *Ferris Wheel* mat, Mimi puppet

Main vocabulary
- elephant, gorilla, panda, polar bear, rhino, tiger

Key language
- Save the (panda).

Teacher's tip: Making a display of our favorite animals

Ask the children to paint or draw their favorite animal. Cut out a large circle to represent the world and cover it in blue and green paper. Stick the children's animals all over the world and display in a prominent place.

Circle time

Hello song and puppet (CD1 Track 2; see TB p 17 & 21)
Opening routines (see TB p 16)
Lesson aims (see TB p 18)

Introduce World Animal Day.
- Explain that there is a special day each year to celebrate animals. Ask the children if they want to celebrate World Animal Day in English.
- Ask the children to name wild animals that they know.
- Use the puppet and flashcards to introduce the new animals. Put the *Ferris Wheel* mat on the floor or board with the flashcards face down (on different colored pods). Use the puppet to turn them over and name them. The children repeat the words.

Game: *Guess and say!*
- Turn the flashcards face down and mix them up.
- Use the puppet to point to one of the flashcards and children guess what it is. Turn the flashcard over and see if they're correct. Repeat several times.

Game: *Say the color!*
- Name the animals on the Ferris Wheel and children name the color. Then the reverse.

Game: *Freeze!*
- Children stand up. Teach them a mime for each animal in turn.
- Name the animals in random order and children respond by doing the mimes. When you say *Stop!* they freeze in position. Comment on these e.g. *What a lovely rhino!* before continuing. Repeat several times.

***Save the rhino* song**
- Say *Let's listen to the song "Save the rhino."*
- Put the flashcards on the board. Children say the words.
- Play the audio. Children listen and point to the flashcards as they hear the words in each verse.
- Children stand up. Play the audio again. Children listen, sing and act out the song doing actions.
- Repeat once or twice.

CD4 Track 42

Save the rhino, (Point a finger upward on your nose)
Save the rhino.
Save the tiger, too. (Mime claws with your fingers)
Save the gorilla, (Beat your hands on your chest)
Save the gorilla.
It's up to me and you! (Point to self then hold out both arms)
Save the polar bear, (Bend over to walk like a polar bear)
Save the polar bear.
Save the panda, too.
Save the elephant, (Make a trunk with your arm)
Save the elephant.
It's up to me and you!

Table time

Student's Book p 95

Listen, point and say.
- Hold up your book. Point to the pictures in turn.
- Play the audio. Children join in pointing to the pictures in their books and saying the words.

CD4 Track 41

It's World Animal Day.
Look at the panda! … And the … elephant … gorilla … polar bear … rhino … and tiger!
Save the animals!

Listen and sing *Save the rhino.*

CD4 Track 42
- Play the song. Children point to the pictures and sing.

Find and circle the animals in the song.
- Children find and circle the animals in the song.

Draw and color an animal you want to save. Say.
- Children draw and color an animal they want to save.
- Children take turns saying the animal they've chosen e.g. *Save the panda!*
- Ask e.g. *Do you like World Animal Day?*
- Say *Happy World Animal Day!* and encourage children to say this to each other and to you.

Activity Book p 95

Look and match. Draw and color to complete the animals.
- Children match each animal to its missing body part, then draw and color to complete the animal.

Circle your favorite animal. Point and say.
- They circle their favorite animal. Then they point and say the words.

Closing time

Learning review (see TB p 18)
Closing routines (see TB p 16)
Goodbye song and puppet (CD1 Track 3; see TB p 17 & 21)

Festivals

World Environment Day

1

2

3

4

4:43 4:44

Listen, point and say. Listen and sing *When we go to the countryside*. Number the pictures in the order of the song. Draw a picture of you in the places you go to. Say. **Language:** beach, countryside, forest, mountains; I go to the (countryside). Let's protect the (beach).

Learning objectives

- Name World Environment Day vocabulary
- Sing and act out the song *When we go to the countryside*
- Participate in celebrating a special day

Materials

- Class CDs, flashcards, *Ferris Wheel* mat, Mimi puppet

Main vocabulary

- beach, countryside, forest, mountains

Key language

- I go to the (countryside). Let's protect the (beach).

Teacher's tip: Choosing where to go

Make the different backgrounds (countryside, beach, mountains, forest) out of colored paper. Have the children paint or draw a picture of themselves having fun. Invite them to choose which background to stick their picture on and to say e.g. *I'm in the countryside.* Get the class to count with you the number of children who have chosen each background.

Circle time

Hello song and puppet (CD1 Track 2; see TB p 17 & 21)
Opening routines (see TB p 16)
Lesson aims (see TB p 18)

Introduce World Environment Day.

- Ask the children if they want to celebrate World Environment Day in English.
- Use the puppet and flashcards to introduce the new animals.
- Put the *Ferris Wheel* mat on the board with the flashcards face down (on different colored pods). Use the puppet to turn them over and name them. The children repeat the words.

Game: *Guess and say!*

- Turn the flashcards face down and mix them up.
- Use the puppet to point to one of the flashcards and children guess what it is. Turn the flashcard over and see if they're correct.
- Repeat several times.

***When we go to the countryside* song**

- Say *Let's listen to the song "When we go to the countryside."*
- Put the flashcards on the board. Children say the words.
- Children listen and point to the flashcards as they hear the words in each verse.
- Children stand up. Play the audio again. Children listen, sing and do the actions in the song.
- Repeat once or twice.

CD4 Track 44

When we go to the countryside (Point to the flashcard)
We have fun (Throw both arms up in the air)
Let's protect the countryside (Wag a finger)
For everyone! (Gesture all around)
When we go to the mountains (Point to the flashcard)
We have fun
Let's protect the mountains
For everyone!
When we go to the beach (Point to the flashcard)
We have fun
Let's protect the beach
For everyone!
When we go to the forest (Point to the flashcard)
We have fun
Let's protect the forest
For everyone!

Table time

Student's Book p 96

Listen, point and say.

- Hold up your book. Point to the pictures in turn.
- Play the audio. Children join in pointing to the pictures in their books and saying the words.

CD4 Track 43

It's World Environment Day.
Look! The countryside … mountains … beach … and forest!
Let's protect the environment!

Listen and sing *When we go to the countryside.*

CD4 Track 44

- Play the song. Children point to the pictures and join in singing the song.

Number the pictures in order of the song. Draw a picture of you in the places you go to. Say.

- Children number the pictures in the order of the song and draw a picture of a place they want to go to.
- Children show each other their pictures.
- Use the children's shared language to ask e.g. *Do you like World Environment Day?* and children respond.
- Say *Happy World Environment Day!* and encourage children to say this to each other and to you.

Activity Book p 96

Follow and draw the paths from the children to the places. Color your favorite place.

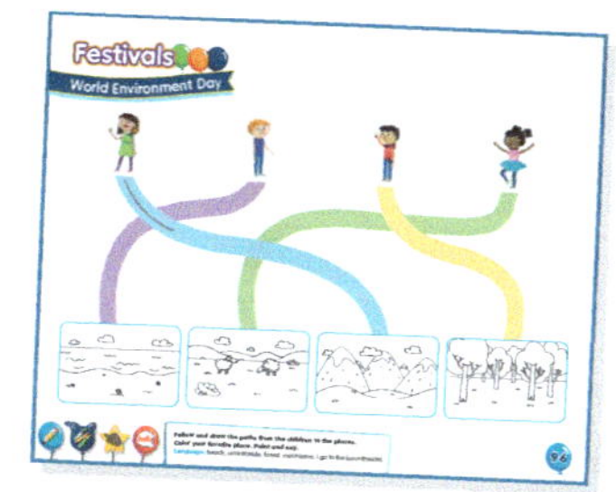

- Children draw paths from the children to the places. Then they color their favorite place.

Point and say.

- Children point and say where they go.

Closing time

Learning review (see TB p 18)
Closing routines (see TB p 16)
Goodbye song and puppet (CD1 Track 3; see TB p 17 & 21)

Project template

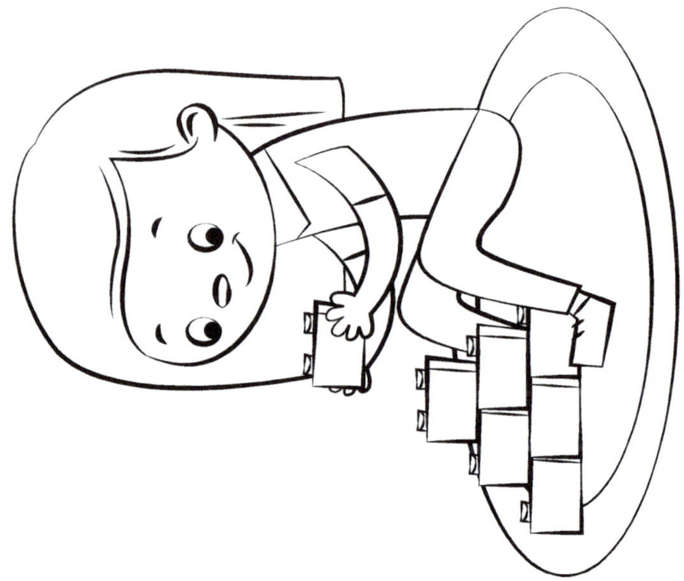

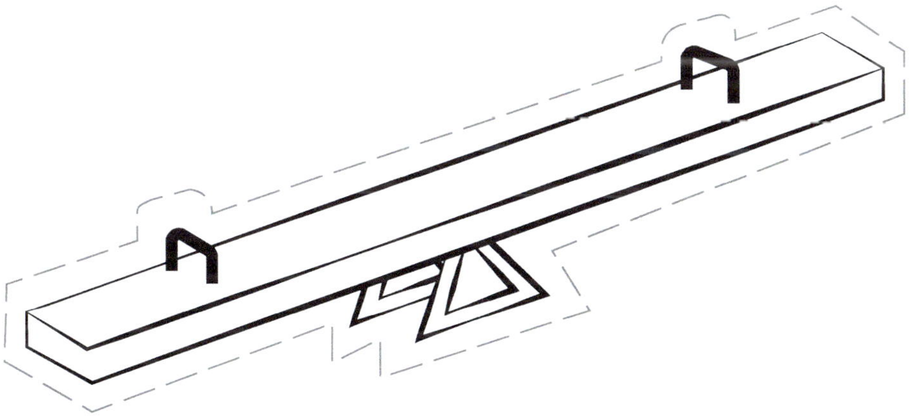

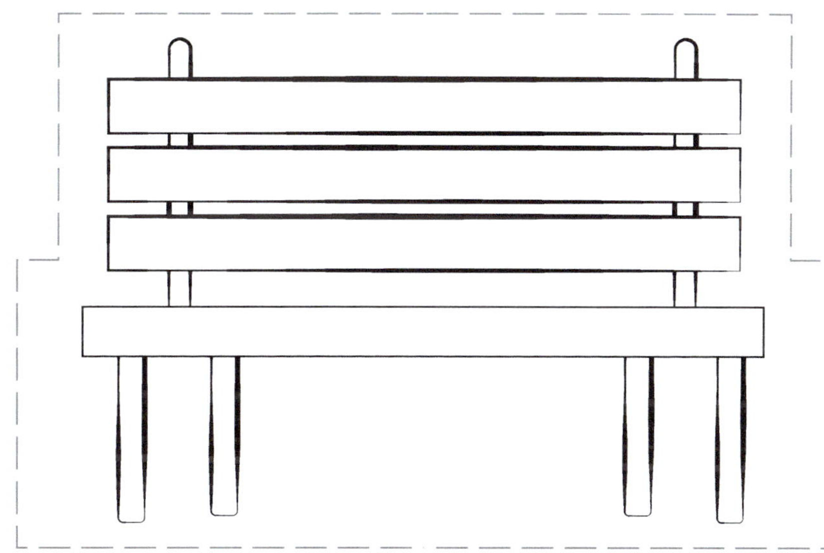

PHOTOCOPIABLE

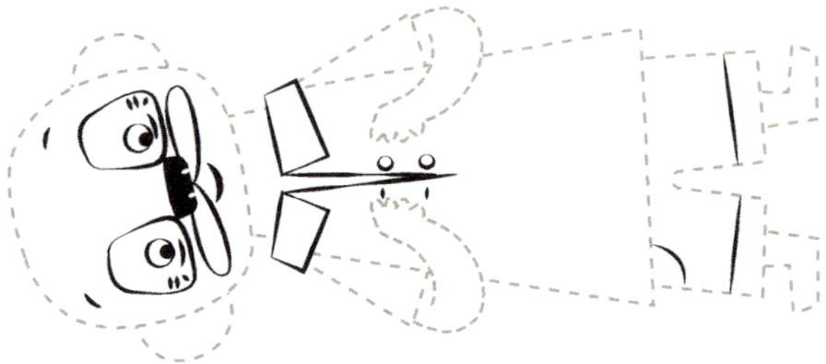

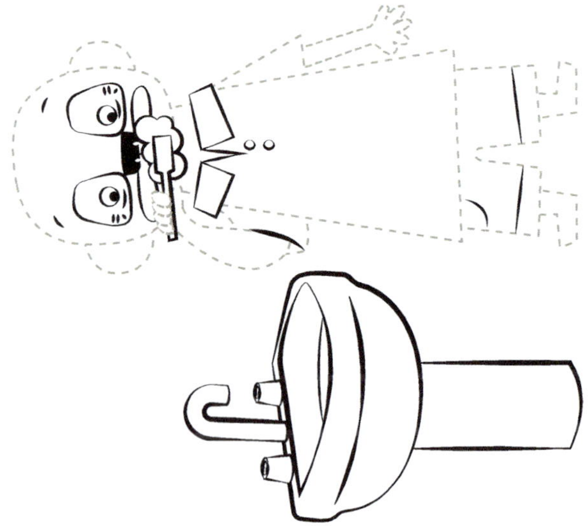

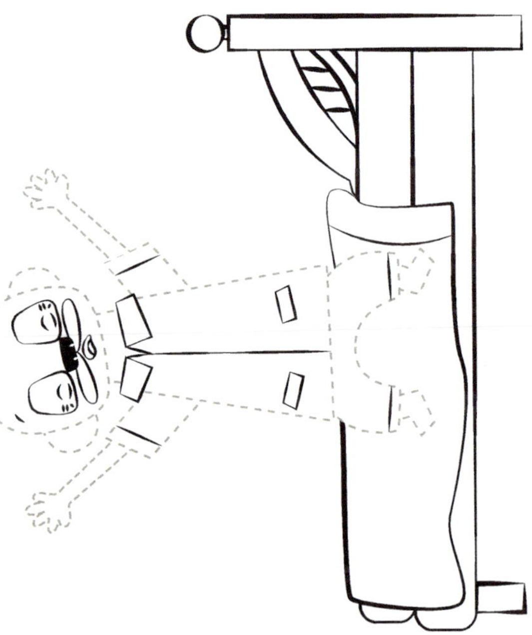

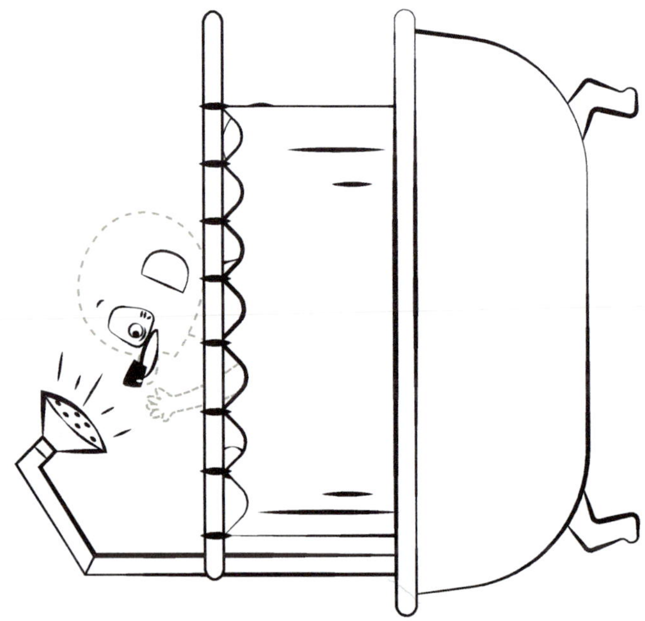

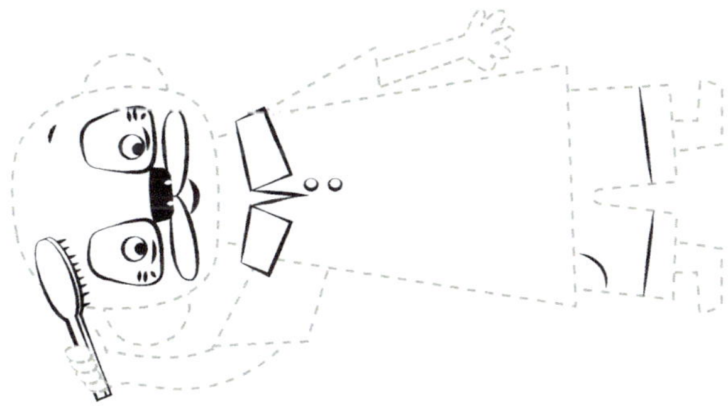

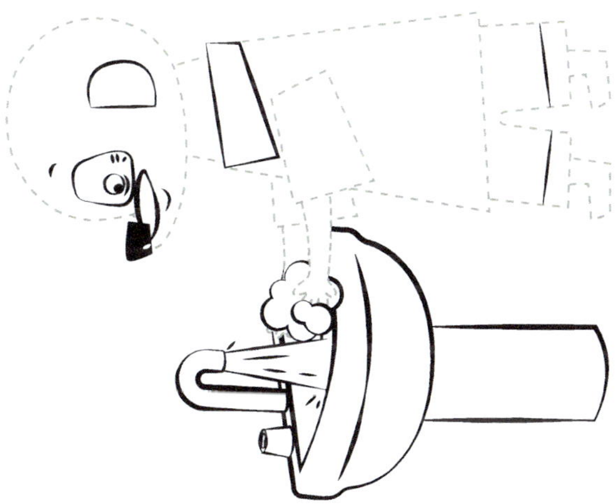

Project template

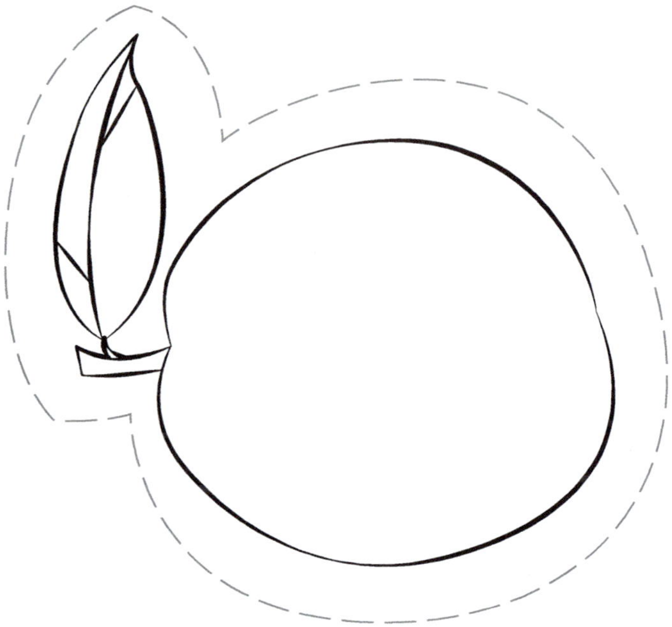

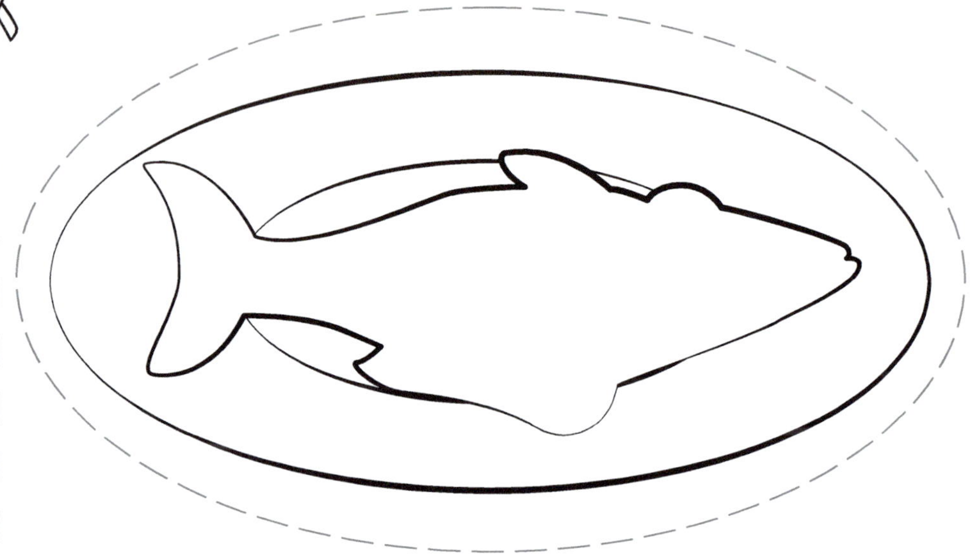

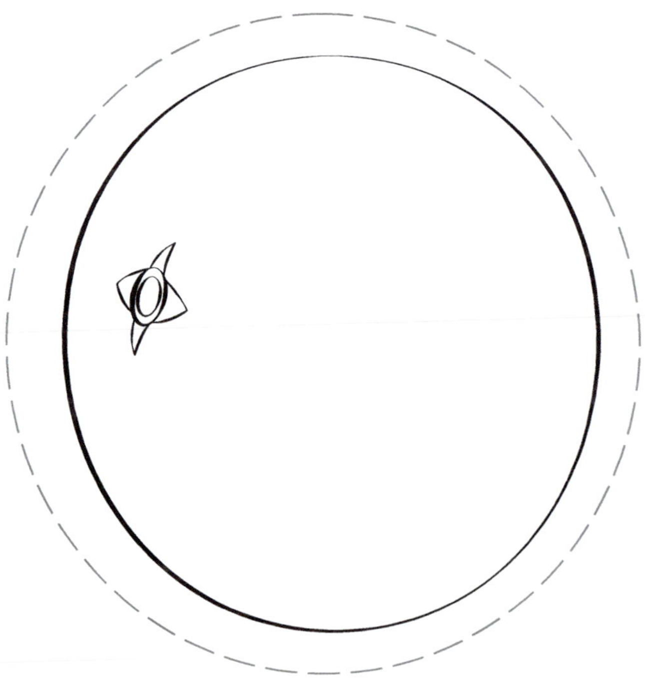

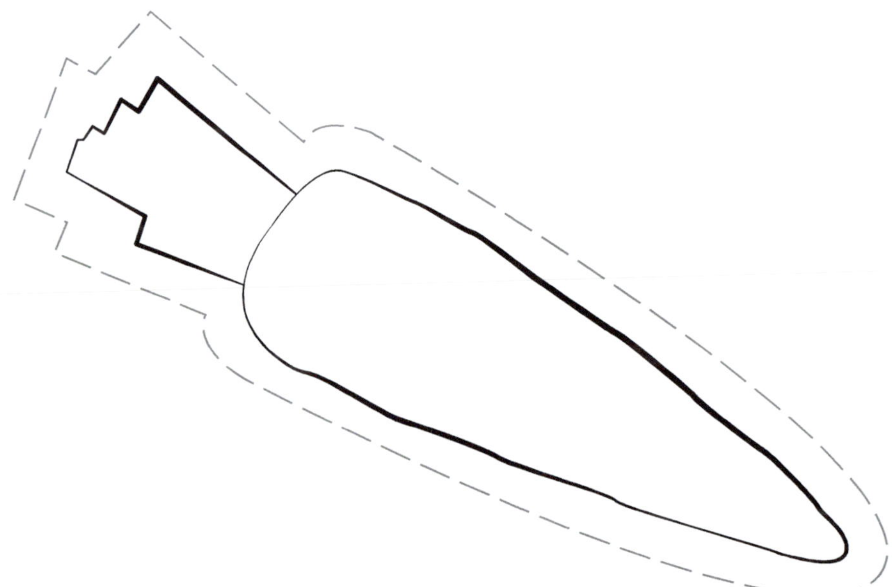

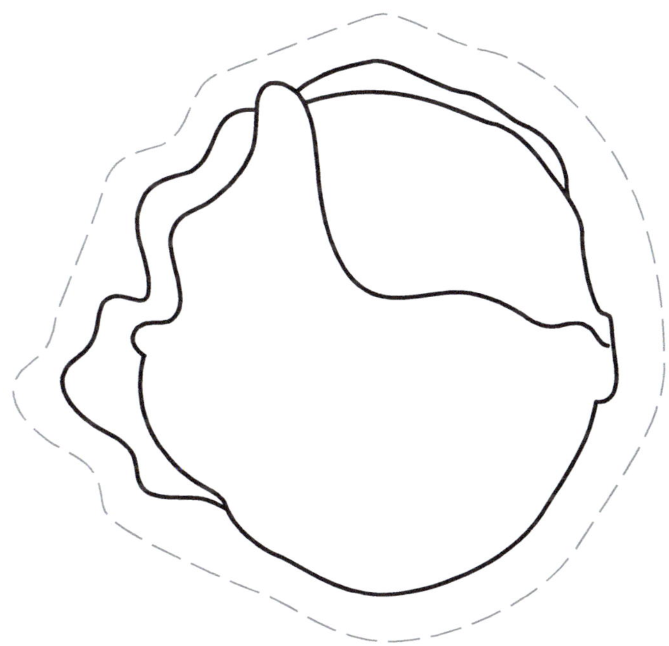

Project template

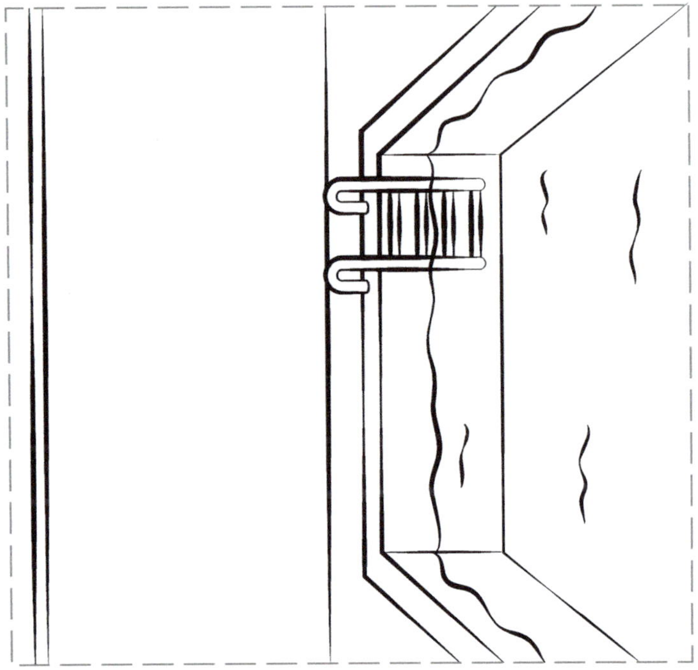

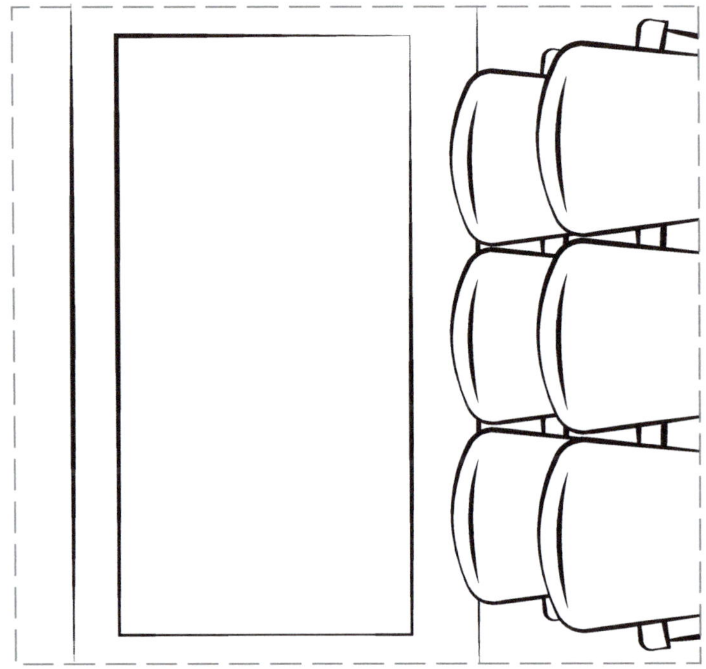

Project template

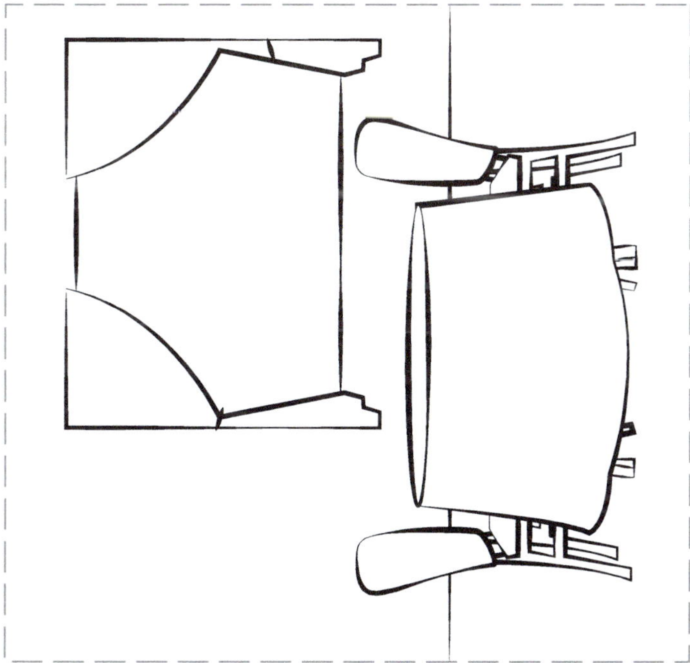

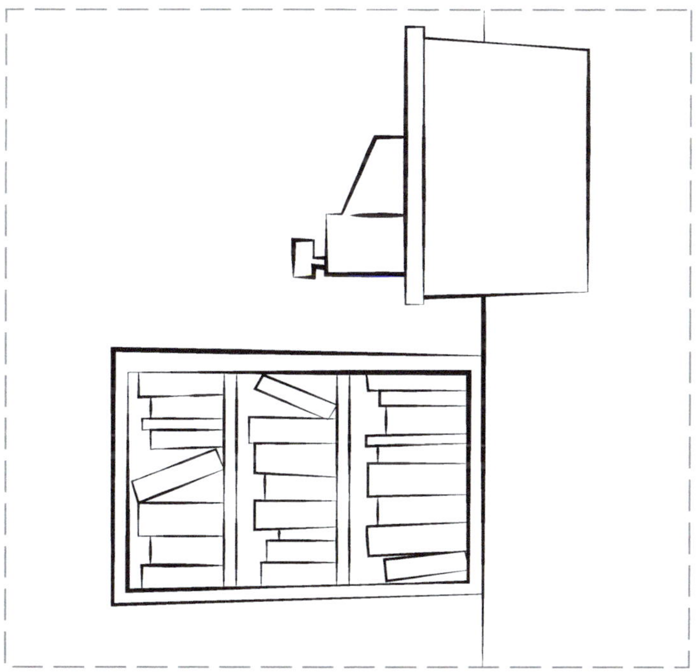

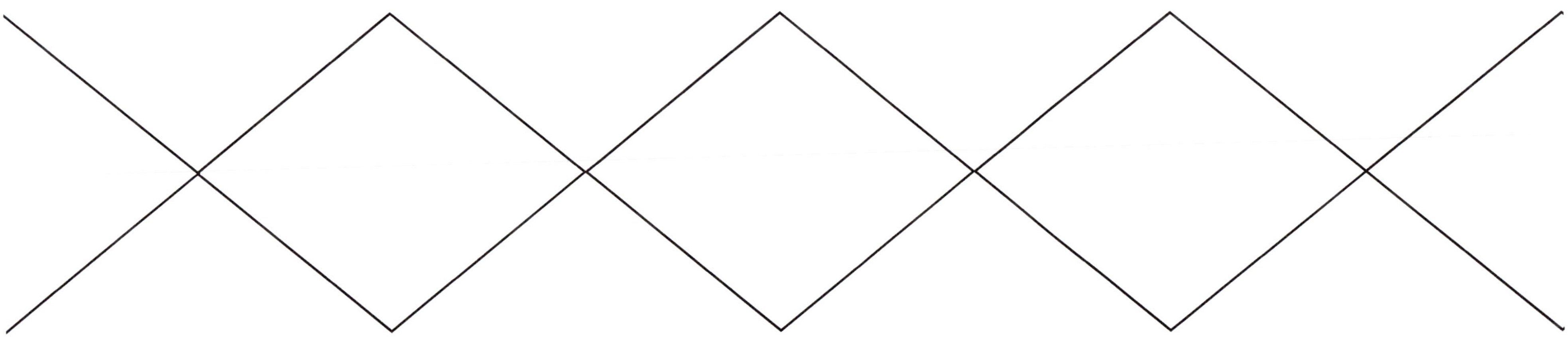

Project template

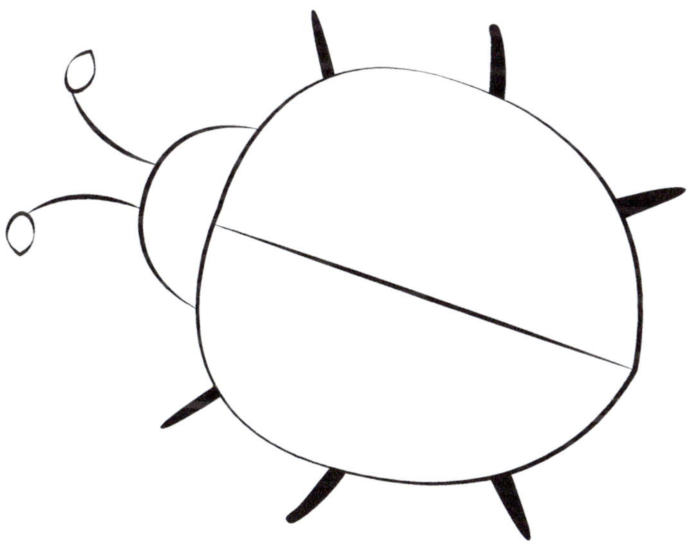

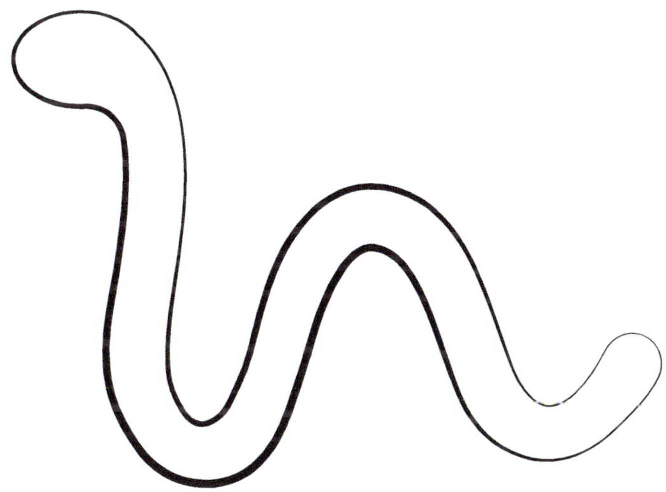